Race and Politics
in the Bahamas

Colin A. Hughes

Race and Politics
in the Bahamas

St. Martin's Press
New York

© University of Queensland Press, St. Lucia, Queensland 1981

All rights reserved. For information, write:
St. Martin's Press Inc., 175 Fifth Avenue, New York, NY 10010
Printed in Australia
First published in the United States of America in 1981

ISBN 0 312 66136 3

Library of Congress Cataloging in Publication Data

Hughes, Colin A.

    Race and politics in the Bahamas.

    Includes index.
    I. Bahamas — Politics and government. II. Bahamas —
Race relations. I. Title.
JL619.A15H83   1981   320.97296   81 8774
ISBN 0 312 66136 3   AACR2

Contents

Illustrations

Maps

Tables

Acknowledgements

This book was originally intended for publication by the Institute of Race Relations, and the IRRs consent to other arrangements is gratefully acknowledged. Much of my reading of Bahamian newspapers took place in London, and I am indebted to the director and staff of the Institute of Commonwealth Studies in Russell Square for their hospitality, and to the staff of the British Newspaper Library at Colindale for their assistance.

The dispatch by Sir G.W. Haddon-Smith is reproduced by permission of the controller of Her Majesty's Stationery Office. Photographs are reproduced by permission of the editors of the *Guardian* and the *Tribune*, Etienne Dupuch, Jr., Publications, Oscar Johnson, Stanley Toogood, and the Bahamas News Bureau. The maps were drawn by Lio Pancino of the cartography section of the Department of Human Geography, Australian National University. Mary Pearson typed the manuscript and Kath Bourke assisted in ways too numerous to itemize. I am grateful to them all.

Three debts are especially deep: to old friends in the Bahamas Democratic League who, a quarter century ago, shared the then unpopular belief that Bahamians need not be divided by racial differences; to my parents who introduced me to the Bahamas; and to my wife who introduced me to Australia.

C.A.H.

1

The Development of a Bahamian Society, 1492-1953

The Bahamas are an archipelago of 700 islands and 2,400 cays and rocks stretching south-eastwards from the coast of Florida to the Windward Passage between Cuba and Haiti. The western end of Grand Bahama is barely sixty-five kilometres from Palm Beach in Florida, and the southern shore of Inagua is almost as close to Cuba and Haiti. Although the islands extend for more than eight hundred kilometres and scatter through 233,000 square kilometres of sea, their total area is relatively small. Only 13,933 square kilometres of land rise above the shallow seas which gave the Bahamas their name. When the writer was a boy the figure had been just 11,396 square kilometres, but aerial photography and more accurate surveys have since added another 2,500 square kilometres to the total. The Tropic of Cancer runs through the middle of the archipelago, and the Gulf Stream flows northwards past the western islands. The sea keeps the winter temperatures high and the summer temperatures low, and the combination of equable climate and the beauty of the sea provides the basis for the tourist economy on which most Bahamians now depend.

Rainfall comes in the summer months from the north-east trade winds; the north-western islands have an adequate fall of up to 1,500 millimetres, but the south-eastern are much drier with annual rainfalls down to 750 millimetres. The islands are low-lying – the highest point is just over 120 metres above sea-level on Cat Island – and composed of coralline limestone so that rainwater either runs off the hard cap rock and is lost into the sea, or else percolates through to lie in underground lakes which rest on cushions of salt water. Excessive extraction for domestic use or agriculture can cause the saltwater to rise through the rock and ruin the fresh-water table; the most densely populated island, New Providence, has to supplement its natural water supply by distilling seawater and brackish water, and by shipping fresh water by barge from nearby Andros. On most islands there is little topsoil, and what little there is lies in tiny pockets in the rock or in deeper "cave holes" so that efficient agriculture has been virtually impossible. Most of the original "cave-earth", which was rich in phosphates, was removed

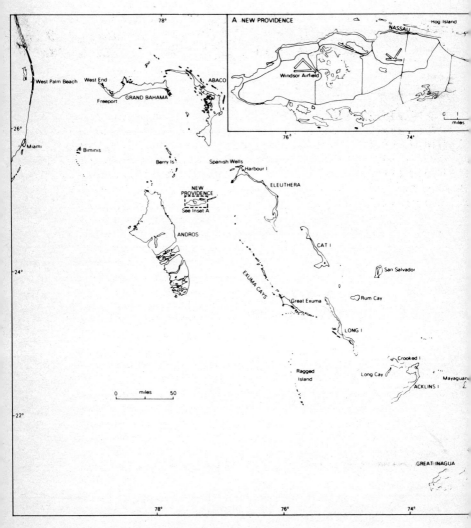

Map 1. The Bahamas

by earlier generations of farmers — who thereby did inestimable damage to the study of the prehistory of the islands. It now appears that modern machinery can break up the cap rock to make the softer underlying material available to extend pasture or agriculture, but for a century and a half the prevailing farming technology consisted of using a machete or cutlass to insert a seed in a pocket of soil and a big toe to tamp the soil down again, supplemented more recently by the use of dynamite to enlarge the pockets. One new governor told the story of being awakened on his first morning in Government House in Nassau by a loud explosion. His first thought of impending revolution was dismissed by the explanation that it was merely the gardener at work.

When Columbus landed at San Salvador in 1492, the islands were inhabited by a group of Arawaks, known locally as Lucayans. As W. K. Brooks wrote in 1887, "The Spaniards had no time nor inclination for the study of anthropology, and their random notes give us little or no knowledge of the people they destroyed."[1] More recently the techniques of prehistorians are beginning to reconstruct a more accurate picture than that which had rested on the fragmentary Spanish evidence. The Amerindian occupants of the West Indies moved northwards from South America in three waves. The first, the Ciboney, about whom very little is known, were reduced to a few groups in Cuba and Hispaniola by the time of European conquest. "They had no pottery and presumably no agriculture and according to enthnographic reports could not converse with other Indians near by. They existed primarily by hunting, fishing and gathering."[2] There is no evidence that they ever occupied the Bahamas. The second wave, the Arawaks, began to move into the Antilles about the time of Christ and appear to have reached the Bahamas between A.D. 800 and 1000 from either Cuba or Hispaniola or both. W. H. Sears and S. O. Sullivan argue plausibly that the first contacts were seasonal visits to the southernmost islands (including the Turks and Caicos groups) to collect salt and shellfish, and that subsequently the central islands were permanently settled. In their view, colonization of the north-western islands would have been inhibited by winter temperatures which would have killed the manioc plants on which Arawak agriculture was based, while the limited rainfall of the southern islands would have similarly discouraged permanent occupation.[3]

The introduction of the *encomienda* system on Hispaniola created an insatiable demand for Amerindian labour, and by 1500 the Spaniards began to remove the Lucayans to Hispaniola to work on the plantations and in the gold-mines and to the pearl fisheries of Margarita near the South American coast. Peter Martyr reported that within twenty years they had carried off forty thousand — a few pages later he says that "twelve hundred thousand" had disappeared — and that by 1516 there remained only "a very small number of them, either in the Spanish colonies or in the archipelago itself".[4] The figure of forty thousand has been generally followed by subsequent writers, for want of any alternative, but seems improbable if settlement was indeed restricted to only the central islands. Whatever the total number, the genocide of the Lucayans was swift and complete. When Ponce de Leon sailed through the Bahamas in 1513 he encountered only one old woman, a solitary survivor of her race, and those who had been taken to Hispaniola quickly died of overwork, disease, and despair. Las Casas mentions one land-owner who killed 90 per cent of his Lucayan work-force within three months, and states that a ship could have sailed from the Bahamas to Hispaniola "without compass or chart, guiding itself solely by the trail of dead Indians who had been thrown from the ships".[5]

The third wave of Amerindians, the warlike Caribs, had moved as far as Puerto Rico when the Spaniards came. Had Europe not intervened in the affairs of the New World, the Lucayans would presumably have fallen victim to them as had the Arawaks in the Lesser Antilles. As it was, the Lucayans' reputation as a gentle people who made their living from the sea and a shifting agriculture of manioc and cassava was preserved by writers like Columbus and Peter Martyr. The Lucayan memory survives in the Bahamas only in a few island names – and more widely in the word for the "hammock" which Columbus first saw at Long Island – and in self-indulgent attempts to link the Bahamian national character to the gentleness of the first inhabitants no present-day Bahamian's ancestors ever knew.

The Spaniards retained some interest in the scattered islands, but they made no attempt to settle, turning south to Cuba and then to the mainland of Mexico and Central America. When Spanish shipping developed the route from Havana up the Florida Channel, freebooters appeared in the western Bahamas, but the first permanent European settlement waited another century. There may have been an abortive French settlement at Abaco in 1625, but the first definite settlement came in 1649 when a group of Puritans broke away from the older colony at Bermuda and landed on the island they called "Eleutheria", place of freedom. Their initial settlements were on two small islands off the northern end of Eleuthera, Harbour Island and St George's Cay, the site of the settlement of Spanish Wells. Other Englishmen colonized New Providence around 1666, and when the first population count was made in 1671 there were 500 free men and 413 slaves on New Providence and 154 free men and 30 slaves on Eleuthera. Thus the slave population, mainly Africans, was already 40 per cent of the total; but in the absence of extensive agriculture, slavery was on a small scale, with the most substantial owner holding only forty slaves.

The early Bahamian economy was peripatetic — logwood and ambergris gathering and salt-raking at Exuma, Inagua, and Turks Island. Following establishment of the great pirate base on Tortuga, only eighty-nine kilometres from Inagua, it was reinforced by piracy. That industry developed steadily, and when Woodes Rogers destroyed their power on New Providence in 1713, there were some one thousand pirates based in the area. Charles Town, the original settlement on New Providence, was destroyed by the Spaniards in reprisal for raids on the St Augustine area of Florida, and on being laid out again in 1695 the town was renamed Nassau to mark the arrival of a Dutch king on the English throne. Continued hostilities with the Spaniards, who sacked Nassau three times in the first decade of the eighteenth century, kept the population small. The settlers and their slaves were frequently carried off or dispersed by the Spaniards, and they did not always return. By 1726 the settled population was much the same as in 1671, while the proportion of slaves had fallen to one-quarter of the total. Lacking the sugar that brought wealth to the West Indies, the Bahamas grew slowly: by 1783 the population was still barely 4,000, of whom 2,300 were Negroes.

The most significant event in shaping the future character of the Bahamian population was the flight of Loyalists and their slaves from the mainland colonies. About one-sixth of the new settlers came from New York, while the great majority had lived previously in Georgia and the Carolinas and gathered in Florida, which had temporarily become a British colony but was about to be returned to Spain. Between 1783 and 1789 the islands' population trebled, and the proportion of slaves rose from half to three-quarters. The settled areas of Eleuthera and Harbour Island were affected only marginally, but the population of New Providence rose from 2,500 in 1783 to 5,600 in 1789, and Abaco and the larger islands to the south-east received their first substantial permanent settlement. In 1787 the Crown completed purchase of the rights of the original proprietors (see below) and made extensive grants of land to the Loyalists, who sought to re-create the cotton-based economy they had known in the southern colonies. The first years were optimistic. Thus the *Bahamian Gazette* on 5 February 1790 reported prospects of a good cotton crop:

> Seven years since lands in the Bahamas were deemed to no value whatever. A fortunate reverse is the case now; and the reason is obvious indeed: for there are examples in plenty of their yielding from 160 to 220 lbs. of clean cotton to the acre i.e., from seven to 10 guineas. And so easily is the labour exerted in raising this produce, that one able field slave can attend six acres. Clearing land is much easier there than on the continent, or in any of the West-Indian islands. The expense of clearing in these islands is not estima-

ted higher than three guineas an acre. In Nova Scotia, five guineas per acre for clearing, we are informed, is esteemed cheap.[6]

The remaining years of the eighteenth century have been romanticized for the Bahamas in terms reminiscent of the ante-bellum South. Thus one account of Long Island, certainly one of the more prosperous islands at the time, tells of

> the great period after 1778 when the Simms, Knowles, Darville, Fox, Mackenzie and Forsyth families, besides many others, built magnificent homes and assumed sway over huge plantations. Their social life was a reproduction of what they had known in pre-Revolution America, but it is recorded that their care for their slaves was marked. They built roads, imported good horses, drove in carriages, lived generally in luxury . . . The freeing of the slaves marked the closing days of a rather splendid era controlled by a well-born and gentle-blooded people.[7]

Such wealth as there was rested on cheap land, imported capital, and the cotton crops of a few good years. By 1805 insect pests and soil exhaustion had taken their toll, and an exodus of white planters from the colony had begun. New land grants after 1802 failed to stop the drift; one estimate of population in 1801 had the total down to 1,599 whites, 752 free coloured, and 3,861 slaves, but this is improbably low when measured against 8,000 slaves in 1789 and almost 11,000 in 1822.

More important for the future of Bahamian politics than the wealth or poverty of white Bahamians in those years was the nature of their relationship with the Negroes, free and slave, who thereafter would make up the great bulk of the population. Much of the speculation about the character of slavery in the Bahamas turns on a passage in Daniel McKinnen's account of his tour of the colony in 1780, appended to Bryan Edwards's history of the West Indies:

> The negroes of the Bahama Islands discover, in general, more spirit and execution than in the southern part of the West Indies. Something perhaps may be attributed to a more invigorating climate as a physical cause; but I believe more is due to the circumstances in which they are placed. Their labour is allotted to them daily and individually, according to their strength; and if they are so diligent as to have finished it at an early hour, the rest of the day is allowed to them for amusement or their private concerns. The master also frequently superintends them himself; and therefore it rarely happens that they are much subject to the discipline of the whip as where the gangs are large and directed by agents or overseers.[8]

Transmuted through the pen of an apologist for the twentieth century *status quo* like Mary Moseley, who edited the Nassau morning paper, the *Guardian,* for most of the first half of that century, this could become a firm statement that "the slaves in the Bahamas, it would appear, had on the whole little cause for complaint as to their treatment",[9] but the point should be that the small size of Bahamian estates meant that supervision was by the slaves' owners, who were more concerned with the preservation of their capital and less with meeting production targets than hired overseers might have been.[10] Slave owners wishing to quit the ruined Out Islands — as all the islands other than New Providence were called — resisted the imposition of a registration system and the concomitant prohibition of movement of slaves between British colonies. Like the slave-owners of the West Indies, they objected to the programme of amelioration sought by British reformers, arguing that the declining value of their slaves reflected the errors of British policy when, in fact, the principal cause was the reduced state of Bahamian agriculture. In 1824 some of the reforms sought by the British government were placed on the statute book, together with some of the better customs already prevailing, and in 1826 almost all British demands were met. Slaves had the right to own property, and marriage both between slaves and free Negroes was encouraged. Nevertheless, violence against whites remained a serious matter.

> Assault on a white person was punished with death, under the statute of 1784. Other abuse of a white person, under the same statute, was atoned for by a fine of £15, or corporal punishment, not limited in amount or character. In 1824 violence towards whites was made punishable at the discretion of the magistrate before whom the case was brought. The statute of 1827 fixed the penalty at fifty lashes for abusive language or threats against a white person. The death penalty for an assault against a white with a dangerous weapon was reenacted in 1830.[11]

Sir Alan Burns cites legislation from 1718 to 1723 which provided a fine of two pounds, payable to the established church, for burning, cutting, or maiming a slave, but also prescribed a whipping of a slave who did not give way to a white person in the street, and he mentions an incident in 1826 when local residents and the governor expressed their sympathy for a white couple who were fined and imprisoned for cruelty leading to the death of a slave girl.[12] A new governor, Sir James Smyth, soon fell out with the House of Assembly and the chief justice over the flogging of female slaves. Smyth twice dissolved the House and had to govern without the assistance of a legislature for eighteen months of his term (1829–33).

The first registration of slaves in 1822 gave a total of almost eleven thousand, but there was also present in the Bahamas by then a substantial number of free Africans who had been taken from slave ships captured *en route* to the New World. Paul Albury estimates their number for the period 1808–38 as "probably about 3,000".[13] They were settled on a number of Out Islands and at several outlying parts of New Providence; many were made indentured servants, but the indentures were terminated in 1838 at the same time that post-abolition apprenticeships were terminated. Inasmuch as they escaped much of the brutal socialization of slavery, they provided a further factor in the Bahamian deviation from the West Indian slave-plantation norm.

When abolition finally came, the imperial commissioners determined that the average price of slaves in the Bahamas between 1822 and 1830 had been £29 18s 1d. The low value of Bahamian exports meant small compensation. Slave-owners received slightly more than £12 per slave, compared with £20 in Jamaica and £50 in the rapidly expanding colony of Trinidad. A total of £128,000 was paid in 1834 for 4,020 attached praedial (i.e., agricultural) slaves on their owners' land, 270 unattached praedial slaves on others' land, and 3,444 non-praedial slaves not on the land. The average slave-owner held 10.7 slaves. Only eleven owned more than 100 each, the largest owner being Lord John Rolle with 376. Most of the compensation went straight into the pockets of creditors and mortgagees, and the ruin of large-scale agriculture in the islands was complete.

Much of the land previously distributed reverted to the Crown because of the grantees' failure to maintain payment of quitrents; by 1835 over forty thousand hectares had reverted. Squatting began during the brief apprenticeship period that followed abolition and continued when apprenticeship was terminated. The legislature defeated the governor's measures to prevent unauthorized occupation of land, but the price for the purchase of land was set too high to permit proper acquisition of title. Complex procedures for ejectment hampered those title-holders who were still in the Bahamas. Many had left, among them W. E. B. DuBois's white grandfather, either turning their land over to the freed slaves as Rolle did at Exuma or simply abandoning it. The former slaves established small farms, using the techniques of clear-and-burn shifting agriculture, and continued to supplement their diet by fishing. By 1845 the governor reported that wage employment in agriculture was confined to a few favoured locations. The salt industry provided some employment at Turks Island — but then the Turks and Caicos Islands were transferred to Jamaica in 1848 because their communication with Kingston was better than with Nassau. The export of pineapples began in 1842, more than a century after the fruit had been introduced in 1720 by a short-lived settlement of Palatine Germans, and some critrus was sent to the United States, but the mainstay of the economy was wrecking, sometimes conducted in circumstances that recalled the piracy that Woodes Rogers had stamped out early in the previous century. In 1856 the proceeds of wrecks accounted for one-half of the colony's imports and two-thirds of the exports; there were three hundred ships licensed for salvage operations, and over twenty-six hundred licensed wreckers in a total population of twenty-seven thousand.

By the middle of the nineteenth century the constitutional system of the Bahamas had assumed the form that prevailed for the next hundred years. The constitutional history of the Bahamas as a British possession had begun in 1629 when Charles I granted the islands, together with the mainland territory of Carolina, to his attorney-general, Sir Robert Heath. In 1649 William Sayle and his associates in the Company of Eleutherian Adventurers received a new grant from the commonwealth parliament; their republican constitution for a governor, a council of twelve, and a senate of one hundred was over-ambitious for the tiny settlements that resulted and remains only a curious fragment of seventeenth-century social contract-making. In 1670 the Bahamas were re-granted to the Lords Proprietor of Carolina, a group of noblemen, who subsequently leased their possession to Woodes Rogers. Rogers took possession in 1718, and in the terms of the colony's subsequent motto "expelled the pirates and restored commerce". In 1729 a new constitutional regime began and the interests of the Proprietors were bought out in 1733.

A General Assembly of twenty-four members was elected in 1729: eight from Nassau and four each from the Eastern and Western districts of New Providence and from the Eleuthera and Harbour Island districts. At that time the white population was distributed among New Providence 633, Eleuthera 134, and Harbour Island 160, so that first Assembly may well have had a better balance of representation to population than any of its successors for the next two centuries and more. In 1784 the Assembly was enlarged to twenty-five members, representing ten districts; Abaco, Andros, Cat Island, Exuma, and Long Island were enfranchised. In 1799 the Assembly's membership was increased again to twenty-nine, with new representatives from San Salvador and Long Cay and from the Turks and Caicos Islands. The exclusion of the latter group from the colony in 1848 cut the membership back to twenty-eight, but a new distribution restored the number to twenty-nine. This electoral distribution remained in effect until 1967, subject only to the division of the four-member Nassau district into two two-member districts in 1886, the City (Nassau having received a charter in 1861 on the strength of its Anglican cathedral) and the Southern District. Eventually four more members were added to the Eastern and Southern districts in 1960 (see chapter 4). In 1841 the governor's council was divided into the Executive Council and the Legislative Council, and the Bahamas attained the full flowering of the Old Representative System.

The first franchise act to survive, that of 1799, shows that all free white males aged twenty-one and over who were freeholders and had paid fifty pounds duties in the preceding year were entitled to vote. In 1807 free Negroes were given the vote, and by the time of emancipation there were four Negro members of the Assembly. An account of the 1834 general election, however, discloses a pattern of politics that was to continue: "The elections in some of the Out Islands were nominal. In some of these only a few electors would assemble to vote and the poll was easily controlled. In closer settlements the poor inhabitants were dependent on the merchants for their necessaries and were generally indebted to the latter, who could control their votes."[14]

The franchise steadily widened until by the end of the nineteenth century it required merely a freehold of £5 or a household tenancy of £2 8s in New Providence and £1 4s in the Out Islands. At the 1864 election there were 5,949 qualified electors, and even when some allowance is made for the right to register and vote in each constituency where the elector had the requisite property, that figure represents approximately one-sixth of the total population, three times the proportion any West Indian colony had reached by the late 1930s. Writing soon after that election about the opening of the legislature — an even more colourful ceremony then than it is now because of the presence of a Zouave garrison — J. T. W. Bacot commented: "The common people who have no vote are not the least interesting part of the show. They are very proud of the Assembly, and of the equality of race proclaimed by their Parliament, and probably each shirtless spectator feels, that although he himself has no vote at present, there is no knowing what a lucky wreck might do for him."[15]

Interest in and identification with the legislature undoubtedly was a feature of Bahamian life that extended past the 30 to 40 per cent of adult men who could vote, and this situation continued into recent times. The white minority kept control of the legislature not through a restricted franchise but by means of corrupt elections. Twenty years after Bacot, another observer complained:

> This mockery of representation is the greatest farce in the world. The coloured people have the suffrage, subject to a small property qualification, but have no idea how to use it . . . The elections are by open voting, and bribery, corruption and intimidation are carried on in the most unblushing manner under the very noses of the officers presiding over the polling-booths. Nobody takes any notice, and as the coloured people have not yet learnt the art of political organization, they are powerless to defend themselves. The result is that the House of Assembly is little less than a family gathering of Nassau whites, nearly all of whom are related to each other, either by blood or marriage. Laws are passed simply for the

benefit of the family, whilst the coloured people are ground down and oppressed in a manner that is a disgrace to the British flag.[16]

The writer was merely a stipendary magistrate who had fallen out with the Nassau whites, so the views of later and more senior witnesses should be added to his testimony.

Sir George Haddon-Smith, who served in the Bahamas immediately before the First World War, subsequently advised the Colonial Office:

> During my two years in that Colony, where I was treated with great consideration by the House of Assembly, I am bound to say that I was not favourably impressed with the advantages gained by the people under that Constitution. The people in the different Islands were not represented for the simple reason that none of the inhabitants could afford the money or time to reside at Nassau, with the result that the members of the House of Assembly were composed of residents in Nassau with little or no interests in the Islands they were supposed to represent. The ordinary member of the House of Assembly usually had his own axe to grind, and it struck me that to attain his end his whole time was taken up in, what is generally known as "lobbying". As for a progressive Government policy it was almost impossible to succeed, as it was invariably opposed by parties whose personal interests were affected by the proposals.[17]

Sir Alan Burns, colonial secretary of the Bahamas in the 1920s and the last official to win election to the House of Assembly, wrote: "The method adopted for the open voting gave every opportunity for bribery and intimidation . . . The police were powerless in the face of a public opinion which regarded bribery as something rather clever. The price of a vote in certain constituencies was well known, and the electors looked forward to an election which promised them money, unlimited rum, and a great deal of fun."[18] The colonial secretary who followed Burns was Sir Charles Dundas. He later returned as governor, and during his term secured the secret ballot for New Providence in 1937; it was extended to the Out Islands under his successor, the Duke of Windsor. "No out-islander could afford half a year or more in Nassau for attendance at the House, and members were therefore of necessity Nassau residents. The candidate fared forth to his prospective out-island constituency with some show of display to impress the constituents. The voters anticipated 'cakes and ale' — to be more precise, rice and rum."[19]

For the voter, peasant farmer or fisherman, white or Negro, an election was a chance to get something, rum or rice and in later years cash, for nothing. The thought that a vote might in some mysterious way change the conditions of his life probably never crossed his mind. Given the sad state of the colonial Treasury except during the brief booms occasioned by the American Civil War and Prohibition, such a prospect was fairly remote. For the candidates an election was a sporting venture, a chance to compete with their peers in a game played by fathers and sons over several generations. Probably only a handful of the more sophisticated or cunning were conscious that the prevailing rules preserved what little privilege the condition of Bahamian society and the economy permitted them. For a comparable style one can turn to the elections of Regency England,[20] although the racial situation of the Bahamas ensured that no local duchess would ever kiss her butcher for his vote — even if a white Bay Street lawyer (Stafford Sands) would carry Negro farmers ashore on his back on their way to vote as late as the 1940s.

The depression into which the Bahamas had sunk by the middle of the nineteenth century was relieved by the outbreak of the American Civil War. The war coincided with the end of wrecking, brought about by the Imperial Lighthouse Service erecting lighthouses along the main shipping routes past the islands. For a few years Nassau harbour was crowded with ships running cotton from the Confederacy and returning with arms and supplies. Local merchants prospered, although the Out Islands suffered as their small exports of agricultural produce were cut off; enterprising Out Islanders moved to Nassau, a process which has been going on in the Bahamas for a century and a half. The defeat of the Confederacy finished the boom, and a disastrous hurricane in 1866 added to hardships.

The period between the end of the Civil War and the end of the First World War can be characterized as one of general depression with limited development in a few areas. The export of pineapples limped along until wrecked by competition from new producers like Hawaii. Sisal, which had been introduced in 1845, enjoyed brief prosperity during the Spanish-American War when the Philippines were off the world market. The modest citrus exports were ruined by the blue-grey fly. Once again such salvation as there was came from the sea, where the sponge industry developed on the shallow banks of the western Bahamas — by 1901 one-third of the workforce, six thousand men in all, went sponging. Although the captains and crews of the sponging sloops had the freedom to decide where and when, and how hard, they would work, the system of financing their expeditions for provisions and gear — up to 1905 in kind, thereafter in cash — left them in the hands of the merchants and sponge agents, mainly local whites or Dodecanese Greeks, who made the advances for and frequently reaped most of the profits from the voyage. The sponging era has been called "the darkest blot of the Bahamas adventure",[21] which somewhat over-states the case. It gave little opportunity for the spongers to become financially independent, but they usually owned their own houses and bits of farming land at their home settlements and were certainly

more independent than estate workers in the classic plantation economies. The peak of the industry was in 1919, when the Bahamas
supplied a quarter of the world's sponges. Its decline was hastened by
the three hurricanes of 1926, after which artificial planting of sponges
was started; overfishing further weakened the industry, and its destruction was completed by a mysterious marine plague in 1937.

Much more significant for the future prosperity of the colony than
any new crop or marine product was the beginning of a tourist
industry, looking to the United States for custom. The first steps to
promote tourism in the Bahamas were contracts with shipping
companies in the 1850s, but a more substantial development was the
building, with government funds, of the first good hotel, the Royal
Victoria, which opened in time to accommodate the blockade-runners.
After the Civil War the number of Americans coming to Nassau fell
away, and the best tourist year of the nineteenth century, 1873, produced only five hundred winter visitors. A second hotel was built at the
beginning of the twentieth century; when it burned down, government
funds were used to rebuild it as the British Colonial, which opened in
1923. A third hotel, the Fort Montagu, was added in 1928, again with
government capital. By 1939 Nassau had twelve hundred hotel beds,
supplemented by several hundred more in private homes available
at the height of the tourist season, which ran from mid-January to
Easter. In the late 1930s some 11,000 to 15,000 tourists came to
Nassau each year, while another 35,000 to 45,000 stopped for a day
while on ocean cruises. Then the outbreak of the Second World War
and German submarine activity in the area drove away the cruise ships
in 1940, and in 1943 the number of "stop-over" tourists had fallen
to 3,500.

The early days of tourism had a limited impact on the economy.
Sponging and peasant farming provided the livelihood of the great
majority of the population; neither was attractive enough to keep the
more enterprising at home. Many left for Florida, where in 1892 the
eight thousand Bahamians in Key West constituted a third of the town's
population. The First World War did nothing to reduce the movement
of whites and Negroes across the Florida Channel, and between the
1911 and 1921 censuses the population of the colony actually fell by
5 per cent. During the war some twenty-five hundred labourers went to
Charleston to work on the wharves; many never returned. Lacking cash
crops to be stimulated by wartime shortages, the Bahamas benefited
less from the war than did the West Indian colonies. Neither did
returned soldiers have the political impact they had in Jamaica,
Trinidad, and Grenada after the war. Some 1,800 Bahamians volun-
teered; 670 served overseas, and 50 died on active service. But white
Bahamians tended to go north to join the Canadian armed forces,

while Negroes went south to Jamaica to join the British West Indies Regiment. One Bahamian soldier, Sergeant Johnny Demeritte, who had lost both legs in the war, figured prominently in the outbreak of racial rioting in Liverpool before the troops went home, an episode that has been neglected by contemporary politicians searching for local black heroes to honour. The present writer, who knew him well as a boy, had to learn the story from an article by an American historian.

For the Bahamas the events of August 1914 were less important than the passage of the Volstead Act in December 1919. When Prohibition began in the United States, existing stocks of liquor were shipped out to the Bahamas, and when these had been smuggled back to the United States, much more was imported, so that by early 1920 the port of Nassau was once again congested. Bootlegging boosted Treasury receipts through the duty paid on imported liquor. It provided employment for the unskilled in repacking the bottles into smaller sacks for easy handling on the high seas, and it founded a new set of modest fortunes along Bay Street for the liquor wholesalers, the shipping agents, and the more daring few who ran their fast vessels up to the three-mile limit and sometimes across it. A small Florida-style real estate boom on New Providence opened another path to wealth, and on 2 January 1929 Pan-American inaugurated air flights from Miami.

Earlier commentators had condemned "the financial intoxication induced by the large sums of money so rapidly and romantically made in the blockade-running days, whose evil result is a distaste for regular habits of patient industry", and the jeremiads were repeated for bootlegging. In a perceptive passage, G. H. J. Northcroft had written in 1900:

> The agriculture of the Bahamas suffers from the fact that the majority of the inhabitants have fallen under the spell of the sea. The Buccaneer strain is more powerful than that of the Loyalist farmers; the seafaring tendency has more than overcome any inherited agricultural instincts; the Bahamian likes better to haul on the halyards, to trim the sheets, or to hold the tiller than to plod at the plough tail or bend over the hoe. Both climate and circumstances make it pleasanter to lounge on a vessel's deck and watch the swift waves curl back from the leaping prow than to experiment with manure or to wage relentless warfare against persistent weeds. Though the roving life of the wrecker has been almost given up the instincts seem ineradicable from Bahamian blood, and its effects are seen in a strong distaste for a laborious life on shore. So the land is neglected to a lamentable extent; far too many go sponging, fishing and turtling; and more money made in these occupations, with large and impecunious intervals between voyages, is preferred to less money made more regularly and certainly by farming, and at much less risk and discomfort.[22]

Leaving aside the question of how many Bahamian farmers ever had an area of soil sufficiently extensive to follow a plough across it, it certainly was the case that no cash crop ever prospered long enough to convince Bahamians that rewards could come from the land as generously as from the sea. Cotton, pineapples, sisal, tomatoes – each produced a decade or so of prosperity followed by collapse, and the staple ground provisions of pigeon peas and guinea corn were so easily grown that only a limited market in them could develop for the small urban population in Nassau.

Most expatriate officials were suspicious of the Bahamians' ready acceptance of tourism as the mainstay of the economy from the 1920s onwards. Tourism was supplemented principally by sponging, which from 1920 to 1930 involved exports between £105,000 and £150,000 a year, but from 1930 to 1939 exports fell to between £52,000 and £90,000 a year, and in 1939 the sponge beds were wiped out by the plague from which the industry never recovered. One exception among the officials was Sir Bede Clifford, who began his governorship in January 1932 when the Wall Street crash had cut back the modest tourist business of the 1920s and the impending repeal of the Eighteenth Amendment promised the end of bootlegging. In his memoirs Clifford quotes his brisk advice to the Executive Council: "Well, gentlemen, it amounts to this – if we can't take the liquor to the Americans we must bring the Americans to the liquor."[23] His first speech to the legislature advocated the revival of tourism:

> It was a choice between the tourist industry and bankruptcy, as it would have taken much longer to build up an agricultural or other industry, even assuming that any such alternative were practical. Geographical and climate advantages were resources as legitimate as soil and minerals and should not be regarded as menial assets the exploitation of which would undermine the moral fibre of the people. They had been successfully developed in agricultural countries in Europe such as France and Italy with excellent results and no ill effects.[24]

A more typical expatriate view, which reports the opinions of both Clifford's predecessor and his successor, comes from Sir Charles Dundas: "I do not think that either Sir Charles Orr [under whom Dundas served as colonial secretary] or I were very good directors of tourism. Our efforts were devoted more to the out-islands, whose inhabitants derived little direct benefit from tourist traffic. Moreover neither of us regarded it as an altogether wholesome influence. Unfortunately it was none the less indispensable to the economy of the colony."[25] Indeed, one can speculate that had the Bahamas been under crown colony rule rather than the degree of internal self-government the Old Representative

System provided, steps might have been taken to discourage the development of tourism in the 1920s.

Although the Second World War cut off the flow of American tourists to Nassau, the Bahamas prospered as a staging-point on the air route down to Brazil and across the Atlantic at its narrowest to the west coast of Africa, and later as a centre of the Empire Air-training Scheme. During 1942 more than four thousand men were employed on the construction of airfields for the American and British governments. Even when the bases were completed, a thousand were employed by the Royal Air Force and the United States Port Engineers, while several thousand men and women were recruited to go to the United States as farm labourers. Modest efforts were made under the direction of the new governor, the Duke of Windsor, to promote agriculture and balanced development on the Out Islands, partly to meet wartime food shortages and partly to arrest the drift to New Providence. In 1942 one visiting expert, later labour adviser to the controller of development and welfare in the West Indies, urged "that Bahamians should look more to the development of their agricultural, fishing and allied resources than sit awaiting the good old times when tourist money fell into their laps",[26] but this advice was predicated on the assumption that there would be less money to spend on tourist travel after the war. A more realistic assessment of the Bahamian dilemma was made by a British economic adviser two years later, who predicted that the tourist trade would revive after a delay but warned: "At the same time more attention than in the past must be directed to the development of agriculture, fishing, forests and allied industries, upon which the economic stability and the standard of living of large numbers of the population depend."[27]

During the 1930s the Bahamas had been spared — or from the point of political development perhaps one should say missed — the wave of strikes and riots that affected most of the West Indian colonies between 1934 and 1938 and led to the appointment of the Moyne Commission, whose recommendations shaped West Indian political, economic, and social reforms in the early 1940s.[28] In June 1942, however, the Bahamas caught up with their neighbours when a dispute over the wages being paid to construction workers on the New Providence airfield led to a strike, the strike led to a march down Bay Street, and the march ended in violence in which most of the shops along Bay Street were looted. At the height of the trouble some two thousand rioters faced thirty-four policemen; two rioters were killed and five wounded, and another two men were killed in subsequent incidents.

The disturbances were investigated by two rival bodies, a select committee appointed by the House of Assembly and a commission of inquiry appointed by the governor, whose rivalry led to a remarkable opinion supplied the House by the constitutional authority A. B. Keith upholding the power of the legislature to summon officials before it and punish them for contempt if they failed to answer questions. The withholding of official witnesses from the select committee gave the governor's commission the advantage, and its report is the more informative document. The commissioners, an English judge and two white Bahamian businessmen, identified the immediate cause as the high rates of pay given to the American construction workers compared with the four shillings a day given unskilled Bahamian labourers. That rate had been fixed by the British and American government to cover all American bases being built in the western Atlantic and Caribbean under the destroyers-for-bases exchange. The Bahamian minimum daily wage had been set at four shillings in 1937, and in August 1941 the House of Assembly resolved that it would not be expedient to alter the rate at that time. There were then no proper trade unions in the Bahamas, where the relevant legislation copied that passed in Britain in the first half of the nineteenth century. In 1940 the Bahamas had declined to come under the beneficial umbrella of the Colonial Development and Welfare Act, for it would have meant legislating to allow formation of trade unions — in fact one union had been started in 1936 and was moribund in 1942, while another, the Federation of Labour, was set up only a few weeks before the riot.

In such circumstances it is not surprising that the commission received conflicting evidence about whether there were deeper, underlying causes of the trouble:

> On the one hand, we are informed to the effect that there are deeplying causes of discontent among the poorer and labouring classes; that they feel that they do not receive a square deal from their elected representatives, who are collectively known as "Bay Street" (in which street or its immediate neighbourhood all the twenty-nine members of the House of Assembly except two have their place of business); that they feel that taxation is not on an equitable basis; that they are not sufficiently represented in official circles; and that urgent reforms are necessary. On the other hand, we are informed to the effect that no political reforms are necessary or advisable, except possibly the imposition of a higher qualification for a member of the House of Assembly; that the members of the House of Assembly are elected on a democratic and entirely satisfactory basis and discharge their mandate to the satisfaction of the electorate; that the system of taxation is the best that can be devised; that all classes are adequately represented; and that any discontent is due to the Administration.[29]

The commissioners concluded that the disturbances were attributable only to labour issues and the prevailing economic depression, and not to racial questions: "There are, no doubt, a few unwise persons of both races who would not be adverse to racial questions being raised; but our examination of 99 witnesses, of every class, leads us to the conclusion that the suggestions of racial differences would be greatly deprecated and resented by the general body of Bahamians."[30]

NOTES

1. W. K. Brooks, "On the Lucayan Indians", *National Academy of Science Memoirs* 4 (1888): 215.
2. C. A. Hoffman, jun., "Bahama Prehistory: Cultural Adaptation to an Island Environment" (Ph.D. thesis, University of Arizona, 1967), p. 14.
3. W. H. Sears and S. O. Sullivan, "Bahamas Prehistory", *American Antiquity* 43 (1978): 3–25.
4. Peter Martyr D'Anghera, *De Orbe Novo,* ed. F. A. MacNitt (New York: Putnam, 1912), vol. 2, pp. 248, 255, 270.
5. Quoted in *Lost Tribes and Promised Lands: The Origins of American Racism,* by Ronald Sanders (Boston: Little, Brown, 1978), pp. 131–32.
6. Reprinted in the *Guardian* of 15 August 1972.
7. H. MacLachlan Bell, *Bahamas: Isles of June* (London: Williams and Norgate, 1934), p. 50.
8. Quoted by, for example, G. H. J. Northcroft in *Sketches of Summerland* (Nassau: Guardian, 1900), pp. 284–85. Some insights into life on a largish estate at San Salvador are provided by *A Relic of Slavery: Farquharson's Journal for 1831–32* (Nassau: Deans Peggs Research Fund, 1957).
9. Mary Moseley, ed., *The Bahamas Handbook* (Nassau: Guardian, 1926), p. 94.
10. Contrast, for example, the situation in Jamaica: "The basic and dominating element in Jamaican slave society was that of absenteeism. This element was central to whole social order and was in some way related to almost every other aspect of society. So central was it indeed, and so much was it the root of all evils of the system, that we may describe the white Jamaican community as an absentee society." Orlando Patterson, *The Sociology of Slavery* (London: MacGibbon and Kee, 1967), p. 33.
11. James M. Wright, "History of the Bahama Islands, with a special Study of the Abolition of Slavery in the Colony", in *The Bahama Islands,* ed. G. B. Shattuck, (New York: Johns Hopkins Press, 1905), p. 456.
12. Sir Alan Burns, *History of the British West Indies* (London: Allen and Unwin, 1954), pp. 472, 634.
13. Paul Albury, *The Story of the Bahamas* (London: Macmillan, 1975), p. 129.
14. Wright, "History of the Bahama Islands", p. 521, n. 447.
15. J. T. W. Bacot, *The Bahamas* (London: Longmans, 1869), p. 103.
16. L. D. Powles, *The Land of the Pink Pearl* (London: Sampson Low, 1888), p. 41.
17. C. O. 321/309/02955, governor Windwards to the secretary of state (25 November 1920).
18. Alan Burns, *Colonial Civil Servant* (London: Allen and Unwin, 1949), pp. 270–71.
19. Charles Dundas, *African Crossroads* (London: Macmillan, 1955), p. 193; for a local reply to a similar view expressed in 1902, see Harcourt Malcolm, *A History of the Bahamas House of Assembly* (Nassau, 1921), p. 55.
20. For example, A. Halévy, *England in 1815,* 2nd ed. (London: Benn, 1949), p. 152, which sounds remarkably like Bahamian elections before 1956.

21. *Bahamian Times,* 16 July 1969; see *The Sponging Industry* (Nassau, 1974), a booklet of an exhibition of historical documents at the Nassau Public Records Office.
22. Northcroft, *Sketches of Summerland,* pp. 183–84.
23. Bede Clifford, *Proconsul* (London: Evans, 1964), p. 194.
24. Ibid., p. 195.
25. Dundas, *African Crossroads,* pp. 158–59.
26. [F. A. Norman], *Report on the Labour Position in the Bahamas* (Nassau, 1942), p. 4.
27. H. J. Richardson, *Review of Bahamian Economic Conditions and Post-war Problems* (Nassau, 1944), p. 6.
28. An incident at Inagua in 1937 is sometimes mistakenly listed among the 1934–38 West Indian riots: Two brothers forced the commissioner and the American owner-manager of the salt works off the island and later murdered a farmer they suspected of being friendly with the American. Only the two took any active part in the incident, but they probably had some local sympathy; both were hanged for the murder. There are no similarities with the mass actions of the West Indian riots.
29. [Sir Alison Russel, H. McKinney, and H. Brown], *Report of the Commission Appointed to Enquire into Disturbances in the Bahamas Which Took Place in June, 1942* (Nassau, 1942), p. 40.
30. Ibid., p. 58.

2

Race Relations in the Bahamas

What in fact *was* the racial situation in the Bahamas by the 1940s? Before attempting an answer to that question, a brief comment on the study of race relations is advisable. The distinguished American sociologist Oliver Cox has warned that: "It is not ordinarily realized that, of all the great mass of writing on race relations, there is available no consistent theory of race relations."[1] John Rex, while declaring that "the problem of race and racism challenges the conscience of the sociologist in the same way as the problem of nuclear weapons challenges that of the nuclear physicist", is equally cautious: "Yet it is important to realize that sociology as a discipline has had some difficulty in coming to grips with this problem."[2]

The present writer has no qualifications to join a debate which has been both wide-ranging in the illustrative material employed and high-flown in the general theories espoused. Such qualifications as can be offered to justify attempting this book derive from the experience of growing up in the place in question at a time when racial distinctions were an obvious fact of life and from training in and practice of the discipline of political science. Another sort of social scientist, whether or not he or she happened to have been born a Bahamian, would no doubt have written a very different sort of book. It is submitted that the Bahamian experience is too deviant, even from the norm of the British Caribbean, to support any attempt to establish new theory or even to go very far towards endorsing established theory. At the same time it may be that the detailed record of one society's change over a quarter-century which is supplied here can become a useful building block for architects with a grander vision.

In attempting to refine the concept of racial differences, a necessary first step to attacking our problem, the work of M. G. Smith is particularly helpful: "In most Negro-white populations, the concept of colour is critical and pervasive, hence we can expect on general grounds that it may have several distinct though overlapping referants. A systematic analysis of the colour concept therefore consists of isolating these different meanings, and of determining the relations between them."[3] Smith himself distinguished five dimensions of the colour concept:

1. Appearance, or *phenotypical colour*
2. Biological status, what might be termed family antecedents, or *genealogical colour*
3. The colour of those with whom the person typically associates, or *associational colour*
4. Conformity to the norms associated with a hierarchically ranked cultural tradition when such norms are associated with colour-differentiated groups, or *cultural or behavioural colour*
5. "An abstract analytic category reflecting the distributions and types of power, authority, knowledge, and wealth, which together define and constitute the social framework",[4] or *structural colour*

Whenever there is reference to racial or colour differences in the Bahamas, it is advisable to ask the purpose for which the concept has been introduced by the analyst, or the use to which it is being put by the man in the street.

Given the long and close association over three centuries between two racial groups in the Bahamas, there has been ample opportunity to develop complex variations within the framework Smith has provided. For the purposes of this book, focused as it is on political change, *structural colour* will usually be the most important dimension because, as Smith says:

> When we speak of structural colour, we imply an allocation of these variables (power, authority, knowledge, and wealth) among color-differentiated groups which obtains presently and reflects historical conditions. Thus structural color connotes the empirical distribution of these variables among the color-differentiated population. If we like, we can distinguish between contemporary and historical scales of structural color, and for certain purposes, such as the analysis of a rapidly changing situation, a distinction of this type may be essential.[5]

Among the variables Smith lists, wealth has had pre-eminent place in the Bahamas. Wealth was more likely to attract power or authority than the other way around. Underlying the colour concept — that is, the idea of racial difference — has been an economic relationship. Without hazarding an opinion on the question whether there was racism before Western capitalism began its expansion into the rest of the world, it is indisputable that the institutions of slavery which shaped Bahamian society produced what Cox called "the purest form of established race relations" by defining an entire racial group, the African slaves, as chattels. In the earliest years of the West Indian and southern mainland colonies, there were whites whose status as indentured servants differed little from that of the African slaves, but quite soon it became racial difference rather than class difference that determined the predominant features of social, economic, and political relationships. In Cox's terms, racial antagonism so suffused other interests that class differences were held in abeyance.[6] After the abolition of slavery, the new order — which Cox called the ruling-class situation — produced a hierarchy dependent in the main on apparent degrees of admixture of white descent.

Given the creation of a multiracial Bahamian society within the legal and social caste distinctions of slavery, it was inevitable that race relations would remain hierarchic in character even after the legal basis for caste had been removed. However, as Smith observes, in multiracial societies in which racial differences have acquired status significance, there will be cultural heterogenity, with the dominant culture having high prestige and the subordinate culture less prestige, but it will also be the case that the hierarchic race relations will reflect that cultural heterogenity and tend to lose that hierarchic character as cultural uniformity increases.[7] In one of his empiricial studies, Smith characterizes two sets of value orientations, one of which is ascriptive and tends to reinforce the prevailing hierarchy of cultural differences by stressing "racial descent and family ties, inheritance of status, property, education abroad, quasi-hereditary organizational position, and associational exclusiveness", while the other favours "individualistic achievements of status, income, occupational and organizational roles, standards of living, and so forth", and therefore tends to cut across and weaken the prevailing hierarchical relationship.[8]

Between the abolition of slavery and the Second World War, Bahamians enjoyed only brief periods of prosperity, which came and went suddenly and unexpectedly. Individuals had opportunities to gain wealth, albeit on a modest scale by the standards of the wider world, and those opportunities rested more on personal initiative than on inherited status. As one governor put it, "Their ways in the past had not bred in the Bahamians the quality of perseverance. They were opportunists, and in the past they had not lacked for opportunities."[9] Their own economic experience, reinforced by the pervasive influence of North American society close to hand, showed what the individual could achieve if he took risks, and so an individualistic set of value orientations ran strongly in the Bahamas. The period of sustained prosperity that began during the Second World War and has continued for an unprecedented period encouraged tendencies already firmly emplanted in Bahamian value systems to develop and thereby undermine the previously dominant hierarchic system surviving from the days of slavery.

The present writer's predisposition to such a view has been reinforced by observations from a study of the settlement of New Plymouth on Green Turtle Cay, Abaco:

New Plymouth's two ethnic groups, whites of British ancestry and blacks of West African ancestry, have long since become culturally similar through the acculturation of the slave population during the period from the sixteenth to the nineteenth century. This accultura- tion process took place in the American colonies until the American Revolution and in the Bahama Islands subsequent to the migration of the Loyalists and their slaves during the 1780s. On Green Turtle Cay, due to such factors as white racism and the socio-economic stratification of the settlement, the process of cultural convergence has never yielded complete cultural homogeneity; each ethnic group possesses a degree of cultural distinctiveness.

Three stages seem to be involved in the process that has kept the settlements' two ethnic groups from becoming completely culturally homogeneous. First, New Plymouth's component populations have been separated from each other. This separation has been in terms of relative physical isolation due to residential segregation, frequently segregated work schedules, recreational segregation, and the like. Beyond this, segregation has existed in terms of social distance when physical separation could not be maintained. Second, differen- tial interaction has taken place. That is, people tend to interact more frequently and more significantly with members of their own group than with members of other such groups. Third, growing out of these twin conditions of separation and differential interaction, differences in culture are maintained or even created. These derive from differences in resources, personal association, and shared ideas.[10]

But, as another field-worker who examined three adjacent settlements at Abaco — Dundas Town, Murphy Town, and Crossing Rocks — writes:

Rigid class lines are not present in the Bahamas . . . but there is social distinction between coloreds and whites, and the whites, by and large, are the wealthier class and the coloreds the poorer class. There is a high degree of vertical mobility in the Bahamas and there seems to be an ever-increasing middle class equally populated by both races. Neither the colored nor the whites are afraid of manual labor and are more interested in achieving success through money than retaining social amenities according to colour.[11]

Until tourist developments extended to the Out Islands in the 1960s, there were few Out Islanders who could have been called middle class by the standards of Nassau. In the large settlements a shopkeeper or two, perhaps the proprietor of the local bar-room, the largest land- owners (where cash crops were available), some boat-owners, and the government's local representatives — the commissioner (who was usually a Bahamian rather than an expatriate), the occasional doctor,

and the school-teacher — enjoyed cash incomes and housing which were
superior to their neighbours' but well below what was available in
Nassau. One student, whose field-work was conducted at Long Bay
Cays in southern Andros, where there had never been resident whites,
concluded:

> Racial interactions are quite different in Nassau from what they are
> in the Out Islands. Nassau blacks are much more resentful and
> antagonistic towards whites. Local observers believe this is because
> of the discrimination urban blacks have received throughout their
> history of association with dominant whites. On the other hand,
> blacks living in the Out Islands have not had first hand realization
> of racial discrimination.[12]

It is unlikely that this student would have come to so firm a conclusion
had she worked at Abaco, Eleuthera, or Long Island.

Just as the numerical ratio prevailing between the two races is an
important factor distinguishing race relations in the Bahamas (and
Bermuda) from the British West Indian colonies, for the same reason
within the Bahamas there have been substantial differences among
the various islands and even among settlements on particular islands.
In the Bahamas as a whole the proportion of the population describing
itself as "white" has never fallen below 10 per cent. For a century
after abolition, local censuses did not ask a question about race, either
from delicacy or acceptance of the artificiality of the answers that
would be provided — so one can only guess at the stages by which the
one-third ratio of 1786 and the 29 per cent of 1826 fell to 11.5 per
cent at the 1943 census when the question was asked once more. Quite
probably the sharpest decline occurred before 1850. In 1869 Bacot
commented that it was difficult to obtain statistics for the Out Islands,
"at one island the white population prevailing, in another the black;
the two races having, at present, a tendency to keep apart, than to
amalgamate".[13] Table 1 shows the figures at the 1953 census. Apart
from New Providence, the only substantial white communities were
located at Abaco, Harbour Island and Spanish Wells, Eleuthera, and
Long Island, though the beginning of economic development at Grand
Bahama and Bimini had introduced a new group of white residents.
The presence of a large "mixed" race proportion at Long Island and the
Crooked Island group marks the earlier presence of white populations
by then much diminished at Long Island and totally fled from Crooked
Island.

For New Providence we can examine the figures for the thirty-six
census collectors' districts into which the island was divided. With
approximately 15 per cent of the population reported as "white",
93 per cent of those whites resided in districts in which more than 20

Table 1. Racial identification of population, 1953.

Electoral Districts	N†	Black	Mixed	White
		%	%	%
New Providence	45,670	70.4	14.9	14.8
Andros, including Berry Is.	7,461	94.7	4.0	1.3
Grand Bahama, including Bimini	5,419	78.4	13.3	8.3
Abaco	3,408	59.8	6.6	33.6
Harbour Island*	1,526	40.1	3.5	56.4
Eleuthera*	6,056	71.5	17.5	10.9
Cat Island	3,201	96.9	2.7	0.4
Exuma	2,919	95.9	2.1	2.0
San Salvador, including Rum Cay	827	88.3	6.2	5.6
Long Island, including Ragged Island	4,076	35.3	50.8	13.8
Crooked Island, including Acklins and Long Cay	2,189	76.2	23.4	0.3
Inagua, including Mayaguana	1,603	90.3	5.9	3.7

* The settlements of Current, Bogue, and Upper and Lower Bluff, which comprised part of the Harbour Island electoral district until 1968, are here included in Eleuthera.

† Excludes "Mongolian" and "not stated".

per cent of the population was white but only 22 per cent in districts more than 40 per cent white. Only two of the thirty-six districts reported no whites, but in a total of seventeen of the districts, whites constituted less than 5 per cent, twelve 5–10 per cent, sixteen 11–20 per cent, and remaining seven 21–30 per cent. Thus while there was a considerable degree of residential segregation of the white population, it was far from complete, being largely confined to a thin line of housing along the northern shore of the island and a substantial, and growing, pocket at Centreville on the eastern edge of the old City of Nassau.

Harmannus Hoetink, calling attention to the differences in the roles of mixed-race groups in the southern United States and in the West Indian colonies settled from north-western Europe (Britain, France, and Holland), attributes them to the presence of a "poor white" class in the United States. Although there were pockets of "poor whites" in the West Indies, notably Barbados, they were not, as in the southern states, more numerous than the slaves. In the Deep South, Hoetink argues, the lowest economic category of whites, fearful of social dominance by successful non-whites, stressed physical charac-teristics in all social relations, even the non-intimate, and their extensive definition of the Negro community came to be accepted by the white elite.[14] In the Bahamas there was a substantial "poor white"element in New Providence and certain of the Out Islands — Abaco, Eleuthera with Harbour Island and Spanish Wells, and Long Island — and the reinforce-ment of close cultural ties, for white and Negro Bahamians alike, with the southern United States.

Two other factors must be mentioned as probable influences on Bahamian departures from the Caribbean norm. One is suggested by a valuable study of communities of sugar-estate workers and fishermen on Antigua in the Leeward Islands of the West Indies by Joel Aronoff:

> The cane cutter's family structure appears to be similar to that model found in the literature on the Negro family in which the family is marginal to the dominant mother-child relationship . . . The family of the fishermen, on the other hand, is an integrated unit in which the father is extremely active and assumes respon-sibility for many tasks in regard to the children which the cane cutter leaves to the mother. Also, it will be seen . . . that the male and female themselves interact over a much greater range of activities than is the case in cane cutters' families.[15]

Aronoff records the greater self-reliance of the fishermen compared with the cane-cutters and their great feeling of personal security. These he attributes to the motivations of the fishermen, who are independent and control their own actions and are therefore self-motivated in a way that the cane-cutters, who "are bound to the vicissitudes of a cane economy, with a crop season of intensive labor and a dull season of major under-employment",[16] cannot be. The fishermen's pay is relatively good and can come in large sums, permitting purchase of big items. They are not exploited physically, or financially, and there are intrinsic rewards in fishing which make the men feel attuned to the job. Finally, there is considerable egalitarianism: "The pot fish crew is an integrated unit of equals. Although there are two main positions, captains and men, in practice the respect which each man receives in the crew is not based on the position he occupies, as in the cutting gang. Rather, the opinion one fisherman holds of another is the result of that man's total behaviour — both on land and sea."[17] The tradition of seafaring runs deep in Bahamian society among whites and Negroes alike. Inter-island transport and the exploitation of the resources of the sea, whether fish, sponges, turtles, or conch, demanded that most Bahamian men went to sea in small boats. One of the strongest objections Bahamian slave-owners had to the system of registration was that it hampered the use of slaves on boats plying among the islands.

The second is a matter of history. William B. Rogers found that the Abaco communities he studied lacked many of the characteristics of "plantation-America" identified by Charles Wagley, and concluded that this was a consequence of brief exposure to the plantation system: "Many of the new plantations collapsed almost immediately and all of them were extinct by 1834. At the longest this is only a period of time of some 50 years which is hardly sufficient time for the institution to become engrained in the culture and have lasting influences a hundred years later. It is true that the plantations brought large Negro populations to the Bahamas, but it is probable that the cultural and societal forms that exist today probably owe more to Africa and the Bahamian adaptive environment than they owe to the institution of the plantation" — although, he adds, "many of the transported slaves were brought from formerly established plantations in the southern United States and consequently their exposure was considerably longer".[18]

A firm conclusion on the point is impossible. Perhaps it would be possible to identify particular settlements which derived from plantations founded by Loyalists whose slaves had been in North America for several generations and make significant comparisons with other settlements whose history was different. Before it was incorporated into the urban sprawl of Nassau, it was said that the settlement of Fox Hill on New Providence, which had originally been formed by Africans taken directly from the slave ships, was different. But population movements in the century and a half since abolition make it extremely unlikely that any settlement, however remote, could provide an adequate test. Thus if one calculates the number of persons born at each Out Island who were living (or visiting) at New Providence at the time of the 1953 census as a percentage of the population of that island, it is obvious that massive mixing of the Bahamian population has taken place. The Crooked Island group leads the table at 76 per cent, followed by Exuma at 68 per cent, Long Island (including Ragged Island) 65 per cent, San Salvador (including Rum Cay) 64 per cent, Cat Island 62 per cent, Abaco 54 per cent, Andros (including the Berry Islands) 53 per cent, Eleuthera 47 per cent, Harbour Island (including Spanish Wells) 39 per cent, and Inagua (including Mayaguana) 38 per cent. The one, exceptionally low, figure that stands out is Grand Bahama (including Bimini) at only 12 per cent, but this has been distorted by the substantial recent growth in both Grand Bahama and Bimini where the population had increased by 75 per cent since the previous census in 1943. If allowance is made for modest movement among the Out Islands as well as into New Providence it appears that between one-third and one-half the Out Islanders were then living on an island other than that of their birth; that scale of movement has continued in the subsequent quarter-century.

Thus while it is possible to identify differing components within the mosaic of Bahamian society, it would be a mistake to put too much weight on close studies of individual Out Island settlements. Figures are available from the 1963 census which show the extent of inter-island mixing by then. Each of the districts listed in table 1 showed between 10 and 15 per cent of the population born in other districts, with three exceptions — Harbour Island and Spanish Wells, with only 8 per cent; Long Island and Ragged Island, with only 7 per cent; and New Providence, with 30 per cent.

At the same time, it should be noted that until the 1960s, despite the substantial exodus of Bahamians to the United States and the frequency of contacts with that country, Bahamian society had experienced little impact from the settlement of non-Bahamians in the islands. Table 2 shows the proportion of those born outside the Bahamas — including many born in the United States whose Bahamian parents happened to be temporarily in the United States or whose mothers had travelled to Miami for their confinements amid better medical facilities — counted at the four censuses up to 1953.

Table 2. Percentage of population born outside the Bahamas.

	1921	1931	1943	1953
United Kingdom	0.3	0.4	0.4	0.9
Other Europe	0.1	0.2	0.2	0.2
Canada	0.1	0.1	0.1	0.3
United States	0.9	2.0	1.6	2.2
West Indies	0.5	1.1	1.3	3.0
Other countries	0.1	0.1	0.2	0.4
N	53,031	59,828	68,846	84,841

Sir Etienne Dupuch has argued that at the beginning of the twentieth century Bahamian society was divided into:

(1) the British official class: "On top of this structure sat the Governor and his English officials, the Governor like a great silent Buddha. In those days it was only necessary for a man to say he was an Englishman. That was his passport. Immediately he became a small Buddha and he was put on a shelf just below the pedestal reserved for the BIG BUDDHA."

(2) the Bahamian whites, divided into "the Government House crowd" who received invitations to Government House, and the rest:

(3)   the coloured majority: "The coloured people were split in groups, determined entirely by degree of colour, starting with black at the bottom, through to off-black, dark brown, light brown, 'high-yaller' and near white."

At the turn of the century, we lived in a very complex society, every man had a place and every man was expected to know his place. Any attempt to cross lines − up or down − was severely frowned upon . . . Each group − right from the top down to the lowest level − played one set against the other.[19]

That sounds remarkably like a typical West Indian situation. Yet on other occasions Dupuch has attributed the introduction of racial segregation to the influence of American tourism in the 1920s, or to be more precise from the connection of Henry Flagler, the promotor of southern Florida, with the first British Colonial Hotel. Both opinions require some qualification. The first place, the British official class, was numerically very small; it comprised only the governor, the three principal officials − the colonial secretary, the attorney-general, and the receiver-general − plus a few senior officials with particular expertise in the police, engineering, and health services. Many departmental heads were normally Bahamians, although recruited from the white and light-complexioned Negro communities. Government representatives on the Out Islands, resident magistrates and later commissioners, were almost invariably Bahamians, and they were the officials who represented "government" to the bulk of the population. Further, whatever their influence in Nassau's polite society, the expatriate officials were curtailed in their political authority by the Old Representative System. The governor's administrative authority was confronted by the legislature's financial authority, which in the absence of British subsidies was complete. Even his administrative authority was eroded by the existence of numerous public boards, composed largely of members of the House of Assembly and their political allies, with statutory powers of their own and the ear of the House on financial questions. Nor was there an expatriate planting or commercial interest to back up British officials, socially or politically. White Bahamian merchants and lawyers held the levers of economic power, controlled such credit as was available to the rest of the population apart from the one bank − a branch of the Royal Bank of Canada − and the import of foodstuffs and export of cash crops and marine products.

For those social purposes which centred on Government House, a tidy three-tiered pyramid may have existed, but elsewhere the expatriate factor was at most marginal. Nor did Bahamians need Flagler to show them how to run racial segregation. An American crudeness of perception may have hammered out some of the complications of West Indian-style elaborations of colour distinctions, but accounts of the preceding half century make it clear that in 1900 Bahamians formed a single society deeply divided into two antagonistic groups by racial differences. So it was too in 1950, but by then the rest of the world was changing and a few Bahamians believed that change was needed in their islands.[20]

NOTES

1. Oliver C. Cox, *Caste, Class and Race* (New York: Monthly Review Press, 1971), p. ix.
2. John Rex, *Race Relations in Sociological Theory* (London: Weidenfeld and Nicolson, 1970), p. 1; for some comment on the problem, see Jenny Bourne, "Cheerleaders and Ombudsmen: The Sociology of Race Relations in Britain", *Race and Class* 21 (1980): 331–52.
3. M. G. Smith, *A Framework for Caribbean Studies* (Mona: University of the West Indies, 1955), p. 60.
4. Ibid., p. 65.
5. Ibid.
6. Cox, *Caste, Class and Race*, p. 344.
7. Smith, *Framework for Caribbean Studies*, p. 63.
8. M. G. Smith, *Stratification in Grenada* (Berkeley: University of California Press, 1965), p. 251.
9. Charles Dundas, *African Crossroads* (London: Macmillan, 1955), p. 154.
10. Alan Gary LaFlamme, "Green Turtle Cay: A Bi-Racial Community in the Out-Island Bahamas" (Ph.D. thesis, State University of New York at Buffalo, 1972), pp. 60–61.
11. William Blackstock Rodgers III, "The Wages of Change: An Anthropological Study of the Effects of Economic Development on Some Negro Communities in the Out Island Bahamas" (Ph.D. thesis, Stanford, 1965), p. 22; much of the material in this thesis is given in William B. Rodgers, "Developmental Exposure and Changing Vocational Preferences in the Out Island Bahamas", *Human Organization* 28 (1969): 270–78, and William B. Rodgers and Richard E. Gardner, "Linked Changes in Values and Behavior in the Out Island Bahamas", *American Anthropologist* 71 (1969): 21–35.
12. Kathleen Burch Clegg, "Political Change in the Bahamas: Its Relation to Modernization" (Ph.D. thesis, University of Texas at Austin, 1975), p. 9.
13. J. T. W. Bacot, *The Bahamas* (London: Longmans, 1869), p. 78.
14. Harmannus Hoetink, *The Two Variants in Caribbean Race Relations* (London: Oxford University Press, 1967), pp. 161–65.
15. Joel Aronoff, *Psychological Needs and Cultural Systems* (Princeton, N.J.: Van Nostrand, 1967), pp. 180–81.
16. Ibid., p. 36.
17. Ibid., p. 141.
18. Rodgers, "The Wages of Change", pp. 24, 25.
19. Sir Etienne Dupuch, *Tribune Story* (London: Benn, 1967), p. 64.
20. On Bahamian history generally, see A. Deans Peggs, *A Short History of the Bahamas* (Nassau: Tribune, 1955), Michael Craton, *A History of the Bahamas* (London: Collins, 1962), and Paul Albury, *The Story of the Bahamas* (London: Macmillan, 1975). A travel book which contains a fair amount of history is George Hunte's *The Bahamas* (London: Batsford, 1975), and

mention should also be made of two slight novels which purport to describe Bahamian politics — Jack Weeks, *The Grey Affair* (New York: Dell, 1961) and Robert Wilder, *An Affair of Honor* (New York: Putnam, 1969) — so that they may be avoided.

3

The Rise of Party Politics,
1953-57

At Whitehall and Westminster no news from the colonies has generally been good news. In the 1940s and 1950s the Bahamas sought no grants from the British Treasury to balance the local budget or advance local development, and chose to remain without Colonial Development and Welfare benefits rather than reform local legislation. There were few British investments in the colony to worry about, but nevertheless the growing tourist industry was making a substantial contribution to the sterling area's dollar pool.

Table 3. Growth in tourism, 1949-56.

	Number of Tourists	Percentage Increase over Previous Year
1949	32,018	
1950	45,371	41.7
1951	68,502	51.0
1952	84,718	23.7
1953	90,485	6.8
1954	109,605	21.1
1955	132,434	20.8
1956	155,003	17.0

The handful of British MPs who had an acquaintance with the Bahamas were socialites rather than socialists, and their contacts were with the Bay Street elite or British or American winter residents, rather than with Negro union leaders or politicians. Because of its high cost of living and entertainment obligations, Nassau had never been an attractive post for ambitious governors seeking to make a reputation before moving on to a bigger and more important colony, and the two governors of the early 1950s were not career men at all. One, Sir Robert Neville, had had a military career in the Royal Marines, and his successor, the Earl of Ranfurly, came from insurance broking in the

Bay Street in the early 1950s (Courtesy of Bahamas News Bureau)

City of London. Neither pressed a confrontation with local politicians, although Neville's extension of the list of those invited to Government House and readiness to talk with local "radicals" earned him unpopularity with Bay Street and a corresponding degree of popularity "over the hill" with the Negro population. Nor did the Bahamas at this time possess a strong colonial secretary, such as Sir Alan Burns had been in the 1920s, who might have pushed his governor into action. While the Colonial Office's long experience of colony-watching must have made it obvious that sooner or later the as-yet-unnamed winds of change that had blown through all the West Indies would eventually strike the Bahamas, official policy, if it existed at all, must have hoped later rather than sooner, and the presence of a Conservative government in Westminster between 1951 and 1964 ensured that the burden of proof for the proposition that change was required would lie heavily on Bahamian reformers.

The Bahamian middle and working classes lacked the Colonial Office's long view of colonial change. But they also lacked the political leaders to challenge the prevailing assumption that the Bahamas were different from other colonies, and even the institutions — such as political parties and trade unions — that might have thrown up such leaders. For the time being most Bahamians were bemused by the growing prosperity that tourism was once again bringing to New Providence and inhibited by the lack of opportunities for political expression. Any reformer would need to show that the existing system, whether in its social, political, or economic form, was unsatisfactory, and that change would be better. First of all he would have to show that change was even possible.

Two main political forums were then available. One was the local press, which consisted of two dailies and one weekly. The morning paper, the *Nassau Guardian*, dated back to 1844; recently it had passed from the hands of the Moseley family, which had run it for a century, to a group of white Bay Street business and professional men. Its bitter rival was the evening paper, the *Nassau Tribune,* founded in 1903, and now owned and edited by the son of the paper's founder, Etienne Dupuch, member of the House of Assembly for the Eastern District of New Providence, and long a critic of the Bay Street establishment. Dupuch was born in Nassau, where his great-grandfather, a Frenchman, had settled in 1840. He served in the BWI Regiment in Egypt and Italy, and like many another colonial soldier was alienated by the racial discrimination practised against coloured troops.[1] His father died at the beginning of the war, and on his return he took over the *Tribune,* where he quickly acquired the reputation of a trouble-maker by attacking established authority. The reputation was intensified by his conversion from the Plymouth Brethren to Catholicism, then a numerically small and suspect denomination in the Bahamas. He left Nassau for a few years to study at a Catholic college in Minnesota and in 1925 was elected to the House of Assembly, where a great-uncle, his father, and an elder brother had sat before him. He held Inagua until 1942, when he was defeated by a vigorous Bay Street effort, but in 1949 won one of the two Eastern District seats for New Providence.

The third paper, the *Nassau Herald,* started by H. W. Brown in 1937, edited for many years by Stanley Lowe and then by Brown again after Lowe's death in January 1953, was, in the eyes of white Bahamians, even more subversive of the natural and proper order of society than was the *Tribune.* In January 1954 Brown sold the paper to W. W. Cartwright and Urban Knowles. In the early 1950s each of the dailies sold three thousand to four thousand copies, while the *Herald,* which appeared irregularly, probably sold fewer than one thousand. Given the concentration of population in New Providence, these figures represent an effective cover of the politically interested. The only other mass medium was the local radio station, ZNS, operated by the government and providing very little political news. Although each of the newspapers took a strong editorial line on most questions of the day, their columns were open to letter writers of all persuasions, and they provide the principal source on which any political history of the Bahamas for this period must depend. It should be noted, however, that Nassau lies close enough to Florida for local radios to pick up Miami stations, and the *Miami Herald* was read by some whites. As air transport grew, New York and even London newspapers were readily available to the politically conscious, as were weekly news magazines like *Time,* and Miami television could be watched despite poor reception. On the other hand, the influential West Indian newspapers, the *Jamaica Gleaner* and the *Trinidad Guardian,* were not readily available.

The other forum was the House of Assembly, elected in 1949. Of the twenty-nine members, eight were employing Smith's concept of *structural colour,* Negro.[2] Five of these sat for New Providence constituencies, and as this island now contained slightly over half the colony's population but had only eight House seats, this bias in favour of the Out Islands almost certainly restricted the number of Negro MHAs. Among the white members, only three or four could be regarded as sympathetic to proposals for social reform, or at least open-minded in their commitment to existing arrangements, and their degree of liberalism did not run to tampering with the ancient constitution or challenging the economic precepts of no income tax, reliance on customs duties for revenue, and minimal government spending. Because of the importance of the House of Assembly, its Speaker occupied an influential position in political affairs through his control of debate and the appointment of select committees by means of which the

House did much of its work. The Speaker since 1946 had been Asa Pritchard, one of the members for Eleuthera.

Under the Old Representative System effective control over Bahamian affairs was divided between the House, with its power to raise revenue and authorize expenditure; the governor and his civil servants, who carried out the day-to-day work of administration; and the hybrid public boards which determined policy in a number of important areas. The principal instrument of executive government was the governor's Executive Council, comprising *ex officio* the colonial secretary, the attorney-general, and the receiver-general, and five members of the House chosen by the governor; although it was possible to choose a member of the Executive Council from outside the House, this was rarely done. One of the five was designated leader of the government in the House, and assumed responsibility for such measures as the governor and the Executive Council wanted brought before the House, but as no principle of collective responsibility was recognized, the leader was an unreliable ambassador either of House to Executive Council or of Executive Council to House of Assembly. In the penultimate resort, by dissolving the House the governor could put local politicians to the trouble and expense of fighting a general election; but like other and better-known systems based on the separation of powers, the Bahamian Constitution survived on the basis of compromise and, in many important spheres, inactivity. If all else failed, the governor could have had recourse to imperial legislation, invoking the House of Commons either to pass a particular piece of legislation applicable to the Bahamas or even sweeping away the old Constitution and imposing one of the new models. While this was a threat individual governors may have used against recalcitrant Executive Councils or Houses of Assembly — for example, to compel introduction of the secret ballot — the political consequences of resorting to West-minster were incalculable. The other chamber of the legislature, the nominated Legislative Council, drew most of its members from veterans of the House put out to grass. Jealous of its own prerogatives and occasionally conscious of a wider view of the national interest than ordinarily prevailed in the House of Assembly, the Legislative Council frequently acted as a brake on House decisions but lacked the will and the opportunity to initiate action. Very few Negroes had ever been appointed to the upper chamber. Apart from small boards of works, elected by Out Island settlements to spend their allocations of a few hundred pounds a year on local roads, docks, and wells, there was no local government in the Bahamas — nor is there to this day.

The first step towards a new sort of politics came in October 1953 with the formation of the Progressive Liberal Party, the PLP. Earlier in the year a "Christian Democratic Party" had been reported, and by

H. M. Taylor (Courtesy of *Tribune*)

Cyril Stevenson (Courtesy of *Guardian*)

September it was claiming five hundred members,³ but it vanished without trace, and the PLP can properly claim to be the first Bahamian political party. The initiative came from W. W. Cartwright, a Negro member of the House for Cat Island, a real estate agent, and publisher of a small non-political magazine. Following three organizing meetings on 2, 9, and 18 October, formation of the party was announced. H. M. Taylor, one of the members for Long Island, was chosen chairman and Cartwright treasurer. Cyril Stevenson of the *Herald* became secretary-general, Clement Pinder assistant secretary, J. S. Carey vice-chairman, and Urban Knowles chaplain. The officers together with Paul Farrington, F. N. Russell, and H. W. Brown constituted an executive board. Charles Rhodriquez, who had been president of the 1942 labour federation, was associated with the party.

A slightly later recruit was Lynden Pindling, a young lawyer who had just returned from London where he had taken an LL.B. at the University of London and been called to the bar. Pindling was born in Nassau in 1930. His father had come from Jamaica to join the Bahamian police, married an Acklins Islander, and left the police force to start a grocery store on East Street. Pindling was the principal author of the party's platform, which extended an invitation to all Bahamians: "The Progressive Liberal Party hopes to show that you big man and you little man, you black, brown and white men of all classes, creeds and religions in this country can combine and work together and supply sound and successful political leadership which has been sadly lacking in the Bahamas." It called for wider representation in the House of Assembly, enfranchisement of women, and reduction of the life of the House from seven to five years, together with the introduction of municipal government for Nassau. On the proposition "that all men are born equal", the party subscribed to the right to full and equal political participation, equal opportunity of employment, security of person, equal treatment in the civil service, and rights of peaceful assembly and freedom of speech, religion, and the press. Its policies would include opposition to communism, better education, agricultural development, lower prices, low-cost housing, and strong immigration controls:

> The P.L.P. pledges that strong immigration controls will be enforced. That while welcoming the outsider who can contribute towards the economy of the Bahamas there will be no compromise on opposing the influx of foreigners which reduce the earning capacity of the Bahamians. The P.L.P. believes that too many persons have been allowed to enter the Bahamas to take work from our people and that it will take a strong hand to control it.⁴

A few days later, a letter to the *Guardian* signed "P.L.P." thought it necessary to deny that the party was financed by the Roman Catholic church or outside interests (a number of the original officers were

Catholics, and a wealthy French-Canadian resident, Alexis Nihon, was suspected of being the party's backer) and pointed to

> the crux of what is wrong with the political machinery in the Bahamas as it exists. First, the lack of civic responsibility of the masses and the economic pressures which leaves them open to bribery, and secondly, the complete political corruption of some of the men who find it necessary not only to buy their way into the House of Assembly, but who tolerate the poverty-stricken condition of the Out Islanders because it gives them a strong weapon in time of election.[5]

Over the next few months the PLP reported formation of a number of branches. In December it enrolled its first woman member, Mrs Lillian Archer, and a party meeting was addressed by Pindling on the subject of the franchise.

A by-election at the end of 1954 provided the first test of the changing political climate. Early in November the president of the Legislative Council, Sir Kenneth Solomon, died, and ten days later the leader of the government in the House, George Roberts, was appointed to succeed him. Roberts's departure from the House entailed a by-election in the three-member Eleuthera constituency, and three candidates came forward. One, the present writer, withdrew before nomination day when the financial demands of the campaign became apparent. The "Bay Street Boys", as the Bay Street merchant-lawyer group were called by their opponents, united behind Trevor Kelly, a man not previously active in political life but owning a lumber yard and mail boats, assets which Eleutheran voters had come to appreciate as part of their due as constituents during Roberts's long service as their representative. His opponent was a lawyer, Useph Baker, whose brother George was already one of the MHAs for Eleuthera and the island's biggest employer through his tomato and pineapple growing and canning interests. Although Baker had the support of only three members of the House of Assembly — his own brother, Etienne Dupuch, and the latter's half-brother Eugene Dupuch, both Catholics like the Bakers — George Baker already had an efficient political machine on the island. Its strength led to revival of an old electoral tactic by the Kelly supporters. A number received conveyances of small lots of land in the constituency, and thirty-five voted on this qualification despite a challenge at the polls by Baker's scrutineers and repeated warnings from the *Tribune,* including one editorial thoughtfully headed "Christmas in Jail?", that such transfers constituted an electoral offence. After an intense and expensive campaign in which each side was alleged to have spent more than five thousand pounds, Baker won by ten votes, 488 to 478, with seventy-seven ballots spoiled. His support in farming settlements at the northern and southern ends of the district outweighed Kelly's majorities in the middle of Eleuthera, where tourism was beginning to take hold. Kelly campaigned for more tourist development and pointed to his membership of the Development Board, which was the public board responsible for tourism, but George Baker employed 250 men and women at the height of the fruit season and had financial arrangements with a hundred independent farmers for whom he packed and marketed. The victors' slogan was "Two bakers are better than one", and George Baker's support carried the day.

The Eleuthera by-election was the last electoral contest in the Bahamas free from racial overtones. H. M. Taylor visited the district briefly as an observer, but the infant PLP took no part in the campaign, though its sympathies would have been with the Bakers. The real significance of the by-election was that an expeditionary force of two hundred "Bay Street Boys" and their supporters had been defeated in a constituency notorious for corrupt elections. A *Tribune* editorial entitled "Goliath has fallen" gave the right biblical flavour.

Bay Street did not take defeat gracefully. As soon as the House of Assembly met, a petition from Kelly challenging the result was presented. It was referred to the elections committee of the House, whose chairman, R. T. Symonette, was the new leader of the House; the balance of the committee appeared to be 4–3 in Kelly's favour. Baker promptly counter-attacked in the Supreme Court, where one of his supporters sought production of the ballot papers with a view to securing evidence for private prosecution of the men who had voted on the disputed conveyances. The chief justice held that he had no jurisdiction to compel production, but the threat of prosecution hung over the thirty-five, who included several MHAs. After some initial skirmishing the elections committee behaved circumspectly. It secured the opinion of English counsel on the legal aspects of Kelly's petition, and in December 1955 announced that Useph Baker had been validly elected. Thus the reformers secured a second victory: proof that the will of the people could be secured against Bay Street machinations.

In January 1955 a small group of Negroes and whites began to meet at the *Tribune* offices to plan an organization in which moderates of both races could come to know each other better and generate policies for political, social, and economic reform. Only three MHAs were involved, Etienne Dupuch himself and two white members not yet absorbed in the Bay Street political machine. Dupuch has given his own account of the first steps, which he attributes to his concern at the formation of the PLP and its "hate propaganda" and to requests made to him to act to prevent racial polarization,[6] but the importance of the PLP as the stimulus has been somewhat magnified by hindsight. At the time the overwhelming dominance of Bay Street seemed a much greater danger to Bahamian racial harmony than did the handful of PLP members. An interim committee of six Negroes and six whites was formed with Dupuch as chairman and the present writer as secretary. A memorandum of principles was prepared, and in February a permanent organization, the Bahamas Democratic League (BDL), was formed. A number of committees drew up proposals which were eventually incorporated in the league's platform,[7] and in the meantime a number of petitions seeking specific reforms was presented to the House of Assembly by Dupuch. Few of the active members aspired to election to the House at that time. A minority thought that a political party should be formed immediately, but the majority were opposed to such a course and saw the league as a sort of Fabian Society, concerned with policies rather than office. As the next general election was more than a year away, a decision could be avoided for the time being. By September 1955 attacks from the PLP and the *Herald* on one flank and the "Bay Street Boys" and the *Guardian* on the other led to agreement that the BDL should contest the approaching election as a party, but the chance of a genuinely multiracial party had already been lost, if it had ever existed.

One of the BDL's first petitions seized upon an issue whose symbolism perfectly encapsulated the problems with which its members were concerned — the Collins Wall. During the 1930s a wealthy merchant named Collins had surrounded his large estate in the eastern part of Nassau with a high stone wall; it was later claimed that one of his motives had been to make work for the unemployed. The land was eventually subdivided into building lots, the mansion became an all-white, privately operated school, St Andrew's, and Nassau's first suburban shopping centre was established in the middle of the area. Most of the new residents were white, although there were a number of Negroes in the southern part of the estate. Immediately to the west and south of the wall were densely settled Negro areas, whence came many who worked as domestic servants or in other capacities in Centreville, as the estate was known, or wished to use its shops. Rather than make a lengthy detour along the main street, they placed ladders at strategic points along the wall and — men, women, and children — clambered over the wall about their daily business. Inevitably accidents occurred; one pregnant Negro woman miscarried after a fall and a Negro boy broke a leg.

In April 1955 the BDL petitioned the House, asking that two gates be opened in the wall to allow pedestrians through. Dupuch, who had presented the petition, was appointed chairman of the House committee to which it was referred, but R. T. Symonette, the other MHA for the Eastern District, in which Centreville was located, warned that landowners were opposed to the scheme, having bought their lots on the basis of the wall being there. Symonette then presented a petition from 100 residents of Centreville asking that the wall be retained unbroken, and argued that there was no occasion for access to the thickly populated areas west of the wall. A new select committee was appointed for the second petition, thereby taking the initiative from Dupuch's hands, and when a third petition, from 350 residents of the Southern District, to the west of the wall, asked that the wall be opened, it too went to Symonette's committee. The *Guardian*, which had claimed that the *Tribune* "would scream its head off about a long standing wall on private property to prove it fights the battle of the average man",[8] made the case for the *status quo*:

> Any action by the House which does not support the position of these landowners will create a most dangerous precedent; it will render future real estate planning and development impossibly insecure; it will cause grave doubts in the minds of all present and future property-owners of the inviolability of guarantees of privacy upon which their purchases were contingent in large measure.
>
> If there is an expectant mother, in this day and age, who displays such total disregard for her own health and that of the child she carries that she "jumps over" a wall — well, a gate isn't going to solve her problems.[9]

The chairman of the Board of Works explained that his board favoured an opening in the wall to improve vehicular traffic flow eastwards, but all petitions died in committee without report. The Collins Wall was not breached until 1959.

Social discrimination, such as was physically represented by the Collins Wall, was more direct and obvious than the discrimination occasioned by the predominance of political and economic power in the hands of a white minority. After all, there had been Negro members of the House of Assembly for more than a century, as well as successful Negro professional and business men, but they were liable to be discriminated against in public places. As early as 18 June 1951 Bert Cambridge, one of the Negro MHAs for the Southern District, had sought a select committee "to consider the advisability of enacting an anti-discrimination and public embarrassment act". His motion was defeated 13–7 when the only six Negro MHAs present and George Roberts voted for the proposal, but scattered complaints about "discrimination" continued. In February 1954 a Negro lawyer, Randol Fawkes, then embattled in disbarment proceedings, announced that he was petitioning the Queen concerning a client, "a black man" who had been sentenced to ten years imprisonment for fraud in the post office following conviction by an "all white jury". Fawkes called this "only one incident in a pattern of social mal-administration experienced by the black people of the Bahamas" and called for a royal commission.[10]

In May 1954 in the House of Assembly H. M. Taylor opposed a grant of an additional £150 to the Imperial Order of the Daughters of the Empire hospitality (for visiting servicemen) committee on the ground that it practised racial discrimination, but the House refused him a select committee on the matter by a 10—5 vote.

When the issue of hotel discrimination finally exploded in November 1955, it did not involve a Bahamian Negro, but instead a Jamaican couple who happened to be stranded in Nassau when their BOAC plane broke down. There had been a similar episode a year earlier, involving a distinguished Barbadian, Hugh Springer, which had given Bahamian Jim Crow hotels wide publicity in the West Indies. This time the premier of Jamaica, Norman Manley, threatened a boycott of BOAC flights to Jamaica, and the governor of Jamaica, Sir Hugh Foot, wrote to the Bahamian governor, Lord Ranfurly, to protest. Ranfurly appointed a committee of three unofficial members of the Executive Council to discuss the matter with the Bahamian Hotels Association and prevent such an incident occurring again, and the *Tribune* warned: "The time has come when discrimination in all licensed public places in this British Colony will no longer be tolerated by the people at whom this indignity is levelled. Our people have been tolerant, patient under years of crushing insult. Their patience is now at breaking point."[11] When the *Guardian*'s man-of-the-people columnist, "Dinghy Joe", compared the good hotel manager with the fisherman who puts on the kind of bait he thinks the fish will bite, a Negro dentist in the BDL, Dr Cleveland Eneas, replied in the *Tribune* that "Dinghy Joe" was

> that Bahamian who will make you believe that the Bahamas attract a very special kind of tourist and is attracting more and more of this unique specimen year by year. He would make you believe that this brand — all 100,000 of them — would suddenly cease to come if some hotels, the Savoy Theatre, and some other places would adopt the policy of being fair and decent and intelligent in accepting as guests and patrons people of a darker race . . . He is that Bahamian who will tell me to sacrifice everything that is principled on the altar of the tourist business. That I must creep and crawl and teach my children to creep and crawl in their own land so that we may attract tourists.[12]

It was a dignified statement of the dilemma that the growing Bahamian Negro middle class, which now could afford to use facilities previously reserved for tourists and whites, such as the better hotels and the best cinema, had now to face.

Taylor gave notice that he would ask whether government (i.e., the Executive Council) by legislative or administrative pressure on the Licensing Authority, would refuse to grant licences to places that practised racial discrimination, but Etienne Dupuch made the running with a resolution:

> Resolved, that this House is of the opinion that discrimination in hotels, theatres and other places in the Colony against persons on account of their race or colour is not in the public interest.
>
> Resolved further that this House is of opinion that a Commission of Enquiry should be appointed under the Commissions of Enquiry Act to investigate all matters relating to such discrimination in the Colony with power to make recommendations for eliminating this evil by legislation or otherwise.[13]

When the House met on 23 January 1956 the gallery was packed and another two hundred stood outside unable to get seats. Dupuch declared that the time had come when the House should state publicly whether there was one Bahamian people or two groups. It was a question that had been avoided in the past and might still have been avoided if developments in communication and transportation had not broken down the colony's isolation.

The resolution was seconded by Bert Cambridge, who confirmed that discrimination did exist: "I have worked in hotels on this island

Etienne Dupuch (Courtesy of *Tribune*)

and I know that common prostitutes are admitted to places in Bay Street because they are white and decent coloured people are refused admission." [14] As other Negro members endorsed the resolution, a leading white member, Frank Christie, moved that it be sent to a select committee. Two other white members added their support for Dupuch: Donald McKinney stated that the racial problem was the biggest question facing the Bahamas and queried whether the effect of discrimination on tourism might not be exaggerated, and Raymond Sawyer thought that a commission of inquiry might be the right body to consider the matter. Christie's amendment was carried 11–9, McKinney and Sawyer voting with the Negro members.

When Speaker Pritchard named the select committee with Christie as chairman and five "Bay Street" members against two Negroes, including Dupuch, the latter rose to protest against the manner of appointing the committee, fearing with good reason that such a committee would bury the resolution. The Speaker ordered him to sit down, and when Dupuch continued to protest, the Speaker threatened to call the police sergeant on duty to remove him. Dupuch repeated his protest, the Speaker repeated his threat, and then Dupuch declared: "You may call the whole Police Force, you may call the whole British Army . . . I will go to gaol tonight, but I refuse to sit down, and I am ready to resign and go back to the people." [15] At this spectators in the gallery began to object, warning that no one should interfere with Dupuch. McKinney hastily moved the adjournment, and the Speaker's procession from the chair was broken up by the crowd surging protectively around Dupuch.

All the Nassau hotels except one, then operated by a committee of its Bay Street creditors, promptly issued statements that their doors were open to all without regard to race. Equally swiftly, Christie's committee reported on 21 February in favour of the first part of the resolution condemning discrimination. On 29 February that portion of the resolution was passed unanimously by the House. Christie tried to make the best of a bad job by arguing that the House was the proper forum for such a discussion, not a commission of inquiry. "The problem had been before Members for years but he [Christie] felt that it had been gradually and satisfactorily dealt with. Representatives of the Hotel Association told the committee that the Association would not participate in discrimination and the committee was justified in concluding that the problem had been overcome." [16] More probably the majority in the House concluded that passing such a resolution was less of an evil than risking a commission appointed by the governor, possibly even a non-Bahamian commission, which might open up wider questions. Dupuch was content to abandon the second half of his resolution, but the PLP later criticized him for that decision when the other Negro member of the committee, Gerald Cash, had wanted to press for legislation as well.

While there had been a definite breakthrough in the field of social reform, the campaign for political reform had proceeded less satisfactorily. Throughout 1954 and 1955 the *Herald* and the *Tribune,* several of the Negro MHAs, and various writers of letters to the *Tribune* and the *Herald* had called for more honest elections and extensions of the franchise. In January 1955 one Negro MHA, Marcus Bethel, secured a committee on constitutional and electoral reform even though it never reported. By the end of that year reformers had agreed on at least three points: universal adult suffrage, which would include the enfranchisement of women, abolition of plural voting, and one-day elections. Bay Street remained unconvinced. When, in April 1955, the PLP proposed petitioning the House of Commons for one-day elections, the *Guardian* objected that the Imperial Parliament should not take away the right of Bahamian voters to exercise their plural votes, and warned that "it would be easier for a determined group bent on winning an election by fair means or foul to get by with its plans if the limited number of election supervisors are thinly scattered all over the islands".[17] In fact, the intention of the supporters of one-day elections was to break the power of the "Bay Street commando force", which probably had mobilized its maximum strength at the Eleuthera by-election and on that evidence could not dominate elections held throughout the whole colony on one day. When the House finally came to the end of its term in May 1956, the provost marshal (the commissioner of police) ordered that all elections in New Providence be held on one day and the Out Island elections spread over a further four days, a very small step in the direction the reformers had sought.

Nor were the reformers always in agreement. When the BDL proposed a redistribution of seats and enlargement of the House so that there would be eighteen New Providence and twenty-two Out Island seats, the *Herald* condemned the idea as pro-Bay Street rigging of the elections. This was a gravely mistaken view of the PLP's interest, for it was not until 1967, when the House had been enlarged on lines very similar to the BDL scheme, that the PLP could win control of the House.

Meanwhile, the PLP grew slowly but steadily. As early as May 1954 it had two candidates, Stevenson and Clarence Bain, campaigning at Andros, and claimed five Out Island branches, two at Andros, and one each at Bimini, Cat Island, and Long Island. When W. W. Cartwright resigned in September 1954, the party acquired its first successful Negro professional man, Lynden Pinding, who succeeded Cartwright as treasurer, and at the same time the party recruited the president of the Taxi Cab Union to its executive board, starting a link with one of the few existing trade unions. In October the PLP held its first outdoor meeting; such meetings became one of the party's most effective means of propaganda.

Despite such activity, at this stage of its career the PLP derived more benefit from the attacks of its enemies than the efforts of its friends. In their printed form these attacks culminated in an article in the *Guardian* by a regular contributor who wrote under the pseudonym of "C. Frank Candour". The article challenged the party's claim to 450 members, doubting whether there were more than 200, and added that even if the party's membership was so high it lacked finance. It went on to bitter and highly personal attacks on leading PLP members, including Stevenson and Taylor.[18] The article was answered by a PLP supporter in a letter which the *Guardian* had the good grace to print on its front page. The writer, Henry Bowen, declared that there was more discrimination in the Bahamas than anywhere else in the Caribbean or even some of the southern United States. He claimed that "C. Frank Candour" was in fact a Bay Street MHA whom he named, an allegation never denied, and warned: "The Progressive Liberal Party is the black man's party, the same as the Chamber of Commerce is the white man's party. If the P.L.P. fails in 1956, God help the Bahamian people."[19]

The personal nature of the attack and its contempt for the PLP leaders — and, because they were among the very few Negro political leaders, for the whole Negro community by implication — did much to rally support for the party. Although later statements that the PLP had been dying and was revived by the intemperate attack overstate the case, the article ranked with Dupuch's anti-discrimination motion in consolidating the racial division in politics before the 1956 election.

The PLP turned to organization in the economic sector as well. In November 1954, the month that the party celebrated its first anniversary with a mass rally, a dance, a march, a convention attended by delegates from Out Island branches, and a banquet with eighty guests at two pounds a plate, the PLP also sponsored a meeting of two hundred employees at the Emerald Beach Hotel, the first new large hotel to be opened for many years. At the meeting, hotel workers were advised not to sign the contracts being offered by management. The opening of the hotel had coincided with the first signs of the death duty real estate boom which lasted through the second half of the 1950s,[20] and the two good auguries led the *Guardian* to write of "the feeling of harmony among all sections of the people and traditions of living which combine the best of both worlds":

> The preservation of this Bahamian way of life is an important asset to a Colony which relies, almost entirely, upon tourism to provide its annual revenue. Indeed, the creation of disharmony and a violent

change in the political climate would serve only to destroy in a very short time the whole structure of our vast tourist industry.[21]

"C. Frank Candour" warned of "an amazing local conspiracy directed against the new Emerald Beach Hotel" as the first step to win control of all Nassau hotels, but no further clash between labour and management developed. At the end of May 1955 Randol Fawkes founded the Bahamas Federation of Labour (BFL) as a federation of unions, and carpenters, stevedores, masons, and painters were soon organized in constituent unions, Fawkes himself acting as legal adviser to the federation. In June, Taylor sought a select committee to consider amending the Trade Unions Act 1943 to allow hotel workers to form a union. The move failed when the chairman of the Development Board, Stafford Sands, explained that hotel workers had been deliberately excluded from the 1943 act because of the danger that a hotel strike would present to the tourist industry. As Sands was one of the leading figures of the Bay Street bloc in the House of Assembly and the engineer of the growing tourist boom, his opinion was accepted without question. Born in 1913, Sands had been called to the local bar and

Stafford Sands (Courtesy of Stanley Toogood)

built up the largest practice as a conveyancer and incorporator of brass-plate companies for overseas owners. He had been elected to the House as a member for the City District in 1937 and by 1945 had risen to be leader of the government, only to quarrel with the governor of the day and resign the post a year later. In 1950 he had assumed the chairmanship of the Development Board, and his energy and enterprise shaped the Bahamas' drive first for tourists and later for financial institutions.

Sands had also been central in establishing a novel development at the northern island of Grand Bahama. After the Second World War the English holiday camp magnate, Billy Butlin, had established a resort at West End, the point on the island closest to the Florida mainland and an old bootlegging centre. It was too remote, however, and Butlin misjudged the habits of American tourists; it closed after a few years. Meanwhile an American, Wallace Groves, who had acquired a timber company which cut pit-props in the island's pine woods, conceived the idea of a free port close to the United States. By 1953, with Sands acting as Groves's lawyer and lobbyist for the scheme, the idea had taken shape, and in 1955 it was embodied in legislation, pushed through by Sands, as the Hawksbill Creek Act. The act authorized an agreement between the government of the Bahamas and the Port Authority (the Grand Bahama Port Authority Ltd), a Bahamian company formed by Groves, under which the Crown granted a conditional purchase lease of twenty thousand hectares at Hawksbill Creek, Grand Bahama, in return for the Port Authority constructing a deep-water port and an industrial estate adjacent to it. This area was technically known as the Port Area, but quickly became Freeport. The agreement imposed certain obligations on the Port Authority — for example, to provide office accommodation and housing for the government officials who would be required by the developing community — but in the main it granted extensive rights: to import all goods, other than consumer goods, required for the construction and operation of industrial and business undertakings free of customs duties, and to export any goods free of duty. With further acquisitions from the Crown and purchases from private land-owners, the area was subsequently built up to 55,440 hectares, 554 square kilometres. Groves retained a half interest in the Port Authority, a quarter interest was acquired by Charles W. Hayward of the British Firth Cleveland group, and the remaining quarter by a group of American investors. The harbour was completed in 1958 and a substantial bunkering facility established, but then for a year or two the Freeport project languished.

The general election of May 1956 was the hardest test of what the reformers could achieve at this stage. The PLP nominated only fourteen candidates; two others fell by the wayside — one withdrew when it was discovered on nomination that he was under age, and another mysteriously failed to nominate and left the incumbent unopposed. Only two of the PLP candidates were certain of victory — Fawkes and Pindling in the Southern District. Another four had reasonable chances:

Signing the Freeport Agreement: *left to right,* A. G. Knox-Johnston (assistant colonial secretary), Sir Robert Stapledon, L. A. W. Orr (attorney-general), Stafford Sands, Wallace Groves, Warren Levarity. (Courtesy of Etienne Dupuch, Junior, Publications)

five others, including Taylor at Long Island, had only an outside chance; and the remaining three were fighting hopeless battles. The BDL, the alternative reform party, could hope only to retain the seats held by the Dupuch brothers and perhaps win a third. Thus it was almost certain that the Bay Street group would be returned, the only question being what losses they might suffer.

The campaign was hard fought, and public meetings in New Providence were noisy affairs with the *Guardian* accusing PLP supporters of disrupting their opponents' meetings, though the accusations were not as frequent nor so well-documented as at later elections. The "Bay Street" campaign turned on two main points. First, its members warranted re-election: "The Bay Street group, which has the majority of members in the old House, is the backbone of the Colony."[22] They were experienced politicians, sound businessmen, men of wealth who provided employment and did countless favours for their constituents. As members of the House and in their private capacities they had brought prosperity to the Bahamas. A series of advertisements illustrated growing prosperity with statistics of the increasing numbers of tourists, buildings, motor cars, bicycles, and telephones, and the "Bay Street" slogan warned, despite the unhappy associations of the metaphor: "Don't sell yourself down the river for a mess of prejudices and promises." Second, on the eve of the election came a warning that the PLP and the BDL would introduce income tax, the PLP doing so perhaps to pay their MHAs a salary. (Between the wars only Jamaica of the West Indian colonies paid its parliamentarians, but in the 1940s payment became general. In the Bahamas the possibility had always been dismissed with the observation that it would be impossible to pay salaries commensurate with the private incomes of the wealthy merchants and lawyers who dominated the legislature.) As the Bahamas had never imposed an income tax, and attracted a number of expatriate residents and businesses as a result, such an innovation was indeed frightening. The *Guardian* particularized the threat by explaining that West Indian colonies had adopted the "British system" of income tax, which meant that a man earning £300 per annum would have to pay £14 13s 4d while someone with £1,500 per annum, then well into the middle class of the Bahamas, would pay £376 6s 8d. The tax would have to be paid every week, like it or not, and the harder one worked, the bigger the tax paid. Moreover, the imposition of income tax would dry up the inflow of British, Canadian, and American investment.[23] The final stroke of the campaign was another personal attack, this time on Cyril Stevenson's matrimonial affairs, in a number of the *Guardian* distributed widely at Andros.[24]

Both party leaders were defeated, Dupuch narrowly and Taylor by a wider margin, but all leading "Bay Street Boys" won comfortably. Although the votes divided almost evenly between them, with close to eleven thousand votes each, what one might call the conservative camp, all whites, had secured twenty-one seats, while the reformers, all Negroes, had to be content with eight. In the racial composition

Table 4. General election, 1956.

	New Providence			Out Islands		
	Candidates	Seats	Votes	Candidates	Seats	Vo
Candidates closely identified with "Bay Street"	4	3	2,800	18*	14*	5,2
White independents pro-"Bay Street"	1	0	282	8	4	2,7
PLP	5	4	4,838	11	2	2,3
BDL	1	0	1,188	3	1	2
Other independents (8 Negro, 2 white)	7	1	2,058	3	0	2

* Including one uncontested seat

of the House there had been no change. But, significant for future political development, a good three-quarters of the votes had been cast for candidates who were clearly identified with one or other of the polarized forces, the "Bay Street Boys" or the PLP, who between them held twenty-three of the twenty-nine seats in the House. Party politics had definitely arrived in the Bahamas. The PLP won both seats in the Southern District, one each in the Eastern District, thereby putting out Dupuch, and in the West, and both seats at Andros, where they had the advantage of a local son candidate in Clarence Bain.

With one-third of the votes at their first election, the PLP had reason to be encouraged, although there was some bitterness at their poor showing in the Out Islands. At their victory march Pindling proclaimed: "A new Negro was born on June 8th; a Negro who had been knocking on the door asking for representation; a Negro who said he would get representation elsewhere if it were not forthcoming; a Negro who said 'If others will not represent us, we will represent ourselves.' "[25] But with an overwhelming majority of seats firmly in hand, the "Bay Street Boys" were not prepared to be conciliatory. Their first task was to organize the new House and elect a Speaker and deputy Speaker who could be relied on. When it seemed possible that Speaker Pritchard could be defeated by a combination of the reformers and dissident "Bay Street" members, the first steps were taken towards forming a definite parliamentary party which could be bound by party discipline. A contretemps occurred when the original candidate for the deputy speakership had to resign because both his and the Speaker's constituencies were the subject of election petitions, and someone was

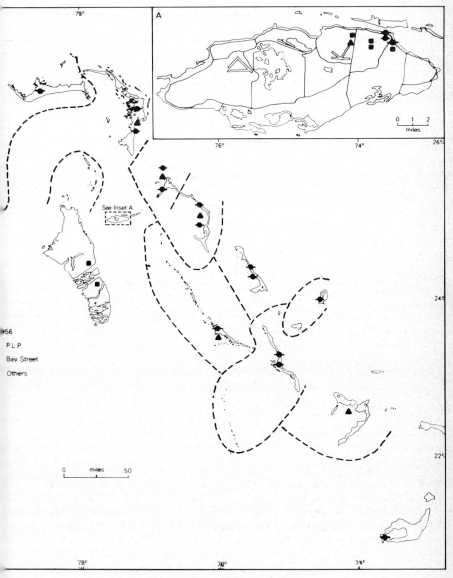

See Inset A

56
P.L.P.
Bay Street
Others

0   miles   50

Map 2.   Results of the 1956 general election

needed to appoint the elections committee; the new deputy Speaker, Raymond Sawyer, was more acceptable to moderates in the House. The elections committee reported after a year, rejecting all five petitions, although a minority report by the one PLP member complained that the committee had relied on police investigations of alleged malpractices and made no inquiries of its own. Various prosecutions failed either because the police were unable to proceed when adjournments were refused, or because confessions had been secured improperly,[26] and in the end the only person convicted of an electoral offence at the 1956 election was the unfortunate PLP candidate bound over for having made a false declaration about his age.

The way now lay open for progress in at least three areas: electoral and constitutional change, industrial action, and — for the PLP, if no longer for the BDL — party organization. Although the three areas frequently overlapped, it will be convenient to treat them separately. In the first two the initiative was taken not by the triumphant "Bay Street" party nor by the PLP but by the colonial government itself. Opening the new legislature, Lord Ranfurly referred to the recent deterioration in human relations in the colony and called for social and political stability. The *Guardian* welcomed his remarks and pointed to "an unreasoning ferment of bitterness and distrust . . . in such an atmosphere there can be no hope of community or prosperity,"[27] without saying that if the choice had to be between community and prosperity which it thought the more desirable. Lord Ranfurly had gone on to say that electoral law was under review, observing that one-day elections were impossible while the company vote and plural voting were retained, and went on: "I do suggest that consideration should be given to the present system of plural and company voting which does not accord with modern democratic practices in other parts of the world, and also to the desirability of widening the franchise."[28] The *Guardian* sniffed at the thought of electoral reform, warning that it would be dangerous to tamper with the company vote and claiming that there was "moral justification for persons with the greatest stake in the country also having a powerful voice in the affairs of that country".

Although it was unlikely that the majority in the House of Assembly would readily agree to electoral reform, it soon became obvious that they would seek constitutional change for a reduction in British control, if only to prevent electoral reform. When Stafford Sands moved for a select committee on the Constitution, as he did annually to prevent any member bent on reform securing such a committee, he commented that a more modern Constitution was required for the Bahamas because of the appearance of party government — even though the "Bay Street Boys" had not then publicly and formally organized.

Various members suggested bits of machinery — having an elected Executive Council responsible to the House, a bill of rights, and adult suffrage — but as the House rose shortly afterwards, nothing further was heard about constitutional matters in 1956, apart from the PLP delegation to the Colonial Office in October.

This came about because crowds of PLP supporters began to attend the evening sittings of the House of Assembly in the centre of the city. On 16 July Speaker Pritchard was booed by a crowd of seven hundred as he left the Assembly building. A short-tempered man at the best of times, he promptly went back to his office, telephoned Government House, and held the mouthpiece through the window so that the governor could hear the crowd's noise. It was then 1 a.m. The governor made a public statement that he had undertaken to protect the privileges of the House and its members, and asked "all Bahamian of good will for their cooperation. They can do this by refraining from assembling in the area during the evenings on which the House is in session."[29] The PLP leadership took exception to this request and sprang into action. Taylor and the party's six MHAs called at Government House, but they also took the dispute outside the colony by cabling the secretary of state to protest that the "people's ancient rights and privileges to see and hear their representatives debate vital issues on the floor of the General Assembly have been challenged and arbitrarily withdrawn by Executive Order". Their cable warned: "This is most undemocratic and in the current stage of political development also highly provocative."

Here was an issue, with an underlying threat of violence, that might induce Colonial Office intervention in Bahamian affairs. A local compromise was easily negotiated whereby the crowd was allowed to stand on the opposite side of Bay Street across from the Assembly building, but Pindling, who had emerged as the parliamentary leader of the party after Taylor's defeat at the polls, told a PLP rally that his party had held out one olive branch in attempting to nominate Sawyer for the speakership. This had been rejected when the Bay Street group insisted on retaining Speaker Pritchard, and it was "pra-pra all the way".[30] As tension built up, the House adjourned early in August for the rest of the year. The PLP opened a drive to raise two thousand pounds to send a delegation to London, a "Crusade for Freedom", to make representations about the House dispute and also to try to secure a say in the selection of the new governor who was to replace the Earl of Ranfurly at the end of his three-year term. The campaign proved more trouble than it was worth when the party had difficulty in raising the money ("Dinghy Joe" in the *Guardian* contrasted the ease with which Bay Street raised the same sum for hurricane relief at San Salvador), and the party's unwillingness to include Fawkes in the delegation contributed to strains that later led to his leaving the PLP for several years. In October, Taylor, Pindling, and another MHA, Milo Butler, visited London and saw the head of the West Indies section of the Colonial Office and the parliamentary under-secretary, to whom they pointed out the defects of the existing electoral system and suggested that universal suffrage would halt corruption at elections. They were told that electoral reform was a matter for the local administration in the Bahamas.

In January 1957 the *Tribune* reopened the electoral debate with a series of articles advocating redistribution, votes for women, and abolition of plural voting and the property qualification for the franchise. In the *Guardian* "Dinghy Joe" answered that "giving a ballot to everybody would be like giving a gun to anyone who is strong enough to lift it",[31] and queried the need for a redistribution when all MHAs lived in New Providence. The first move to change the ground rules of the political game came on the constitutional side rather than the electoral. At the end of April Sands's select committee on the Constitution defied precedent and reported. It proposed an amendment to the Royal Instructions so that the Executive Council should consist of the lieutenant-governor if any (a curious provisions for a non-existent office never satisfactorily explained), the usual three senior officials, and six members of the House of Assembly and the Legislative Council elected by the House to hold office until removed by an absolute majority of the House. This reformed Executive Council would assume the governor's responsibility for naming members to the public boards annually. The select committee justified its recommendations: "The present divisions of the Executive side of Government into a series of almost 'water-tight' compartments without sufficient liason and cooperation, coupled with the present method of appointing unofficial members of the Executive Council, makes it almost impossible either to plan comprehensive policies for the development of the Colony or to carry out policies after such planning has been complete."[32]

All parties agreed on the desirability of constitutional advance, but the "Bay Street Boys" wanted to obtain the maximum degree of self-government free from governor's and Colonial Office controls which were already intruding into labour relations, while their opponents wanted electoral reform before any diminution of Colonial Office control began. The majority pushed the report through 18–7, the only racial note in the debate coming when Milo Butler called the committee's report an insult to Negroes who had already been slighted by the governor's failure to appoint any of their number to the Executive Council. The House had not reckoned on the Legislative Council, which advised against the report: no change in the Constitution was necessary or desirable, and if a change was to be made there should be an electoral mandate.

In the meantime a minor episode had done little to endear the "Bay Street Boys" to the Colonial Office. In February 1957 a visiting Colonial Office official, F. Kennedy, had attended a PLP reception at a Nassau hotel in the company of the acting colonial secretary, F. A. Noad. When Stevenson proposed a toast "Our guests", Kennedy responded civilly with the toast "The PLP". The majority in the House took strong exception to such sociability and legitimation of the PLP. Questions were asked, and eventually a select committee appointed to look into the affair. Noad was blamed for Kennedy's supposed indiscretion, and when he retired at the end of his contract the House voted a gratuity only one-half that which might have been expected, the shortfall being assumed to be punishment for his part in the incident.

While the "Bay Street Boys" sought to advance on the constitutional front, the PLP pressed on in the labour field. In September 1956 Butler and Fawkes visited banks on Bay Street to demand equality of opportunity for Negro staff. At two banks they were told there was no discrimination in employment, and at the third the manager was absent and no reply was available, but the act was more symbolic than part of a sustained campaign. At a party rally Butler and Fawkes threatened to close any Bay Street shop that did not employ Negroes – not really the main question, which was whether Negroes were employed in responsible positions or not – but again no confrontation developed, and when a strike started at the new development of Freeport over recognition of the Grand Bahama branch of the BFL, even the *Guardian* agreed that the developing company should be prepared to train local labour and recognize its rights. In March 1957 Fawkes returned to the subject of organizing hotel workers and sought a select committee to investigate conditions in the industry so as to liberate workers from the "chains" that bound them. Stafford Sands replied that he would welcome an inquiry, for conditions were the best in the Caribbean, to which Pindling replied that although wages might be high, so was the cost of everything. Both Sands and R. T. Symonette repeated the argument that it was established legislation that prevented unionization, legislation that had been passed so that no small section could upset the whole industry.

One problem for the PLP was the unsettled state of the BFL. In November 1956 a new group of union leaders were chosen, and in May 1957 the executive dismissed Fawkes as legal adviser. A few days later he was also expelled from the PLP. Taylor explained the expulsion at a public meeting on the ground that Fawkes always wanted to have his own way, as when he insisted on being included in the London delega-

Randol Fawkes (Courtesy of *Tribune*)

tion even though he was the only member of the party executive to support his inclusion. Fawkes remained outside the PLP for several years, but at a stormy meeting of the BFL in June a counter-coup reinstated him in that organization, and by a vote of 46—43 he was elected president at the head of a new slate of officers.

Two episodes give the PLP occasion to claim that they were hard done by. In July 1957 an attorney wrote to the Speaker to complain about a judgment debt of seventy pounds owed by Cyril Stevenson which had been met by a dishonoured cheque; the communication was referred to the qualifications committee of the House. Stevenson quickly produced a receipt for the amount, but Pindling pressed a motion of no confidence in the Speaker resting on allegations that Speaker Pritchard had discriminated in the appointment of House committees, had publicly declared his opposition to trade unions, and had failed to recognize the PLP in the House even though on opening day Pindling had told the chair that he was parliamentary leader and presented the party's platform for the information of the House. When the motion was debated, Pindling commented that the Stevenson business "could have been conducted in a more gentlemanly and friendly manner". The Speaker, who rejected PLP suggestions that the deputy Speaker should preside during the debate, demanded that Pindling withdraw the word "ungentlemanly", and Pindling, given the choice between apologizing or discontinuing his speech, sat down. This was the first of many clashes between PLP members and Speaker Pritchard which reinforced PLP claims to their supporters outside the House that the rules of the House were rigged against free debate.

Another incident, this time outside the House, arose from the death of one of the Abaco MHAs. A mistake in a telegram from the returning officer frustrated a PLP move to fly a party of voters to Abaco to enrol. When the colonial secretary told the local returning officer that he should provide another registration period, "Bay Street" lawyers warned against this and he refused. The "Bay Street" candidate won the by-election easily, 627—85, but the suspicion of sharp practice confirmed fears that fair elections were still difficult to secure.

At the end of October the new governor, Sir Raynor Arthur, flew to London for further discussions on the House of Assembly proposal for constitutional reform. He was pursued by a six-member mission of "Bay Street Boys" and by Pindling for the PLP. Late in November the secretary of state gave his decision in reply to a question in the House of Commons. The Colonial Office would not consider changes until satisfied that they had general support in the colony. The secretary of state added that he had agreed, as a matter of practice and in accordance with the usual conventions of consulting majority opinion, that the governor would normally consult the leader for the government in the House on the selection of members of the Executive Council and chairmen of the public boards, while the chairmen of the boards would be consulted about the selection of members. As this was already current practice, there was no real gain for the majority group. The critical question was whether the governor would accept the advice that he was given, and when the list of appointments to the boards appeared at the end of December 1957 there had been few changes. Fifteen of the twenty chairmen were reappointed, and ten of the boards had no change in personnel at all, although the *Tribune* reported later that the majority had won one victory in replacing the chairmen of one board where a substantial construction project was at stake. This was trivial compared with what was happening in labour affairs.

NOTES

1. Sir Etienne Dupuch, *Tribune Story* (London: Benn, 1967), p. 27.
2. In fact these eight would cover a wide range of *phenotypical* and *genealogical* colour, while a number of the twenty-one here called "white" might well be classed as of mixed racial descent in some other society. Where it has been found necessary to use such a classificatory adjective in this study, it relates to *structural colour.*
3. *Guardian,* 29 September 1953; there had also been talk of a party at the 1949 election.
4. Ibid., 22 October 1953; the full text of the platform appeared as an advertisement in the *Guardian* of 26 October 1953.
5. Ibid., 2 November 1953.
6. Dupuch, *Tribune Story,* p. 139.
7. See *Tribune,* 20 March 1956.
8. *Guardian,* 30 April 1955.
9. Ibid., 13 May 1955.
10. Ibid., 9 February 1954.
11. *Tribune,* 3 January 1956.
12. *Guardian,* 12 February 1956.
13. *Tribune,* 24 January 1956.
14. Ibid.
15. Ibid.
16. Ibid., 1 March 1956.
17. *Guardian,* 24 April 1955.
18. Ibid., 31 October 1954.
19. Ibid., 1 November 1954.
20. As real property owned outside the taxing jurisdiction was not liable to death duties, a number of aged residents of the United Kingdom and a few in the United States purchased Bahamian land and buildings. After their deaths, their estates were resold to the original vendors at a small loss but considerable tax saving.
21. *Guardian,* 12 November 1954.
22. Ibid., 28 May 1956, letter signed "Truth".
23. Ibid., 8 and 12 June 1956.
24. Ibid., 14 June 1956.

25. *Tribune,* 30 June 1956.
26. For an account of contemporary election practices, see the *Guardian,* of 24 October 1956.
27. *Guardian,* 11 July 1956.
28. Ibid., 10 July 1956.
29. *Tribune,* 20 July 1956.
30. Ibid., 24 July 1956; *pra-pra* is a Bahamianism for wrestling unrestrained by rules.
31. *Guardian,* 12–13 January 1957.
32. *Tribune,* 29 April 1957.

4

General Strike and General Election, 1958-62

One consequence of the growing number of tourists, most of whom arrived by air, was that New Providence's original airfield became inadequate for the increased traffic. Fortunately there already existed a larger airfield some miles to the west, Windsor Field. It had been the Windsor Field construction workers who had rioted in 1942. This former military field was reactivated at a cost of £550,000, some of which was recouped by the sale of land in the area of the older airfield — another minor grievance involved the repurchase rights of owners whose land had been appropriated during the war, but no Bahamian Crichel Down resulted. The official opening of Windsor Field had been scheduled for 16 November 1957, but before the ceremony could take place a long-standing dispute between the Nassau taxi-cab drivers and other transport interests erupted.

The drivers had formed a union as early as 1946, and for some years they had grumbled about the tour companies whose chauffeur-driven automobiles competed with them for tourist traffic. The longer journey to and from Windsor Field should have meant increased fares for the taxis, but the Nassau hotel operators negotiated an agreement with a local bus company and a large white-owned taxi company to supplement their own limousines which also ran a shuttle service to and from the airport for hotel guests. On 1 November a hundred taxi-drivers used their vehicles to block entry to the new airport. The blockade was lifted after twenty-four hours, but during that period a number of tourists had been prevented from entering the colony when their flights were turned back, and subsequently a number of drivers were charged in the Magistrate's Court with obstruction and three with assault. An eight-week truce was then arranged, during which the taxi-drivers possessed a monopoly of traffic to and from the airport, and by the end of December it seemed that agreement had been reached on most points in issue. When the remaining questions were referred to an arbitration tribunal appointed by the governor, the union objected to all three members and sought, rather unrealistically, to have Randol

Fawkes chosen as arbitrator. The colonial secretary replied that the governor was not prepared to alter the panel.

The protracted negotiations had given the union time to win support for a broader confrontation, and on 13 January 1958 the BFL called a general strike in support of the taxi-drivers. A wide section of the working population responded — construction workers, hotel staff, airport porters, bakers, garbage collectors, and employees of the Electricity Corporation. The start of the strike coincided with the opening of the legislature, and as members of the House entered the Assembly building on 13 January preparatory to filing across the square to the Legislative Council chamber to hear the governor's speech, Fawkes and the PLP MHAs were cheered by the crowd. When Milo Butler called out: "These are your representatives . . . Get rid of white man rule in this country,"[1] the crowd turned to booing certain white members, and when the governor arrived he too was booed as he inspected the police guard of honour. His speech warned that recent events might have set the economy back for years, and he pleaded for protection of the tourist industry on which "we all, whatever our stations in life, ultimately depend".[2]

The next day British troops from Jamaica flew in to keep order, and a frigate arrived with technicians to operate basic services, if required. Although speakers at a combined Taxi Cab Union and BFL rally told their supporters to remain orderly and advised them to stay home if martial law were declared, some of the whites feared the worst, including a repetition of the 1942 riot. The *Guardian* quoted one PLP speaker as having demanded: "Give us what we want and nothing will happen. Don't give us what we want and everything will happen."[3] One of its news stories prophesied hysterically: "Rumours of impending riots were everywhere Tuesday afternoon as the city seemed ready to erupt. Along Bay Street merchants threw up storm windows in the first measure against the expected blow. Police said they expected trouble. Gangs of men were reported drinking heavily preparatory to marching on Bay Street. Looting was feared. Riot squads were alerted. Injury and bloodshed seemed inevitable."[4]

In practice the strikers and their supporters confined themselves to peaceful picketing and a boycott of Bay Street-owned shops. Barrooms were closed by a magistrate's order, and there were relatively few violent incidents: one hotel bus was dynamited, and an attempt was made to cut the electricity supply to the waterworks. Potentially the most explosive incident occurred in a clash with pickets outside Speaker Pritchard's shop, following which three pickets were charged with intimidating him and one of the Speaker's sons was charged with causing harm by running down a picket with an automobile. Much later there were other incidents: the troops' canteen burned down, dynamite was thrown into the grounds of an hotel, and finally the *Guardian* building burned down, but no criminal charges resulted from any of these events.

The strikers won some support overseas. The ICFTU sent a donation of two thousand dollars and a series of Jamaican trade union leaders, representing the regional ICFTU organization, arrived to give encouragement. Two of them, together with a representative of the British TUC, Martin Pounder, played a helpful part in negotiating a settlement. The strike ended after nineteen days, but a number of the strikers had already sought a return to work. The governor undertook to create a Road Transport Authority to regulate the industry, and in a radio broadcast asked the community to forget the past. During the strike, pressure had been applied to secure the intervention of the British government: as soon as the strike was threatened, the *Tribune* asked for a royal commission; and when the strike began, the PLP cabled the secretary of state for the colonies to send a representative to the Bahamas. In the later days of the strike the secretary of state told the House of Commons that he was indeed considering appointment of a royal commission but would prefer to make his decision when the local situation was calmer.

The 1958 general strike is a major landmark. For the *Guardian* it was not a labour dispute at all, but "the carefully engineered outcome of all the race and class hatred that has been preached for years in this community".[5] However, the PLP's part in the strike was much more hesitant than the party's enemies claimed. Although Pindling took part in the preceding negotiations as legal adviser to the Taxi Cab Union, and PLP speakers supported the BFL and Taxi Cab Union leaders at mass meetings, the party's official statement was cautious:

> A spokesman for the Progressive Liberal Party declared today that whilst the Party is not directly responsible for the strike or the policies of labour, it cannot remain aloof from the present situation. The Party is deeply concerned, it was stated, with the problems affecting labour, and it continues to urge its members and supporters to use the boycott against those who seek their enslavement.[6]

Later, during their running debate with Fawkes, PLP leaders claimed that the party had held back at Fawkes's request that the party not intervene in union affairs, but it is also probable that the party leadership was alarmed at the extent to which Fawkes was making the running in a crisis, and alarmed too at the threat to the economic stability of the colony inherent in a general strike. The most immediate consequence of the strike was that it brought Bahamian problems to the front pages of the world's press for a day or two, and shook the Colonial Office off the fence it had straddled so long. It also did something to cement relations between the PLP leaders and their West Indian counterparts. Fawkes and Pindling sought the support of the chief ministers of Barbados, Jamaica, and Trinidad to their demand for a royal commission, and the Jamaican House of Representatives unanimously passed a resolution to that effect.

Whatever the political implications of the general strike, it was obvious that something would have to be done about the colony's antiquated labour legislation. The House of Assembly addressed itself to the matter — which had already been under spasmodic consideration for a year or more. The *Herald* warned its readers that Foster Clarke, chairman of a select committee considering new legislation, would amend the act to enslave Negro hotel and domestic workers still further, but it seemed more likely that the House majority could no longer defy the Colonial Office and would try to improve the legislation. An English draftsman was imported by the majority group to advise on the bill, and the resulting draft was published for public information. At Clarke's invitation, Pounder returned to Nassau to advise local trade unions on the implications of the bill, and in April the labour adviser to the secretary of state visited the Bahamas for a fortnight to give further advice. In July the House passed the bill, Pindling conceding that most of the English recommendations had been adopted. Even Fawkes grudgingly allowed that it was a step in the right direction.

Although the legislation necessary for a healthy trade union movement, including the colony's biggest industry, had at last come into being, trade union affairs were far from satisfactory. The governor, Sir Raynor Arthur, warned the BFL's Labour Day parade against mixing labour business with politics, but the two were inevitably interwoven. When seventy-seven workers were laid off at a new hotel being built near the Emerald Beach Hotel, almost three hundred struck in sympathy. The strike lasted twelve days, and was broken only when a hundred strikers crossed the picket line to return to work. On the last day of the strike Milo Butler was on the picket line with Fawkes; the PLP stated that he had been there in a private capacity, but the two militants were escorted off together by the police. While the strike continued, a group of unionists who had broken with Fawkes and the BFL started a new organization, the Bahamian Trades Union Congress, claiming that they would seek "democratic unionization" but denying any intention of trying to attract existing unions away from the BFL. The PLP did not declare their support for the new body, but the *Herald* gave it considerable publicity, and as the party leaders were then engaged in a public dispute with Fawkes it seems probable that the breakaways had tacit PLP encouragement.

After the strike had been broken, Fawkes denounced the PLP, and the party leaders countered with a series of public meetings to give their side of the case. They explained that for months after November 1956 they had tried to win Fawkes back to the party, but when in September 1957 a meeting was finally arranged he proved unrepentant and demanded that the party change its name to Progressive Labour Party, a step which the *Herald* dismissed as an "insane idea" which would be a breach of faith with the party's supporters. In the midst of his wrangle with the PLP, Fawkes was bound over to keep the peace for three years following a union-organizing visit to Andros for which he was convicted of trespass and insulting behaviour. He then held a public meeting to attack the Bahamian magistrate who had convicted him, and was duly charged with sedition. The PLP, again forced to follow in his turbulent wake, rallied around with an appeal for funds for his defence. In November he was discharged by the Supreme Court on a legal submission that vilification of an inferior court did not constitute sedition under the Bahamian criminal code unless there was also an incitement to a breach of the peace.

While union affairs went badly for the PLP, the prospects for electoral reform improved. At the end of March 1958 the Colonial Office announced that the secretary of state, Alan Lennox-Boyd, would visit the Bahamas, apparently the first occasion on which so weighty a British representative had taken a hand in Bahamian affairs on the spot. The majority group in the House, by then organized as the United Bahamian Party (UBP) (see below) welcomed the news and observed that its mission to London in the preceding November had extended an invitation to the secretary of state. The visit in April lasted a week, and Lennox-Boyd managed to visit three Out Islands as well as New Providence. The *Tribune* took the opportunity to warn that this was the last chance the colony would have to put its house in order, otherwise there would be a royal commission, and went on to make Bay Street flesh creep by referring to the possibility of a Labour Party victory at the next British general election, after which all reforms would be imposed by the Colonial Office. As he left, the secretary of state said firmly that "no one should be in doubt as to the ultimate authority of the Imperial Parliament" and called for passage of the pending labour legislation and for measures of electoral reform. These, he said, should confine plural voting to one residential and one property vote per elector, should extend the franchise to all adult males — but not to females because there was no evidence of any demand for this, and should create additional seats for New Providence with the consequent by-elections being held without delay.[7]

All Bahamians had a good word for Lennox-Boyd, and even the UBP welcomed his proposals. Its new platform had included a promise of adult male suffrage, and the party's spokesman on constitutional affairs, Stafford Sands, expressed the hope that the necessary legislation might be passed by the end of 1958. Thus it was generally expected that the by-elections for the additional New Providence seats could be held in the spring or summer of 1959, and the PLP named its four candidates in the expectation that there would be two more seats for the Southern District and one more each for the East and West. On 21 April the select committee on the Constitution, chaired by Sands, issued an interim report; its members unanimously agreed to reduce the plural vote to a maximum of two, to abolish the company vote, and to create four new seats for New Providence. However, the *Guardian* warned against haste and the expectation that the by-elections could be held before the end of the year. Widening the franchise opened new opportunities for electoral malpractices; proof of age and proper identification would be required together with a new electoral register, and all this would take "a considerable amount of time".[8] The governor set off for a fortnight in London, where the secretary of state had told the House of Commons that equality of representation was impossible in the Bahamas and rejected a Labour Party demand for a dissolution of the House of Assembly and a general election.

The first inkling of further difficulty came with press reports that the UBP hoped to win three of the four New Providence seats on new boundaries.[9] In August the House adopted a majority report from the select committee which called for a survey of the potential electorate in New Providence, but not a minority report by Fawkes which sought the immediate enfranchisement of women. When he opened the legislature in December 1958 the governor declared he was confident that there would be no delay in providing the necessary legislation, but no final report came from Sands's committee until the beginning of February. The survey of male British subjects aged twenty-one and over had disclosed 416 residents in the City District, 2,629 in the Western, 4,937 in the Eastern, and 6,639 in the Southern. Accordingly the majority of the committee recommended that the Eastern and Southern districts should each be divided into two new districts by an impartial committee, and incidentally and noncontroversially that all New Providence boundaries be rectified to run down the middle of streets rather than follow compass bearings as they had done since the last redistribution in the nineteenth century.

On 9 February 1959 the House adopted the majority report, whereupon the five PLP members walked out of the chamber, the first time such a gesture of protest had been made in the House. A *Guardian* editorial called for disciplinary action against the five for leaving the chamber without the Speaker's permission, and Speaker Pritchard wrote to demand a written apology, failing which the members would be named. A small PLP rally had already endorsed the walk-out, and

PLP demonstration against New Providence boundaries: *left to right*, Clarence Bain, Lynden Pindling, Arthur Hanna, Charles Rhodriquez, Spurgeon Bethel, Milo Butler. (Courtesy of *Guardian*)

when they had received the Speaker's letter the five MHAs told a second rally that they would defy his ruling and refuse to apologize.

As the new crisis developed, the secretary of state intervened by offering to appoint an impartial committee on boundaries should one be necessary and clarifying his intention on plural voting. Lennox-Boyd went on to warn that if suitable action were not taken in a reasonable period he would consider legislation by the imperial parliament. When the House met, Pindling challenged the Speaker's authority to discipline the five unless he acted at the time of the offence. A week later the Speaker withdrew his demand for an apology on the advice of the legal adviser to the House, who had concluded that the House rules had not the force of law and contained no power to suspend members, but only to reprimand or censure them.

On 26 February 1959 Sands presented a second interim report from his select committee, which met the secretary of state's points. The PLP at once opened "The Drive for Freedom Fund" to send another delegation to London in "a last minute attempt to prevent a wicked and iniquitous Bill from becoming law",[10] and a letter was dispatched to Lennox-Boyd complaining that his intervention had complicated rather than clarified the situation. It had been the PLP understanding, it was claimed, that only freehold owners would qualify for the property vote, but the secretary of state had indicated that leasehold would be included.

> We have been misled. It is now obvious that every effort is being made to compensate the majority group for the loss of the company vote and the multiple plural vote.
>
> We wish to state this: that if our recent statements are the basis upon which the new legislation is to be drafted, we cannot accept such terms and will be left with no alternative but to withdraw our original agreement in principle and renew our demand for universal adult suffrage now, based upon one person, one vote.[11]

The implication of the inclusion of a leasehold franchise was that Sands's own constituency of the City would be strengthened by the votes of businessmen who leased offices and shops there while residing elsewhere, mainly in the Eastern District.

Two minority reports had been appended to the select committee's latest report. One, by Fawkes, wanted enfranchisement of women and abolition of all plural voting; the other, by Stevenson, sought both these changes plus a further seven seats for New Providence and transfer of election petitions to the Supreme Court — that is, adoption of the BDL proposals of 1955 his *Herald* had so roundly condemned at the time. Sands refused to delay further action until the PLP had had an opportunity to meet with the secretary of state, and the House sat out a PLP fillibuster to adopt the majority report after twelve and a half hours debate and rejection of a move for a royal commission.

On 17 March a PLP delegation consisting of Pindling and Stevenson saw the secretary of state, and renewed the request for a royal commission on constitutional reform. If their demand was not granted, they said, the tempo of agitation in the Bahamas would have to be increased, and in both Nassau and London Pindling was quoted as having threatened that there might be demonstrations during the forthcoming visit of the Duke of Edinburgh. On their return to Nassau the PLP leaders told their largest rally since the general strike that the by-elections would be held on the old boundaries, and when the amending legislation came before the Legislative Council the attorney-general had the bill referred to a select committee. He explained that it had been rushed through the House too quickly for the government to move amendments there, but the matter had since been referred to the secretary of state and the amendments to be moved had been approved by him and by the governor. The amendments provided that a redistribution should take place after the by-elections but before the next general election, speed in getting the four new members elected being the most important consideration. Election petitions should be heard by the Supreme Court. A tenancy of twenty-four months, rather than the six months set by the House, would be required for the property vote, and a House amendment to the law of evidence which would have protected voters and candidates' agents against the evidence of accomplices would be struck out on the ground that it would make convictions for corruption more difficult to obtain. The Legislative Council agreed to all the amendments, and returned the bill to the House, where Sands sought leave from service on the select committee, reputedly to avoid the indignity of having to accept the secretary of state's changes. The House accepted the new version and defeated a move by the PLP, supported by Fawkes and the other Negro independent, Gerald Cash, to tack on the enfranchisement of women and a reduction of the life of the House to five years.

Having won a considerable victory by the postponement of the division of the Eastern District, which would have given the UBP one of the new seats, the PLP had an unexpected political windfall. On 10 October 1959 the *Herald* printed a document supposedly written by an American journalist working for the *Guardian*. According to the document, its author, Peter Knaur, had also spent ten months as a propaganda adviser to the UBP. Much of the report, which had an air of authenticity and was never repudiated by the UBP, was unexceptional, but some of its comments on the nature of Bahamian society were insulting to the Negro population:

The Negro people, in trying to ascend in society, will usually try to do so in ways respected by the white man. Irrespective of ratio, this is the white man's society, and the Negro does not have the self-confidence to destroy it.

The "Knaur report" wrote off one-half of the Negro population as either committed anti-PLP or anti-UBP and suggested that the other half could be wooed and protected from PLP attempts to create a racially tense situation:

> Many of the really altruistic acts which members have done in the past for the populace of the Colony should be given publicity even if it means embarrassment to the donor. Also all levels should be used for this bridge: Legislative – A Select Committee to study the care of the aged in New Providence. Party – A Committee to help expectant mothers. Individual – Drive through Grant's Town to visit an "old friend", to see people and be seen. With the proper publicity such acts are amazingly effective politically.[12]

The report impeached the credit of such UBP-sponsored charities as Community Welfare Ltd, which since the 1956 general election had provided a travelling medical service for Out Islands lacking a resident doctor and more recently a job placement bureau in Nassau. More seriously, as the *Tribune* commented, "it reflected an attitude of mind that dies hard among a *very* small group of people in this community . . . an idea of racial superiority that has defeated every effort to weld our people into a solid unit of Bahamians."[13]

The situation was not helped by the *Guardian*'s efforts to brazen out the disclosure in a front-page editorial which asked:

> Race hatred? You can search Peter Knaur's writings – including his report – from end to end and you will find none. The *Herald* makes much of Peter Knaur's remark "This is a white man's society". Think carefully. Does anyone seriously think that it is not? Is it an African society? Anyone who says so is insulting the people of the Bahamas who for centuries have been British – in name, in language, in custom, education and culture. In everything, in fact, except origin.
>
> Does the *Herald* advocate that the streets of Nassau should echo to the beat of the tomtom, or witness the primitive rites of voodoo and black magic? Not even the *Herald* advocates that.
>
> And why? Because the people of the Bahamas have had centuries of civilization. There can be no comparison between them and their brothers across the ocean who are for the most part only one generation removed from savagery.
>
> This is why Peter Knaur said "This is a white man's society". But he meant it in a sociological, not a racial, sense.[14]

The *Tribune* warned the *Guardian* to stop criticizing Africa, and

Nkrumah in particular. The *Guardian* retorted that the PLP was using African developments to catch votes while Ghana rushed towards dictatorship, and threw in details of a recent ritual murder in Africa for good measure.

Again we must retrace our steps briefly. Following the 1956 general election the majority group had organized briefly to ensure the election of the right Speaker and deputy Speaker, but the matter had been taken no further. Several times the *Guardian* wondered aloud whether it was not time to form a party, but not until December 1957 did anything occur. Then a draft letter was prepared to solicit members, but was leaked to the *Tribune* before it could be sent.[15] On 1 March 1958 formation of the United Bahamian Party was announced, and all twenty-one white members assumed the UBP label. On 8 April a *Guardian* editorial explained: "On political and economic questions those who now sit in the Assembly as members of the U.B.P. have always been in full accord, so with their principles firmly established the adoption of a party name has been done simply to keep up with the political times." In June, the party held an organizing meeting to adopt a constitution, in September it issued a manifesto, and in December it elected officers. R. T. Symonette, leader for the government in the House, became chairman, and another MHA, Foster Clarke, secretary. Stafford Sands was given the post of public relations officer, and one of the two Negro members for the Southern District defeated by the PLP in 1956, Bert Cambridge, became vice-chairman, In practice the formal constitutional arrangements of the UBP usually meant little save an opportunity to display the party's Negro supporters to advantage and accommodate some younger whites who had not yet secured seats in the House. The party was effectively the group of members who had worked together in business and politics for many years with Symonette and Sands co-equal *de facto* leaders of the party. In the New Year's honours list for 1959 Symonette was knighted, the first time such an honour had gone to a serving leader for the government.

With the advent of a second party in the House of Assembly, the anomalous position of the public boards became more pronounced. When the new boards were nominated for 1959, three PLP MHAs accepted places; two, Pindling and Sammy Isaacs, refused, as did Fawkes. The PLP claimed that following the secretary of state's visit they had been offered a place on the Development Board advisory committee, which usually sat on an equal basis with the board, but had held out for a place on the board itself. In the end a Negro formerly in the BDL went to the advisory committee, thereby ending the complaint that all members of the board most important to the colony's welfare were invariably white. Party division in the House left the Governor's Executive Council also in a curious position, for it

Roland Symonette (Courtesy of *Tribune*)

included Eugene Dupuch of the now defunct BDL and since June 1958 another Negro member of the House, the independent Gerald Cash, together with Symonette, Peter Bethell, and Raymond Sawyer, all of the UBP. Sawyer's appointment in June 1958 had vacated the deputy speakership, which went to R. H. Symonette, son of the leader for the government.

At the end of 1959 the governor used the Crown's prerogative powers to reform substantially the Legislative Council, making it a more effective body and thus a better counterweight to the House, increasingly controlled by the UBP. An amendment to the Royal Instructions replaced life membership with appointment for an initial term of ten years, with a maximum of a further ten years' extension, and two additional places were created. The receiver-general joined the attorney-general as *ex officio* members, and the enlargement, coupled with vacancies, allowed the appointment of four new unofficial members. One was a UBP member of the House, C. W. F. Bethell, occasioning a by-election for Grand Bahama, and the others Etienne Dupuch of the *Tribune* and two white lawyers, Donald McKinney, who had also lost his seat in the House in 1956, and Leonard Knowles.

The House came back smartly. In its reply to the governor's speech, the House observed: "The house respectfully submits that a larger measure of self-government at Board level would immediately reduce the unnecessary burden placed on Your Excellency's Council and would also produce a greater degree of efficiency in the affairs of Government."[16] The reply also criticized the governor for having changed the tenure and composition of the Legislative Council without first advising the House, and the House then proceeded to reject several Executive Council-sponsored measures and appointed a select committee to investigate the efficiency of government departments, a slap aimed at the new Civil Service Commission, which had the hopeless task of trying to produce an effective civil service while competing with a booming private sector for the very limited pool of educated manpower in the Bahamas. Most significant of all were the remarks made by Stafford Sands moving for his usual select committee on the Constitution: "I would rather serve under a Bahamian who was my worst enemy than under another man who was my friend. I am convinced that this Colony can only reach its fullest flowering under self-government."[17] His motion was seconded by Alvin Braynen, who a few days earlier had resigned from the UBP so that he might be free to vote as he wished in a "transitional period in the Colony", and supported by PLP speakers.

The by-election at Grand Bahama on 24 February provided the first test of party support since the official appearance of the UBP. Both parties sent strong teams of supporters to the island for a hard-fought and expensive campaign, and the *Herald* earned a niche in the history of libel by its attack on the independent candidate, whom it accused of "claiming there were only three ladies in [the settlement of] West End. He named the three",[18] for which the editor-publisher, Cyril Stevenson, subsequently paid a hundred pounds damages. The first count gave the victory to the PLP, but on a recount with 145 ballot papers rejected the result became Harold De Gregory (Independent) 236, Warren Levarity (PLP) 231, Dawson Roberts (UBP) 200,

Charles Williams (Labour, a party formed by Fawkes in June 1959) 72.
The PLP protested against the outcome to the governor and were told
to lodge a petition with the court if dissatisfied. After some difficulty
in raising the thousand pounds security, they did so, and on 24 May
a recount by the Elections Tribunal of the chief justice and a stipen-
diary magistrate made it Levarity 269, De Gregory 262, Roberts 245,
and Williams 72. In addition to securing another seat in the House, the
PLP had the satisfaction of seeing the UBP vote reduced to little more
than a quarter of the total, and as at Eleuthera the Negro public were
shown that they could retain victories won at the polls.

A more direct confrontation of the two political parties would come
later in the year at the New Providence by-elections, but first we might
sample the exchanges about race and politics being passed in 1958,
1959, and early 1960. During the general strike, the PLP — or at least
its mouthpiece, the *Herald* — continued to pitch its appeal at all
Bahamians regardless of race. Thus one article during the strike called
on all Bahamians to awake: "When I say Bahamians, I mean all of you,
the whites, blacks, half-ways, and you Abaconians, for you too are
Bahamians are you not? . . . You coloured people of this island are not
alone in this struggle, for there are white people who are shoving for
the same purpose, although few have the guts to voice their feelings in
the open."[19] A few months later an article by H. M. Taylor asked the
question: "Is the P.L.P. a Negro Party?" and concluded that it had to
be because no whites had the courage to support it. When the Negro
sought freedom for himself he found whites in the front line opposing
him, and other whites passively benefiting from every Negro defeat.
Racial exclusiveness, Taylor declared, had not been the original intention of the party, and the plank attacking Jim Crowism had not been
inserted in the platform until the party's second convention lest it be
misrepresented as meaning the PLP stood only for the Negro. The
plank read:

> The "Jim Crow" practices now being carried out in the Bahamas are
> cause for serious concern and are strongly condemned by the Party
> as un-democratic, un-British, un-Christian and against the principles
> of the United Nations Universal Declaration of Human Rights.
> Having this in mind the Party pledges to eradicate this evil. In the
> firm belief that no human being should be regarded as second or
> third-class citizens because of race, colour or creed, the Party pledges
> to enact proper anti-discrimination and anti-segregation legislation to
> bring the Bahamas into line with other progressive countries in the
> world. We believe: (1) It is the inherent right of all citizens of any
> country to develop their own social environment, to maintain their
> own associations and to form their own social gatherings. (2) That a
> public business, licensed by Government, should not be the medium

of private associations, and all such places should be bound by law, if necessary, to make their services available to every person in the country regardless of race, colour or creed. To this end the Progressive Liberal Party will strive.[20]

The issues of discrimination on which PLP MHAs and the *Herald* seized were a mixed bag. Some involved private acts: a new bank had not invited Negroes to a reception; a white woman blocked a public pathway; a Negro woman had been refused service in a new restaurant. Occasionally there was the act of a white official: a white police officer had spoken rudely to a Negro sergeant's wife when she arrived to collect his pay; police had tried to break up a PLP meeting — "It was always our opinion that it was a mistake to (employ men) who had police experience in British colonies where the people were ruled by the whip and the boot."[21] Sometimes it was action by the white-dominated House of Assembly: there was a "diabolic plan" to introduce a thousand white families to New Providence to offset the growing Negro population; the House refused to vote expenses for a PLP member selected for a Commonwealth Parliamentary Association course. Probably the most effective issue given the PLP was the action of the House in voting only £5,000 for drought relief at Andros at the time that it voted £10,000 for the assistance of racehorse owners affected by a dispute over the management of the track between Raymond Sawyer and the PLPs reputed patron, Alexis Nihon, and £120,000 to provide accommodation for the British troops stationed in Nassau since the general strike. The *Herald* reported the decision under the caption: " 'Conchy Joe' Representatives Vote to Feed Horses — Vote to Starve Negroes" and urged: "Every Negro in this Colony must never forget this brutal act of some Bahamian legislators. It should forever be indelibly engraved upon their memory so that in future years when these same men seek office again they will be reminded of their inhumanity to man, of their hatred for Negroes and their treachery to their country."[22]

In fact, since Dupuch's 1956 resolution overt acts of social discrimination had become rare. When in May 1959 Stevenson secured a committee to prepare legislation to end discrimination, he was able to cite only three reported instances, and one of these proved an anticlimax when the club owner in question, a member of the House, complained that one of the PLP MHAs had fallen off his bar stool in the supposedly offending premises a few weeks earlier. Rather more effective was the evocation of past injustices; thus a letter from Clarence Bain, the other MHA for Andros;

For as long as I can remember, the social and economic life of these islands has been directed by the people nicknamed Conchy Joes, and it appears that many are being hit very hard to see responsibility being shared and their group getting less powerful. It cannot be said that these Conchy Joes ever owned slaves in the direct sense, but indirectly they have had the way of life of these islands so manipulated that the Negroes worked and developed the wealth of the country while the Conchy Joes reaped the reward.[23]

The point about slave-owning was a subtle one; the attack on the present white leaders was that they were former "white trash" or had some admixture of Negro blood, that they had made their money only through bootlegging or sharp practices of the one generation, not that they were personally the descendants of the old slave-owners.

On occasion PLP leaders continued to deny the accusation that they preached racial hatred or were anti-white:

There is no desire in this Party to persecute people because of the colour of their skin. It is not the desire of their party now or at any time after it has attained majority status to persecute people of the white race. It is not our desire to bring the white race down; it is our desire to raise our people up.

We preach race because it is necessary in order to educate our people in the proper way. It is necessary to make our people realise that there are some good things about the Negro . . . Over the years the whites have been taught to support their own people, politically and otherwise. This is all we are asking our people to do.[24]

An incident a few months later showed how far race relations had deteriorated. In January 1960 the matron of the public hospital, an Englishwoman, was attacked in her quarters. When the *Tribune* launched a reward fund of a thousand pounds to apprehend her attacker, the *Herald*, which had been critical of the administration of the hospital for some time, complained that the matron might have provoked violence:

The only reason people are getting excited about this incident is that an English woman is involved. The same thing could have happened to women in the Southern District, and nobody has opened their traps. In their minds there is plenty of difference between English womanhood and coloured Bahamian womenhood. When a coloured Bahamian is involved they couldn't care less and they discuss it with a shrug by saying that it was probably her own fault.[25]

A week later a letter to the *Herald* attacked hospital staff for allowing themselves to be fingerprinted in the search for the attacker.

To such emotion the PLP's opponents could only reply that race relations in the Bahamas were not bad, and prosperity was growing every day. After the Notting Hill riots in London, the *Guardian* conceded that Bahamians would inevitably feel some perturbation at such happenings, but observed that it was a matter of great satisfaction that Bahamians preferred to remain at home.[26] Much was made of a report, commissioned by the House, by the First Research Organization of Miami on levels of living in the Caribbean, which provided impressive proof of what the UBP had claimed — that Bahamians were better off than Jamaicans, Trinidadians, Barbadians, and Guianese.[27] For the by-elections the *Guardian* repeated the successful message of 1956:

> The people who will suffer from the evil results of the P.L.P.'s campaign of race hatred are the coloured people of the Colony — the people to whom the policies of the Majority Party have brought material prosperity undreamt of a few years ago. They, the very people the P.L.P. pretends to champion, are the ones who will find jobs non-existent, money vanishing to a trickle, the grim spectre of want at the door.[28]

Nevertheless the UBP noted a reluctance of many whites to register for the election, while the PLP scored an impressive success in March when five prominent young Negro business and professional men joined the party. Three, Paul Adderley, Orville Turnquest, and Livingstone Coakley, later played key roles in the party. The PLP was further strengthened when a leading member of the People's National Party of Jamaica came to Nassau to speak for its candidates. With the Southern District safe for the PLP, the only question at issue was whether the UBP could, under the old boundaries, salvage one of the four seats. The poll on 20 May showed that it could not. In the Eastern District the two PLP candidates led in each polling division. In the Southern District the UBP, despite its nomination of two Negro candidates, one of whom was the former member, was not a serious competitor, while Fawkes's support was shown to be personal.

Table 5. By-elections, 1960.

Eastern District		Southern District	
Taylor (PLP)	2,020	Bethel (PLP)	1,936
Hanna (PLP)	1,947	Dorsett (PLP)	1,850
Johnstone (UBP)	1,526	Stubbs (Labour)	812
Cole (UBP)	1,348	Wright (Labour)	698
Farquharson (Labour)	88	Bodie (Ind.)	184
		Cambridge (UBP)	149
		Weir (UBP)	142

The *Tribune* called the result a "crushing vote of 'no confidence' in the ruling U.B.P.", and the *Guardian* agreed:

> The average voter here went to the polls not so much to support the individual P.L.P. candidates as to vote against the present leadership in the Colony. The fact that it is that very leadership that has brought them to their present condition of prosperity means nothing to them. They've proved that. The majority of population in this Island want to be governed by their own kind. The voters, by and large, have absolutely no conception of what the business of government entails. They voted in the majority on the purely emotional basis of racial affiliation.[29]

The PLP, now with ten MHAs in place of the five with which it started the year in the House, declared its economic policy on a statesmanlike plane: tourism would be supported and investors could be assured that there would be no income tax and no retroactive expulsion of non-Bahamians.

No sooner had the new members taken their seats than one of them, Arthur Hanna, moved to amend the Elections Act to provide for universal adult suffrage, a five-year term for the House, and abolition of the property vote. UBP spokesmen accepted the principles of adult suffrage and a five-year term but baulked at abolishing the property vote, which was defended on the grounds that it enabled Out Islanders resident in Nassau to continue voting at their home islands and that it compensated for the lack of local government. Hanna's proposal was referred to the Constitution committee enlarged for the purpose. Meanwhile the new boundaries for the divided Eastern and Southern districts were drawn by Sir John Nicoll, a former governor of Singapore, appointed by the secretary of state. They bore some resemblance to the UBP's earlier scheme, but Pindling's attempt to secure their defeat failed 15–12 and thereafter the PLP switched its emphasis from the boundaries question to securing the vote for women.

This was a long-standing issue. As early as 1952 a petition to the House had attracted six hundred signatures, and on 21 October 1954 the *Tribune* published a letter from one of the organizers of the original petition, Sylvia Larramore, repeating the demand. Although both the PLP and the BDL adopted the principle and encouraged women members, little happened until after the general strike. The secretary of state's curt rejection of the suggestion because of lack of demand spurred the campaign, and in September a new organization was formed. In December 1958 a new petition with almost three hundred signatures went to the House, and in January 1959 the members in a rare gesture of conciliation adjourned to the nearby magistrate's court to hear the movement's spokesman, Doris Johnson, put the suffragette case. Again nothing happened until September 1960, when the PLP

launched a new campaign to send a delegation to London. When two
women members of the movement and H. M. Taylor, whose inclusion
in the delegation had been opposed within the party, saw the secretary
of state in November, they were told to await the recommendations of
the select committee.

In June of that year Sir Raynor Arthur came to the end of his three-
year term and prepared to leave the colony. In a reflective speech to
the Chamber of Commerce he denied that there was any cause for racial
feeling in the Bahamas, and warned against the emergent party system
being allowed to divide on racial lines. A white party could not hope to
win an election and a Negro party would find that its *raison d'être*
would disappear just as the British Labour Party "which based its
appeal to the electorate on class hatred has suddenly found itself out on
a high limb because class distinctions have disappeared and this appeal
evokes no response from the public".[30]

The PLP convention that December was reduced to one day by a
hurricane, but it attracted thirty-five delegates, including twenty from
Out Island branches. The new recruits joined the executive board of the
party, together with one white, an Englishman named John Purkiss, and
a new party body appeared, the National Committee for Positive
Action, which included a journalist then employed by the *Tribune,*
Arthur Foulkes. The PLP agreed that merchants should be taxed more,
but reiterated its condemnation of income tax. Meanwhile the UBP,
under some pressure, elected a young lawyer, G. A. D. Johnstone, as
chairman, and chose a new party secretary and a new executive committee which excluded all the party's parliamentary members. In
December a UBP meeting approved votes for women 63–2, and at the
end of the year the new public boards included more PLP members,
including Taylor on the Development Board advisory committee. Amid
such convergence of policies, the year ended on a note of levity as
Fawkes sued Stevenson for libel, claiming twenty-five thousand pounds.
Defence witnesses alleged that Fawkes had proposed that the House of
Assembly be blown up and that he had paid to have dynamited the
house of the magistrate who bound him over to keep the peace, but the
jury awarded him two hundred pounds.

The new year, 1961, found the UBP more amenable to change than
ever before. R. T. Symonette stood down as parliamentary leader of
the party — but not as leader of the government in the House of
Assembly — because of demands on his time. Donald D'Albenas, a
Canadian merchant who had lived in the Bahamas for many years,
succeeded him, and the selection of a new deputy leader and new
parliamentary party secretary showed a deliberate attempt to move
away from the image associated with men who had sat in the House
since the 1920s and 1930s in favour of the younger men who had

already taken over the party's executive committee. In policy matters the UBP was equally conciliatory. The opening of the legislature had been picketed by a small group of suffragettes, and the select committee on the Constitution reported immediately in favour of votes for women, but with effect from 1 January 1963, which could be in time for the next general election provided there was no earlier dissolution. The committee's report was signed by the seven UBP members, but the six PLP and independent members refused to sign and Pindling presented a petition seeking immediate enfranchisement of women. A month later a House committee recommended that no further public beaches should be sold to private interests – the control of one beach near Nassau disputed between the public and private ownership may have had some effect in the New Providence by-elections in 1960 – and the UBP executive committee went further and recommended that the government start acquiring beaches and picnic grounds for public use. The party executive also asked that the Collins Wall be opened at another two places, and a House committee approved eighteen thousand pounds for the purpose.

The PLP remained sceptical of the sudden change of heart:

> Make no mistake about it, Bahamians. Our struggle was never more clearly defined. Regardless of what anyone may say, this struggle is white against black, and we did not produce the rules – they did.
>
> The Negro majority is now engaged in a death battle with the white minority. Before any efforts can be made towards racial harmony in this country, we are going to have to destroy their vicious and twisted concept of racial superiority; bring them crumbling to the ashes of defeat, smash their smug little harbours of arrogance and complacency.
>
> Only then will we be able to start all over again – on terms that are truly equal – to build a decent society where racial divisions are of no consequence and where the colour of a man's skin bears no relevance to his position in any segment of that society. This, of course, is an ideal, and it is possible that it will never be attained. But the task cannot even begin until everything represented by the United Bahamian Party has been obliterated.[31]

In particular the PLP was concerned at the growing number of non-Bahamians being brought to the colony to meet the need for trained personnel. At the beginning of 1961 the colony was unable for the first time to meet the demand for farm labourers to go on recruitment to the United States, and some hundreds of Haitians were brought in to work on new commercial farms started by American interests at Grand Bahama. As tourist spending rose from $11.4 million in 1950 to $51.5 million in 1960, according to the First Research Corporation of Miami report, and as Nassau emerged as a major tax haven – there were eight banks and seven major trust companies by 1960 — so the demand for clerks and stenographers, cooks, and supervisory workers began to out-strip the supply of trained Bahamians. The PLP declared that it was the first duty of Bahamians to secure employment for Bahamians, and if there were not enough Bahamians qualified, to send them abroad for training.

In August 1961 the party's youth organization, the National Com-mittee for Positive Action, launched its own monthly paper, the *Baha-mian Times,* edited by Arthur Foulkes. In its second number the *Bahamian Times* observed that the Bahamian "knows from bitter experience that the European appearance and accent has opened doors that have been shut to him for many years"[32] and later claimed that there were countless cases where Negroes qualified to fill certain positions were passed over for the light-skinned foreigner. "Bahamian Negroes are not only interested in a seat at the cinema or the corner restaurant; they are even more interested in positions of responsibility and jobs which pay."[33] Stevenson suggested that a body more represen-tative than the Executive Council should have the final say over the issue of work permits.

In February 1961 Clarence Bain sought a new select committee to consider anti-discrimination legislation, citing three clubs on Out Islands that discriminated in accommodation and the banks in Nassau which practised job discrimination. The UBP defended itself on the grounds that it was impossible to legislate good will and no racial barriers existed "to prevent the social, economic or professional advancement of anyone living here".[34] Despite the narrow UBP majority in the House, the PLP managed to win few points itself; one came when Pindling secured improved facilities for the straw-work vendors in the city after they had been moved on by police. Various PLP members raised issues without getting anything more than a committee appointed: the abolition of special juries (there had been nine Englishmen on the jury in *Fawkes* vs. *Stevenson*); a board to control real estate agents; pure food legislation; withdrawal of British troops; price control; low-cost housing; Swiss-type banking legislation. More advantageous still to the PLP should have been some of their direct defeats in the House: a motion to remove the limit on the number of taxi-cab licences carried 15—14; retention of fees at the Government High School; a resolution to open Out Island air services to tender carried on the Speaker's vote which threatened the local BOAC subsidiary, Bahamas Airways, to the advantage of United States carriers supported by UBP members.

By far the most serious matter before the legislature in 1961 was the growing financial crisis. Opening the legislature in January, the new governor, Sir Robert Stapledon, warned that the sudden advent of prosperity "throughout the islands of a large undeveloped archipelago" had presented the Bahamian government with "challenging problems, particularly in the field of taxation, of education and of health, of communication and other common services",[35] and his budget introduced in March allowed for a deficit of £748,000, due mainly to declining revenue. By the time the Appropriations Bill had been passed in July, the deficit looked like being close to £4 million, yet the only increased taxation authorized by increased excise on petrol and diesel oil was committed to road works.

Expert reports on the colony's educational and hospital systems pointed to lamentable defects. In his opening speech, Stapledon had cited the difficulties in teacher training; 57 per cent of head teachers were untrained, as were 72 per cent of other teachers in New Providence and 96 per cent in the Out Islands. Untrained teachers were ineligible for admission to training colleges in the United Kingdom, and the local training college, which had had a stormy political career some years earlier, would have to be reopened. When the new academic year started in September the shortage of both teachers and schoolrooms was exposed. At one preparatory school in the Southern District twelve teachers faced 607 children organized in sixteen classes, two to a classroom. At the local senior school there were twenty-five staff for 1,060 students; the largest class had 98 children, and three classes had to meet in the school yard. In June two officials of the Commonwealth Development Finance Corporation reported on the colony's financial position. They pointed to the lack of a ministry of finance and recommended revision of all sources of revenue, but even the PLP was unable to agree on such a drastic move. Proroguing the legislature in August, the governor warned that the Executive Council would have to decide which projects could be paid for out of existing revenue, which would deprive the House of its jealously held controls over expenditure.

When the legislature reopened in January 1962 the governor immediately introduced his new budget, barely balanced at £9.2 million. With the general election drawing closer, both sides moved to the attack. When the PLP invited the UBP to co-operate in abolishing or reforming the Legislative Council and securing an Executive Council elected by the House, the deputy Speaker, R. H. Symonette, charged that the PLP wanted the UBP to do the work now so that they could take over as dictators later. He claimed that certain PLP members had been meeting with lawyers of the United States Teamsters Union and warned that the PLP was showing "the earmarks of Communism, undermining authority and overthrowing the Constitution".[36] The specific allegations were easily disposed of by the PLP, who started equally specious counter-charges that the deputy Speaker had claimed that Negroes were incapable of governing themselves. In a more elaborate story, the *Herald* purported to expose a UBP plot to induce a depression and blame the PLP for the consequences. As evidence the *Herald* cited parts of a letter it claimed to have secured which advised white employers to lay off staff and say that business was bad because of the PLP. The letter indicated an incredible degree of cynicism on the part of the supposed authors. The UBP leaders denied that any such letter had been issued and offered a thousand pounds for a copy. The letter itself soon dropped out of the debate, although the PLP continued to claim up to polling day that any economic difficulties had been deliberately started by their opponents. In April they seized on a statement by Stafford Sands that "permanent residents" from Europe would be sought; they warned that the colony's doors were being flung wide open to convert Nassau into a new Johannesburg and the colony into a new Kenya "where Negro Bahamians would be fortunate to get jobs as servants in the homes of their white European masters".[37]

The PLP's attention had not yet been drawn seriously to the development at Freeport, where the inflow of non-Bahamians was to present such problems in a real, rather than fantasy world. In 1962 extension of the harbour was begun in association with a cement works established by U.S. Steel, but industrial development had been very slow, in large part because of the lack of facilities for the workforce which would have to be imported. So in 1960 the Port Authority switched its emphasis to residential and tourist development, and in 1960 the agreement was amended to treble the area and allow the company to sell land for residential purposes which had originally been granted for industrial uses, and under the amended agreement the Port Authority was required to build at least one first-class hotel. Wallace Groves then entered a new partnership with a Canadian investor, Lou Chesler, who had been successful in large-scale real estate developments in southern Florida and elsewhere, and about forty thousand hectares were conveyed to a new company, the Development Company, in which the Port Authority owned half the shares and Chesler, personally or through other companies, controlled the other half. By 1962 there were some fifteen hundred residents at Freeport, and a thousand Bahamians who lived elsewhere on Grand Bahama worked there. Under the original agreement the Port Authority granted licences to industries, businesses, and professional people who worked at Freeport. The Port Authority and its licensees were allowed to import skilled, semi-skilled, or unskilled labour if they were not available, subject only to a proviso that if unskilled labour was sought for Freeport an application had to be made first to the Bahamas government. If the chief industrial officer was unable to recruit the required workers within thirty days, permission would then be granted to import them. In return, the Port Authority undertook to use its best endeavours to employ Bahamians, provided they were prepared to work for wages and conditions prevailing elsewhere in the Bahamas, and to train Bahamians for employment at Freeport. The PLP had opposed the 1960 amendments and warned that they would seek to review the agreement when they obtained office, but for the time being Freeport attracted little attention in the political arena.

Despite the ostensible agreement of both parties on the need to transfer more power from the hands of expatriate officials to elected Bahamians, there was only one further change implemented before the election. In April the House unanimously agreed to reduce its term from seven to five years in the future. Registration of women began on 2 July and after a slow start seems to have enrolled most of those eligible. A dispute with constitutional implications grew out of the clash between the commissioner of police and the chairman of the House select committee on the police force, R. M. Solomon, which led eventually into a commission of inquiry into Solomon's charges of misconduct by the commissioner. The commission exonerated the commissioner on most counts and criticized Solomon for having made the allegations, but the whole affair displayed clearly the unsatisfactory division of responsibility between the governor and the House of Assembly with the Executive Council, divided between officials, UBP members, and independents uneasily in the middle.

One racial incident which narrowly missed turning into a fully fledged riot should be mentioned as illustrative of how racial tension had intensified in Nassau. On 1 August a nine-year-old Negro boy (selling, ironically, copies of the *Guardian*) was ejected from the air-conditioned liquor shop where he sought to carry on his business. When he tried to re-enter, the twelve-year-old son of a white employee blocked his way, and the younger boy fell to the ground. He was taken to the hospital to be treated for a bump on the head and then sent hom, but in the meantime a rumour — one is tempted to say the classic rumour of race riots — spread that he had been killed. A crowd gathered outside the shop and was addressed by Milo Butler. Eventually the riot squad was called out, and one curious tourist was fined three pounds for failing to move on. By early afternoon the first anti-British letters had been delivered by hand to the *Tribune* office calling for the deportation of the whites concerned; another letter later reported hearing someone demand: "We need to get about a dozen white people and string them up."[38] The *Tribune* found proof that Communists might already be active in the colony in the speed with which the incident developed. Ultimately the white boy was charged with assault, but the case was dismissed by the juvenile panel unanimously, and it was claimed that the younger boy had thrown a soft drink in his face earlier in the day.

Early in October the legislature was prorogued and then dissolved. Both parties issued lengthy policy statements, the UBP's comprising 26 points and the PLP's 126, with relatively little difference between the lists.[39] Each promised an early constitutional conference, although the PLP spelled out in some detail the sort of changes they would seek. Each promised to protect Bahamians from imported labour, although the UBP spoke only of "unfair competition" whereas the PLP undertook that no non-Bahamian would be given permission to work so long as there were "sufficient Bahamians capable and qualified in efficiency to fill such positions". The UBP announced its commitment to fostering co-operation and good will between all classes and races to ensure freedom and equal opportunity for all "for the enjoyment of the economic and social advantages offered by the Bahamian way of life", while the PLP promised to promote racial harmony by outlawing discrimination. The UBP offered a review of taxation "with a view to increasing Government income without placing burdens on the poor man, while preserving the Colony's traditional freedom from direct taxation", and the PLP undertook to "stimulate revenue" and provide a balanced budget and increase capital reserves.

On policies there was little to choose between the two alternatives, but the UBP warned that the PLP candidates were inexperienced and irresponsible, and the PLP claimed that they were of the same race as the bulk of the electorate, or as Milo Butler put it, "We have been run by the U.B.P. and their forefathers for 300 years and it is time we ran ourselves . . . There are 88 per cent of the population who look like you and me and only 12 per cent who look like the U.B.P. people . . . No rhyme or reason why people who look like that should go on ruling us."[40]

The election was marred by violence at a number of UBP meetings, which both the *Guardian* and the *Tribune*, now solidly behind the UBP, blamed on pro-PLP "goon squads". The *Herald* denied any responsibility. Late in October the Cuban missile crisis provided the first real threat to Bahamian security since the German U-boats of twenty years earlier; the *Herald* endorsed President Kennedy's handling of the crisis, but the Public Works Department thoughtfully provided fall-out shelter plans, and UBP harping on the damage revolutionaries like Castro could do to their country took on a new dimension. The *Herald,* which had originally hailed Castro's success "Batista Overthrown: U.B.P. Next",[41] had been discreetly silent on events in Cuba for some time. Still closer to home was the definite recession in the Bahamian economy, and in particular the building industry, which developed as investors held back for the results of the impending election. Building permits for the first ten months of 1962 were down by £1 million, or 20 per cent, over the comparable period of 1961, and although this indicator was unreliable because only two-thirds of permits are normally used, it was one Bahamians had grown accustomed to watching. Further, by early November there were some 1,700 registered unemployed, including 240 from the building industry, which had previously experienced a shortage of labour mitigated only by the supply of illegal Haitian immigrants.

As polling day neared, both sides fell back on well-worn techniques. The *Herald* harked back to the "Knaur report" and asked why a party claiming to represent the Bahamian people should have only two Negro candidates: "This is what is meant by racialism. Through their candidates and by inference in all their propaganda, the United Bahamian Party tells the voters of their country that a Negro society is best governed by white politicians and that Negroes do not possess the ability to govern themselves."[42] When Eugene Dupuch observed that the PLP had created a monster – that is, racism – which they could not control, a PLP supporter posted a sign "Let the Monster Live, Good Lord", and promptly had his tenancy of twenty years standing terminated by his UBP landlord. His victimization figured prominently in PLP propaganda.

Milo Butler was quoted as saying, "All these years these people have had their feet on our necks – now you have a chance to throw them off. 300 years ago our pride was ripped out of us slaves in a nasty manner. They beat us until we lost our pride and our language. Now if a man of the other race should kick you, you should kick back, and then you will know you have your pride back."[43] He was answered by an editorial in the *Tribune*:

> We hear a great deal about slavery . . . and about Uncle Toms . . . but what are the facts? Slavery was a terrible institution . . . but do you know that there is still an active Anti-Slavery Society in England . . . because slavery was never completely stamped out in Africa? Before Europeans started the trade in slaves African tribes fought among themselves. Warrior tribes preyed on the more peaceful tribes. They killed them . . . they ate them . . . and they led them away into slavery. After a trade was started in the export of slaves the Europeans were the traders . . . but the Africans themselves caught their black brethren and sold them to the white man. By no act of their own were the slaves freed. They were freed by the conscience of a Christian society . . . after which Britain kept a squadron of the Royal Navy on patrol along the coast of Africa to suppress the trade . . . and European governments did everything possible to suppress a continuation of the trade among Africans themselves.[44]

The *Guardian*'s editorial reply looked to the present rather than the past:

Take a drive through the most populous sections of New Providence, through the areas where the P.L.P. would have you believe the Negro is kept in "slavery" by the white "masters". Did you ever see so many "slaves" driving around in automobiles? Did you ever see the "wages of slavery" accomplish the construction of so many large, modern buildings? Did you ever see so many "slaves" who own their own businesses, from banks to garages to grocery stores? Did you ever see so many "slaves" supporting from their own earnings such large, healthy families? Did you ever see so many happy, well-fed, and in many cases self-employed "slaves"? Could any of this have been accomplished while one Bahamian's foot was placed squarely on the neck of his countryman?[45]

The *Guardian* reflected on the fate of Ghana and Guiana, Cuba and the Congo, where the people "all fell for the demagogic claptrap of political opportunists who promised them freedom, glory and riches", and as in 1956 printed a special supplement, "Success in Tourism Brings Prosperity to all Bahamians", which set out the striking proposition that since 1949 the Bahamas had spent £126 million on imports and received only £14 million for exports and £4 million for contract labour in the United States. The expenditure of £4.7 million for tourist promotion had netted £87 million in tourist and foreign capital expenditure, whereas the next two items in the Bahamian balance of payments were crayfish tails worth £1.5 million and tomatoes worth £0.8 million.

There were rumours that United States gambling interests were in contact with the PLP, that on election eve a large airplane had landed mysteriously on an Out Island to meet the local PLP candidate, and even the hoary old tale of the property-owner mowing his lawn who, aware that a passer-by was watching him closely and asking why, was told that if the PLP won the other man had selected that house to take over. There were two "intercepted" letters, the first ostensibly written by a young woman to a friend in Canada advising her how to bluff the immigration authorities and once in the Bahamas get a job, the second to a man in south Florida to the same effect, against which the UBP ran a story that a UBP supporter had been refused a prescription at the public hospital. When the chief medical officer investigated and found no foundation to the story, the *Herald* claimed that the woman admitted telling it to a UBP candidate "as a joke".[46] The PLP alleged that the UBP was orchestrating unemployment and lack of public works, to which the chairman of the Board of Works replied that the board's weekly pay cheque for casual labour was up over earlier months.

When the PLP met the charge that they were inexperienced by pointing out that the UBP leaders had been young once, the *Tribune* answered that they had served an apprenticeship under experienced parliamentarians, whereas the PLP leaders wanted "to sweep all seasoned direction out of government".

> They want to break down all the safeguards that have guaranteed us stable government — and there isn't a single man in the P.L.P. with any experience of executive government — there isn't a single man in the P.L.P. with any experience in big business — examine their records and see how many have made any brilliant success of their own affairs. These people don't want to come in to learn government — which is the biggest business in the world — they want to take over a happy and prosperous country with perhaps the most delicate economy in the world. In short — they want to experiment with your bread and butter.[47]

Other editorials and letters to the editor developed the themes: the PLP were inexperienced, they were in politics for personal gain, they would impose heavy taxes. One of the strongest statements came from a correspondent implausibly signing himself "A Coloured Carpenter":

> But let us look and see where we get our bread from, not coloured people, because the blind can't lead the blind. We are all poor and we have to go to the white man for jobs. We know that if we work for a coloured man he can't pay us off, so don't let us look at where we fall. Now to you ladies, every morning you have a job to go to and somebody will do you a favour, but for whom are you working? There may be a few of you working for coloured men, but the majority of you are working for the white man, and even you that are working for the coloured man, you are not fully satisfied with your salary or working condition. So if the P.L.P. gets the majority of seats in the House of Assembly, you know that only they and their families will be taken care of.[48]

The election on 27 November was an overwhelming triumph for the UBP. In New Providence the PLP won five seats easily in the Western, South Central, and Southern districts, where one seat went to Fawkes, but the UBP held the two seats of the City easily, and Symonette and Eugene Dupuch, moved from Crooked Island and running as an independent, defeated Taylor and Isaacs of the PLP in East Central. In the Eastern District a very close vote returned one PLP incumbent, Hanna, and one new UBP member, Johnstone. Thus in New Providence, despite the sizeable majority of the total vote the PLP secured, the seats were shared PLP six, UBP four, independents two. In the Out Islands the PLP held their two seats at Andros easily, but lost Grand Bahama to De Gregory, who ran again as an independent. Elsewhere they managed to make only one contest close, Inagua, where a son of Etienne Dupuch, Bernard, won the seat his father had held in the 1930s. Of the twenty-one Out Island seats, the PLP could manage only two; independents won four and UBP fifteen. On balance, the new

UBP leaders: *left to right*, R. H. Symonette, Trevor Kelly, Stafford Sands, John Bethell, Roy Solomon. (Courtesy of Etienne Dupuch,

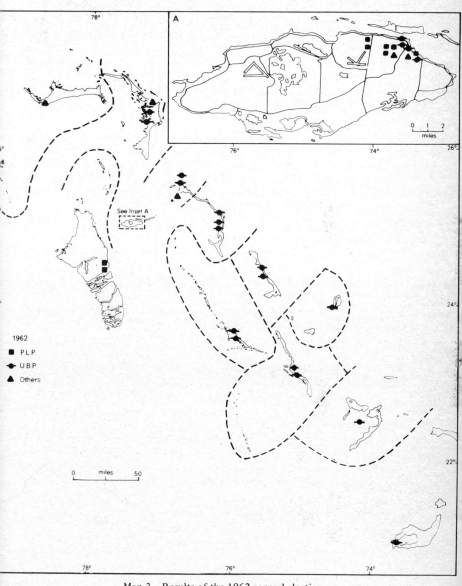

Map 3. Results of the 1962 general election

House could be categorized as UBP nineteen, pro-UBP independents four, idiosyncratic independents (Braynen and Fawkes) two, PLP eight — a net loss of two seats for the PLP. Each side had its own arithmetic of the vote; thus the *Herald,* under the caption "P.L.P. won 6,000 votes more than the U.B.P.", gave the totals as PLP 31,752, UBP 25,433, independents 9,646, and Fawkes Labour 3,004. Any such calculation must be unsatisfactory, because it adds together votes cast in one-member, two-member, and three-member constituencies, although on balance one could properly say that the maldistribution of electorates produced a grave distortion of what was a roughly equally divided electorate.

The *Herald* lamented: "We confess that we were not merely disappointed with the results of the election, but shocked and surprised as well . . . Particularly, we were amazed by the lack of support in the Out Islands, with the remarkable exception of Andros. It would appear that a great task lies before us in opening the eyes of a people kept so long in darkness that they are unwilling to emerge."[49] The *Guardian* was equally perceptive in attributing the UBP's success to the enfranchisement of women it had so long resisted. A long letter from Eugene Newry of the PLP's National Committee for Positive Action concluded: "The average white person voted UBP because subconsciously he was aware that the PLP by talking of Negro history was bringing to the surface buried guilt feelings which are naturally very unpleasant. He wants to forget his ancestors' past and rightly so."[50] What was harder to explain is why so many Negroes voted for the UBP.

Some of the explanation no doubt lies with the growing prosperity, closely linked to the rising number of tourists. Apart from 1958,

Table 6. Growth in tourism, 1956-62.

	Number of Tourists	Percentage Increase over Previous Year
1956	155,003	17.0
1957	194,618	25.6
1958	196,658	1.0
1959	264,624	34.6
1960	341,977	29.2
1961	368,211	7.7
1962	444,870	20.8

the year of the general strike, the increase had been spectacular, and even the loss of momentum in 1958 was quickly recovered. Moreover, some of the benefit was beginning to spill over from New Providence onto other islands. By 1962 almost 110,000 of the total arrived at an Out Island, two of which were linked by air with the United States; in 1958 and 1959 there had been only 20,000 tourists landing at an Out Island. But as there was cause to expect that the boom would continue – as indeed it did for another seven years – the PLP was faced with the same choice as after the 1956 election, whether to continue plugging away at electoral and parliamentary politics or turn to something stronger.

NOTES

1. *Tribune,* 14 January 1958.
2. *Guardian,* 14 January 1958.
3. Ibid.
4. Ibid., 15 January 1958.
5. Ibid.
6. *Herald,* 25 January 1958.
7. *Guardian,* 14 April 1958.
8. Ibid., 22 April 1958.
9. *Tribune,* 13 May 1958.
10. *Herald,* 28 February 1959.
11. *Tribune,* 18 March 1959.
12. *Herald,* 10 October 1959.
13. *Tribune,* 14 October 1959.
14. *Guardian,* 16 October 1959.
15. *Tribune,* 17 December 1957.
16. Ibid., 9 February 1960.
17. *Guardian,* 26 January 1960.
18. *Herald,* 13 January 1958.
19. Ibid., 25 January 1960.
20. Reprinted in the *Herald,* of 27 February 1960.
21. *Herald,* 4 October 1958.
22. Ibid., 28 June 1958; the Loyalists dubbed the earlier Bahamians "Conchs" after their staple seafood delicacy, *Strombus gigas.*
23. Ibid., 28 February 1959.
24. Ibid., 23 May 1959.
25. Ibid., 3 February 1960.
26. *Guardian,* 12 September 1958.
27. See for example, the *Guardian,* of 26 February 1959 for the cost of a "market basket" of groceries in notional hours of work for various occupations in each territory.
28. *Guardian,* 4 April 1960; another substantial report was commissioned from the Economist Intelligence Unit and issued in December 1958.
29. *Guardian,* 25 May 1960.
30. *Tribune,* 10 June 1960.
31. *Herald,* 10 October 1960.

32. *Bahamian Times,* September 1961.
33. Ibid., January 1962.
34. *Guardian,* 9 February 1961.
35. *Tribune,* 12 January 1961.
36. Ibid., 1 February 1962.
37. *Herald,* 25 April 1962.
38. *Tribune,* 17 April 1962; see also the editorial in the *Tribune* of 15 December 1962.
39. Texts of platforms in *Tribune,* 5 October 1962, and *Guardian,* 6–7 October 1962 (UBP); *Tribune,* 13 October 1962, and *Herald,* 22 October 1962 (PLP).
40. *Guardian,* 31 October 1962.
41. *Herald,* 3 January 1959.
42. Ibid., 24 November 1962.
43. *Guardian,* 31 October 1962.
44. *Tribune,* 20 November 1962.
45. *Guardian,* 31 October 1962.
46. *Herald,* 10, 17, and 24 November 1962.
47. *Tribune,* 24 November 1962.
48. Ibid., 25 November 1962.
49. *Herald,* 1 December 1962.
50. *Tribune,* 21 December 1962.

5

White Power, 1963-66

A few weeks after the election, the secretary of state for the colonies, Duncan Sandys, arrived in Nassau for the Kennedy-Macmillan talks held at Lyford Cay at the western end of New Providence. He was met by a PLP demonstration at the airport and by a *Guardian* editorial which declared that the time had come for internal self-government, as both parties had supported the idea in their election programmes.[1] Sandys conferred with representatives of the UBP, the PLP, and the Legislative Council separately and invited all groups to come to London for constitutional talks. Meanwhile, the UBP took a firmer grip on the existing machinery of government: UBP representation on the Executive Council was increased and PLP supporters were dropped from public boards. As 1963 progressed, four of the five independents in the House joined the party, and early in 1964 the last fell into line. The party appointed as its constitutional adviser Major-General Sir Ralph Hone, previously head of the legal division of the Commonwealth Office, and when the conference opened on 1 May the UBP was well prepared to press its case for internal self-government.[2] After the conference Hone became government adviser in Nassau and drafted the details of the new constitutional arrangements.

The model agreed to in London completed the transformation of the Old Representative System, already eroded by the rise of disciplined parties, into a fairly standard form of pre-independence responsible government successfully used in the West Indian territories that had already achieved independence. The UBP sought to preserve some of the old public board system by providing that those concerned with "governmental functions" should assist the new ministers with such functions and executive powers as might be assigned by statute or by the minister concerned, subject to the minister's responsibility to cabinet and the legislature. Such a deviation from the current Westminster model met the disapproval of the Colonial Office, and the conference report noted "that such of them as operate in the normal field of Government responsibility will exercise only consultative and administrative functions".[3] Jamaica had had a brief experiment with something similar at a comparable stage of constitutional development after 1944, advisory committees composed of members of the legislature and attached to ministers, but they quickly disappeared. In the Bahamas too, the logic of ministerial government quickly asserted itself, and the hybrids were abandoned, although other old boards, which were in reality social welfare committees (e.g., of prison visitors), licensing authorities, or public utility corporations continued much as before, sometimes purged of parliamentary members, sometimes chaired by a parliamentarian who had missed ministerial office.

In other respects the report provided for a cabinet of no fewer than nine members, including a premier and a minister of finance, no less than one nor more than three sitting in the upper house; the governor would designate and remove ministers on the advice of the premier. The attorney-general would remain an official, the colonial secretary would become chief secretary, and a new office of secretary to the cabinet would be established. The governor would be given power, at his discretion, "to designate a Minister whom he may consult on such matters relating to the police force as he thinks fit and, with the prior approval of the Secretary of State, to delegate to a Minister such responsibility relating to internal security and the police as he may deem fit and upon such conditions as he may impose", provided the legislature was informed first. The Legislative Council would become the Senate; a minority of its members would be party-appointed, five on the advice of the premier and two on the advice of the leader of the opposition; the other eight would be appointed by the governor "after consultation with the Premier and any such other persons as he may in his discretion decide to consult". Serving members of the Legislative Council would continue as members of the Senate, save that the remaining life terms would be altered to ten-year terms under the new Constitution. The Senate's powers over legislation would be restricted, to a delay of fifteen months over ordinary legislation, to requesting amendment of ordinary money bills and to delay for two months, and in the case of a special class of money bills (to be known as Taxation Bills) imposing an income tax, a capital gains tax, a capital levy or estate duty to requesting amendment and to delay for fifteen months. A dispute between the Senate and the House would be resolved by the attorney-general. The deviation from the British Parliament Act of 1911, which shaped intercameral relations in most colonial constitutions, came to be explained as a guarantee given to local and expatriate investors rather than a resurgence of upper chamber Toryism at this time.

The present House of Assembly would continue until dissolved in the ordinary course; its successor would be enlarged to thirty-eight members, eighteen to twenty-two representing Out Island constituencies and sixteen to twenty representing New Providence. The machinery and principles of electoral distribution had been one of the main sources of disagreement at the conference: the solution was a standard British model — a Constituencies Commission comprising the Speaker as chairman, a judge of the Supreme Court as deputy chairman, two members nominated by the premier and one nominated by the leader of the opposition, and acting at least every five years. Subject to the formula for New Providence and Out Island representation, the commissioners should be guided "by the consideration that the number of registered voters per member should be as nearly equal as is reasonably practicable and the need to take account of special consideration such as the needs of sparsely populated areas, the practicability of elected members maintaining contact with electors in such areas, size, physical features, natural boundaries, local government areas, geographical isolation and inadequacy of communications". However, the conference went on to pre-empt the commission's discretion to some extent by fixing the New Providence–Out Island ratio for the next election at 21:17, observing that this would largely limit the commission to redrawing the map of New Providence to allow for its extra seats and should the commission choose to recommend variation in the Out Islands it would be guided by the criteria and ensure that each existing Out Island constituency return at least one member (a rider preserving the seat at San Salvador). The UBP had sought to leave the franchise to the local legislature, but the Colonial Office agreed to PLP demands for the abolition of the property vote and this was included in the conference report.

Other provisions of the Constitution should follow the common model: statutory commissions to protect the public service, judiciary, and police from political interference; and constitutional safeguards to protect fundamental rights. The original UBP submission had contained an elaborate set of proposals for "fundamental rights and freedoms of the individual" derived from the constitutions of Trinidad, Jamaica, British Guiana, and Malta. The provision for protection from discrimination on grounds of race, membership of a particular community, place of origin, religion, or political opinion came from the British Guiana (Constitution) Order in Council, s.11, and prohibited discrimination "either expressly by, or in the practical application of, any law or any executive or administrative action of the Government of the Bahama Islands", subject to various riders, one of which was the exclusion of entry into, movement or residence within, or employment in the Bahamas. The PLP lodged a minority dissent on three points: appointment and tenure of senators chosen by the governor in his discretion, the ratio of New Providence and Out Island seats, and omission of a requirement for single-member constituencies.

For most of 1963 the PLP appeared chastened by its electoral failure the previous year. International politics had a momentary attraction when Taylor, no longer an MHA, and Stevenson held a press conference in Miami to denounce the Bahamian government for suppressing a report that Cuban forces had entered Bahamian waters to seize eight Cuban refugee fishermen at Elbow Cay on 21 February.[4] Bahamians had become vaguely aware that Cubans, both those who had remained under the Castro regime and those who had fled to south Florida, where they formed a growing and belligerent community, were poaching Bahamian fish and shellfish. There were also rumours that anti-Castro groups were using isolated cays and islands as staging bases for hit-and-run raids on Cuban territory, and so the Taylor-Stevenson story had the ingredients of a major incident. They were censured by the PLP National General Council for making such a statement without party authority, and it could be suspected that their motive was influenced by a wish to keep members of the old guard in the centre of the stage which was being usurped by the new guard of young professional men, mainly lawyers, who now dominated the parliamentary party. The Bahamian government, backed by a British frigate, pursued an even-handed policy of arresting poaching vessels and charging would-be raiders with illegal possession of unlicensed firearms; the Cuban *émigrés* in Florida proved more of a nuisance than did their compatriots who stayed at home. In April police and a party of Royal Marines captured nine Cuban *émigrés* at a cache of arms on Andros, and another party of Cubans were caught on their boat in the Exuma Cays.

It will be recalled that in 1960 Freeport had turned from industry to tourism as a mainspring for development. However, that too proved insufficient to maintain the massive injection of capital that was required to convert the raw and rather unattractive Freeport area into a desirable place to visit or settle. In 1962 the decision was to revive the idea of a casino which had been floating around for some time. There were already two small private clubs, the Bahamian Club on New Providence and the Cat Cay Club near Bimini, which were exempted from the provisions of the Penal Code which prohibited gambling, but the clubs were exclusive and contributed nothing to the attraction of the run-of-the-mill tourists who made up for their limited spending power by sheer numbers. A company was formed, owned jointly by Lou Chesler and Wallace Groves's wife, to operate a casino at the Lucayan Beach Hotel, then under construction, to attract more tourists to Freeport and use its profits to subsidize other hotels. On 1 April 1963 the Executive Council granted an exemption certificate to the company, Bahamas Amusements Ltd, to operate an unlimited number of casinos, provided each was in or operated in conjunction with a hotel at Grand Bahama, for a period of ten years. Later the circumstances surrounding the change of the government's previous policy of hostility to casinos were examined by a commission of inquiry (see below). The PLP issued a statement condemning the grant of the exemption certificate without consulting the legislature and "in spite of the known widespread objection to gambling by the legislature and the public". A deputation called on the governor to register the protest,[5] and also complained about the absence of a direct tax on gambling income, but did little to mobilize public opinion on the issue. Not until 1963 did the government give serious attention to the rising tide of expatriates within the Bahamas. Then the existing Immigration Act, which dated back to 1928 and merely controlled entry without making provision for employment controls, was replaced. The new Immigration Act which became operative on 6 January 1964 defined a new status, that of the "belonger", who was deemed to belong to the Bahamas and have the same rights as the Bahamian-born. It also provided for certificates of permanent residence which might be endorsed so as to prohibit employment without the approval of the Immigration Board, and for entry permits which were endorsed for employment as specifically set out on the permit. The arrangements of the Hawksbill Creek Act were specifically exempted from the operation of the new legislation.

Issues that had an overtly racial flavour were few and far between. One concerned the text-books used in Bahamian schools. It began with a PLP attack on *Pleasant Paths* to *Geography, Book II*, which Paul Adderley claimed would produce a feeling of inferiority among black children. Godfrey Kelly, chairman of the House education committee, moved a resolution regretting that it had been introduced into board schools and calling for its immediate withdrawal. Then Lynden Pindling moved for the withdrawal of an old adventure story set in the Bahamas, Richard Le Galliene's *Pieces of Eight,* which had been used in literature classes in recent years but was not currently prescribed. Written at the turn of the century, it contained references to the "darkie population", described Grants Town as "darkest Africa where everything was black" and Andros as a place where there were a "nasty lot of nigger cabins"; among those to whom the novel had been dedicated was the father of three UBP parliamentarians.[6] The *Guardian* agreed that *Paths to Geography* should be condemned, but criticized the PLP for using the occasion to have a five-hour debate on racism and objected to withdrawing *Pieces of Eight* merely because it described the ancestors of students in unacceptable terms. The *Tribune* met the PLP attack on a different quarter – Pindling's objection to a passage from *Uncle Tom's Cabin* in the *Royal Reader* and to "Uncle Tom" himself:

> But today people of the P.L.P. stripe try to debase this fine charac-
> ter. If a coloured person is not a tough – if he is not a ruffian – if

he shows any gratitude for benefits received — if he possesses the qualities one would expect of a man born and reared in a Christian society — then he is an Uncle Tom and a traitor to his race. A coloured man is expected to hate anything white — although white people fought and died for his causes — and they are still leading the battle for the full establishment of his rights in a free and democratic society.[7]

Not surprisingly the editorial was answered, and when one correspondent gave an example of offensive material in *Paths to Geography* which explained how whites had the best of everything, the *Tribune* answered that this was just a statement of fact which should not make coloured children feel inferior but should spur their ambition.[8]

Public service appointments always held racial implications. When the expatriate attorney-general retired, a Bahamian, Kendal Isaacs, succeeded him, the first Bahamian to hold the post for half a century; but when the expatriate commissioner of police moved on, the local man was passed over and the salary doubled to attract the former inspector-general of colonial constabulary on the grounds that the force had been demoralized by the recent commission of inquiry into the previous commissioner's conduct. Adderley sensibly sought a committee to consider a scheme for overseas training for public servants to replace existing *ad hoc* departmental arrangements. The Board of Education was convulsed for much of the year over its attempt to discipline a senior lecturer at the Teachers Training College, Carlton Francis, who had attacked the quality of a course he attended at the University of the West Indies: after protracted inquiries, litigation, and demonstrations, Francis resigned from the public service and later turned to politics.

Early in October Sir Roland Symonette announced the composition of the cabinet which would take office the following January. He would be premier and Stafford Sands minister for finance and tourism; there would be nine other ministers and three more without portfolios, although with specified responsibilities. The last arrangement was changed before the new Constitution came into force so that the three became full ministers with departmental duties. A fifteenth minister would be named to act as leader of government business in the Senate. The report of the constitutional conference had not referred to the subject, but Symonette had at once indicated that ministers would not be paid salaries: "We felt this would insure that the people in the new government, as in the old system, would have enough money to be beyond the kind of financial pressure sometimes brought to bear on a country's administration."[9] When the PLP later sought a committee on parliamentary salaries, the idea was ridiculed.

However, the dangers of a system of unsalaried ministers soon appeared. It was announced that Symonette was going onto the board of Mackey Airlines, one of the air carriers between south Florida and the Bahamas. Pindling moved in the House of Assembly:

> It is the opinion of this House that the traditions of the United Kingdom Parliament be observed in all matters relating to the possibility of conflict between Ministers' private interests and their public duties and that the Ministers concerned should choose either to terminate such private interests as may appear likely to conflict with their public duties or to resign the appointment as Minister and refrain from holding office in the government.[10]

UBP members denied there was a conflict of interest, and Sands, declaring that his hands were clean, pointed out that the PLP delegates at the London conference had agreed to ministers retaining their private businesses. The press report of the debate does not show that any member drew the distinction between retaining and enlarging business interests.

The problem reappeared at the beginning of 1966 when Sands, who had been knighted in the New Year's Honours of 1964, was appointed a director of the Royal Bank of Canada, the oldest bank represented in Nassau. Adderley attacked the appointment, and asked the premier to secure Sands's resignation from either the bank or else the finance portfolio. A government press release argued that Sands's presence on the bank's board could only be to the advantage of the Bahamas:

> Since the Colony depends upon the attraction of outside development capital to underwrite the major part of its growth, it is the feeling of Government that the Minister's appointment to a directorship of one of the leading banking houses of the Western Hemisphere can only be to the advantage of the Bahamas . . . The Royal Bank of Canada has been the Government's bankers for many years and the interest of the bank and the Government are thus closely identified. It seems, therefore, that the Colony can only gain from the close liaison which will be achieved between the Government and its bankers through the position of the Minister of Finance as a director of the bank.[11]

The summer of 1962 had been the first for many years to experience substantial unemployment, although summers have been traditionally the off-season for tourists. During the election campaign the state of the economy had been clouded by partisan claims, but once the UBP were firmly in the saddle it became apparent that there were difficulties. Government revenues were sluggish, and it seemed that a loan or additional taxes might be required. The colonial secretary attributed the current difficulties to revision of United States tax laws concerning offshore companies which were combing out some of the smaller and shakier companies, reduction in the duty-free allowance of American tourists returning home, the general financial situation abroad, and the "unsettling effect" of the election.[12] Some relief was provided by the negotiation of a twenty-year lease for an underwater testing base at Andros in return for which the United States government would make available loans of £3 million for sewerage works in New Providence and £5 million for harbour improvements; the £150,000 a year the British Admiralty would pay the United States for use of the base would also be made available to the Bahamas for public works.

Despite a rise in the number and value of building permits issued in the first months of 1963, when summer came unemployment again became an issue. At the end of June the PLP sent two thousand of the supposed unemployed marching down Bay Street, and their supporters disrupted a UBP rally called to publicize the government's policies on employment. By the end of October 1,900 had registered with the government's employment agency, but as half of these were domestics and only 250 in construction and general trades, it appeared that there was little wrong with the demand for labour. Randol Fawkes, who had rejoined the PLP, led the Transport Agriculture Distributive and Allied Workers street sweepers and garbage collectors seeking a weekly wage of twenty pounds into a dispute with the Board of Health, and the *Guardian* gloomily supposed the PLP was on its way to another 1958 debacle,[13] but industrial relations continued placid.

The eighth annual convention of the PLP was held in September 1963 and displayed the new direction the party was taking. Taylor and Stevenson, still under a cloud over the Elbow Cay incident, stood down from the chairmanship and secretaryship, and although Taylor was elected a life member and honorary chairman it was clear that his influence in the party was ended. Pindling became chairman; Orville Turnquest, another lawyer and MHA, defeated Cecil Wallace-Whitfield, also a lawyer but unsuccessful in his bid to enter the House, for the secretaryship, a third MHA, Spurgeon Bethel, won the party's treasureship from the incumbent. Only one of the founding fathers, Charles Rhodriquez, retained a senior party post, as first vice-chairman; one more lawyer-MHA, Arthur Hanna, won the second vice-chairmanship. The party's one white, John Purkiss, defeated Wallace-Whitfield for the assistant secretaryship, but he quit the party a few weeks later in protest over its acceptance of the new Constitution. At the end of the year Pindling as leader of the opposition had to nominate two senators: he chose Rhodriquez and Clifford Darling, president of the Bahamas Taxi-cab Union.

Taylor, who had expected to be named, resigned from the PLP, charging that the present leadership had "betrayed the ideals of the founding fathers". He pointed out that under his leadership the party had grown from six members to five thousand, but the party's success had contributed to his loss of personal influence. Pindling was at once a man of the people, darker in complexion than Taylor, less Anglicized than other university graduates like Adderley and Turnquest, and still a successful professional man with whom the rising Negro middle class could identify. Had Taylor held his seat in the House, his removal might have taken longer and been more awkward, but it is impossible to believe that he could have retained control of the new forces within the mass party which had emerged and now possessed the support of half the voters in the Bahamas. In January 1964 Pindling set up a shadow cabinet. With only seven reliable members in the House, excluding the erratic Fawkes and the suspect Stevenson, his men had to match twice their number, and Pindling designated seven unsuccessful candidates as "parliamentary secretaries".

The new parliament opened on 20 February with the first speech from the throne presented on the advice of cabinet on internal matters. The UBP provided an ambitious programme with some emphasis given to welfare services, for which Eugene Dupuch had ministerial responsibility. The tax base would be enlarged by a new tax on gambling, by an increase in the previously nominal shop licence fees, and by extension of the real property tax, which then covered only 2,600 taxpayers. Sands's first budget speech on 15 March pointed proudly to a net balance of £2.5 million in the Treasury; although the budget entailed a deficit of £1 million, most of that was to be explained by a re-voting capital items from the previous year. The first financial measure, imposing the gambling tax as a licence fee on the three casinos, ran into trouble in the Senate, where it was challenged as retroactive and leaving a discretion with the executive rather than the legislature and was eventually rejected.

One racial incident about this time illuminated an aspect of the colony's economic history. As already noted (see chapter 1), following the abolition of slavery freed slaves and their descendants occupied many large tracts of land abandoned by their previous owners, who had received crown grants late in the eighteenth and early in the nineteenth centuries. Destruction of title deeds by hurricanes and insects, intestacies and illegitimacies, the departure of individuals and families to other islands or the United States, and inadequate property descriptions in such title deeds as there were produced a conveyancer's nightmare. As the post-war growth of tourism revived land values, the legislature adopted a modified form of a Canadian arrangement whereby titles could be "quieted" by the courts: someone claiming ownership could make *ex parte* application to the Supreme Court, advertise his claim, and if no adverse claimant came forward to dispute his application he would receive an indefeasible certificate of title from the court. The sort of clear-and-burn agriculture practised by Bahamian peasant farmers did not easily establish the proof of continuous occupation required by the common law of possessory title developed with reference to England's green, pleasant, and closely cultivated land. Thus many farmers who had roamed over a particular tract for several generations, cutting a field here and there and then abandoning it to revert to bush after a few seasons, found themselves defeated by the lineal descendants of those who had obtained a crown grant or a "proper" conveyance decades earlier but had had nothing to do with the land in living memory.

In 1963 an application by Cat Island Farms Company Ltd, owned by one of the two UBP MHAs for the district, Harold Christie, was opposed by some twenty-five local farmers, some of whom defied a court direction to stop cultivating the land pending a final decision as to the title to the land. In June 1964 three women were committed to gaol for periods of twenty-one to twenty-eight days for contempt of court and refused leave to appeal to the Privy Council. A deputation of the farmers was taken to Government House by Milo Butler, and during a solemn moment in the House commemorating the service of George Roberts, who had died the previous day, Butler shouted, "Three Negro women have been sent to gaol and nobody cares a damn about them." [14] The deputy Speaker, Alvin Braynen, promptly named him, but no one moved for his suspension.

In November, when legislation to establish a Court of Appeal was before the House, Butler returned to the attack. Negroes were being kept down; they could not rise to the top of the public service – instancing the hospital and the Education Department; the Supreme Court had denied the women leave to appeal because they were Negroes, but if it had been "one white prostitute", leave would have been granted. [15] The following week the adverse claimants lost their case. At the end of the year the puisne judge who had committed the women to gaol retired and went into private practice in Nassau; when his work permit expired, there was a PLP government in office and his application for renewal was rejected. When the Court of Appeal Bill was again before the House, Adderley said that there had been monumental injustices in the past, some of them based on racial discrimination. Butler was more direct: there should be at least two Negro judges: "They want to have all white judges so they can all sit down and work out how to put our people in prison. I want an opportunity to have a judge sit down at my tea table so that I can tell him what I want done." [16]

The visiting minister for home affairs of Malawi told the ninth PLP convention, "You here must rule. In saying this I am not saying that you must chase away foreigners. No; if they are businessmen they must take care of their business; but in politics you must rule." He repeated

Nkrumah's advice to seek first the political kingdom. Butler, moving the vote of thanks to "this wonderful delegation from the old home-land", spoke of "these brave men who are prepared to die knee deep in blood to free their country".[17] The convention saw two significant moves. Pindling stood down as chairman, and his candidate, Wallace-Whitfield, defeated Adderley 40–26. Jeffrey Thompson succeeded Turnquest as secretary. Hanna sought to change the party's name from Liberal to Labour, and when Adderley objected that it would be a betrayal of the voters who had supported the party, Pindling observed that he could not see what harm it could do to the party – but the matter was not pursued.

On 4 February 1965 the Constituencies Commission reported to the House. New Providence was divided into seventeen single-member electorates; only two were safe for the UBP, and another four or five were marginal. For the Out Islands, Cat Island and Harbour Island would each lose one seat, while Andros and Grand Bahama would each gain one and would be divided into single-member constituencies, which would give the UBP a chance of winning one Andros seat. Hanna, the PLP representative on the commission, did not sign the report and wrote a minority report complaining of "substantial departures" from the principles agreed at London and laid down in the Constitution. When the proposals were debated in the House in April, PLP speakers attacked the decision to proceed without waiting for census figures, and claimed that the new City District boundaries had been drawn to produce a privileged district. When Butler exhausted his fifteen minutes of speaking time in committee, he refused to sit down; he was named and eventually carried from the House by four policemen. Hanna followed suit by stating that he would be suspended and then refusing to resume his seat after his appointed time; he too was carried from the chamber. It was claimed that the incident was premeditated, the evidence being that a press photographer was conveniently present to record Butler's removal.[18] When the House met again, PLP supporters picketed the building. After some debate it was agreed that the suspensions had been legal but operated only for the day; the two offenders were readmitted and the debate on the Constituencies Commission resumed in committee, Butler making a bitter speech lasting forty-five minutes with the assistance of two extensions of time.

Before the House met next, on the 26 February, Sir Roland Symonette broadcast to "correct certain misrepresentations" about the commission's report, although he declined to pass an opinion on its work, saying that was a matter for the House. He warned that efforts were being made to create disturbances – apparently a leaflet had called for people to "storm Rawson Square":

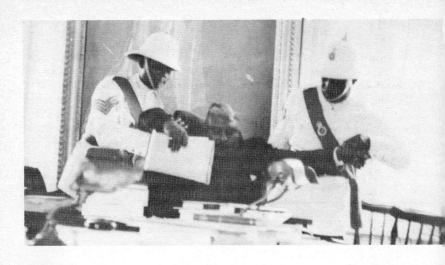

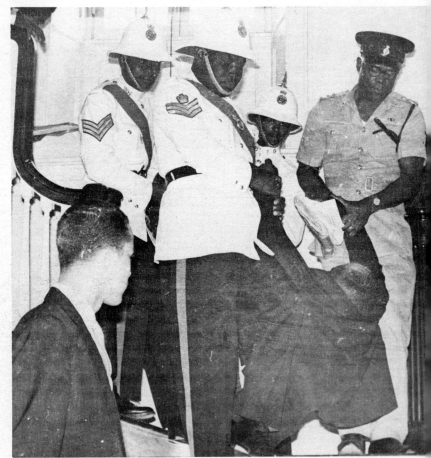

Milo Butler being removed from the House of Assembly (Courtesy of *Tribune*)

Everyone will suffer if violence is permitted to take place. We have for many years now been building a prosperous country. We have before us the opportunity to continue on this course. But everything can be ruined in a moment of careless and violent conduct. Do not be persuaded to take part in disturbances which will injure yourself and your family.

It is my intention and that of my Government to conduct the business of the House of Assembly in a proper and dignified manner. This will be done regardless of what pressures are brought to bear upon us. We do not intend to yield to any form of intimidation. We do not propose to give way to threats. We will not be influenced by violence and disorder.[19]

A large crowd had gathered outside the House and booed UBP members as they entered. A force of police with the commissioner himself in attendance added to the feeling of impending drama. Pindling sought to defer the redistribution proposals going into committee and was defeated; Spurgeon Bethel sought a national registration campaign to determine the distribution of voters more accurately and then a redistribution conducted by a United Nations special commission, and he too was defeated. Pindling then stated that the government did not intend to do anything to meet their objections: "We tried to lay our cards on the table; we tried to get the Premier to indicate whether he would be prepared to amend the draft, but it appears that it is the intention of Government to push this matter through. This only shows that they mean to rule with an iron hand. If this is the intention of Government I can have no part in it. If this is the way you want it, then this is the way you will have it."[20] Whereupon he picked up the mace, which, he declared, "is supposed to belong to the people of this country", and threw it through an open window into the crowded square below. Butler followed by hurling the two hour-glasses out, and all PLP members present (Stevenson not being there) walked from the chamber. Pindling, once outside the building, climbed onto a Post Office van, told the crowd what had happened, and invited them to join him in a sit-down in the adjacent intersection of Bay and Parliament streets. The police started to drag demonstrators away, and after twenty minutes of this a magistrate read the Riot Act and the riot squad moved up, at which the crowd dispersed. The House approved the report and rose at 1 p.m., but members stayed in the building for some time to avoid the confrontation with the crowd.

A subsequent *Tribune* editorial claimed that throwing the mace through the window might have been the signal for a demonstration which did not eventuate.[21] That is unlikely, for had Pindling wanted to widen the incident it could certainly have been arranged. The TUC general secretary called for a boycott of Bay Street shops, but little came of it. A fund was started to replace the mace, which raised eight hundred pounds, but it also produced a letter to the *Tribune* which read: "The Mace was destroyed by Mr Pindling who represents a part of the Southern District which are all coloured people. Mr Pindling did not receive one vote other than coloured, and in the people's opinion he did what he did fighting for the people's right. Many of us think that any black man who donates one single penny to that fund should be run out of the country."[22]   R. H. Symonette, who as Speaker had chaired the Constituencies Commission, explained that the commission had taken the 1963 census data into consideration and drawn boundaries to produce 1,600 to 1,740 electors in each district, but Pindling announced that the PLP would petition the United Nations and, if the Committee on Colonialism decided to act, would conduct their own voter count.

On 20 May one Leon Rolle, aged twenty-four, was fined five pounds for disorderly conduct at a public beach by abusing a white occulist as a Conchy Joe and threatening violence to all Conchy Joes. The *Tribune* reported that government buildings at the airport had been daubed with slogans like "Foreigner go home. Ice Pick riot war on U.B.P. soon" and, in a more philosophical vein, "Bad Government make bad laws, bad laws made bad people". On 24 May the PLP held a protest march of several thousand down Bay Street and heard a speech from the American Negro politician Adam Clayton Powell, who was reported to have said:

> Black Bahamians are not free so long as Bay Street is totally controlled by Conchy Joe. Until black Bahamians run Bay Street, the full dimension of absolute freedom is an unknown quantity for you, a prize eluding your outstretched hands. Until you black Bahamians help run the Government, or better still, run the Government yourselves, you will remain second-class citizens. The Bahamas government was never more distorted by political trickery. The stench of non-representation has been removed, but the foul odour of misrepresentation remains. This is why the Bahamas is a classic example of "perfumed colonialism". Sprinkle some Bay Street tokenism in jobs, let a few black people surface to the top – listen you police, you civil servants – but keep the rest under water and let them drown or struggle to survive. That is perfumed colonialism. That is the Bahamas.[23]

Stevenson had resigned from the PLP following the mace incident – and in an open letter indicated that he had had nothing to do with the party for the previous eighteen months. In a passage thought to refer to the loss of Taylor and Stevenson, both light complexioned, Powell said:

> The greatest weapon you have is unity. Don't argue among yourselves. Stop quibbling among yourselves on the basis of light skinned and dark skinned Negroes. Don't bicker amongst yourselves on the

basis of privilege or under-privilege. Stop bickering amongst your-selves on the basis of education or lack of education. Stop quibbling among yourselves about what you wear and what you don't wear. Realise this — I don't care whether you are as fair as the noonday sun, or black as the face of western midnight, when you come out there and face that white man he says you are a Negro.[24]

PLP leaders outside the House of Assembly: *left to right,* Clifford Darling, Paul Adderley, Orville Turnquest, Arthur Hanna. (Courtesy of *Tribune*)

One step to cool the situation came from the governor, who issued a press statement that a new electoral register would be started. The register would show whether there were any great discrepancies in the numbers of electors in the New Providence constituencies, and if there were, "no doubt the Commission [would] wish to give the matter its further consideration".[25] When the House met on 1 July, PLP members were absent and the meeting censured Pindling and Butler for the destruction of the mace and the hour-glasses. On 15 July Adderley and Bethel reappeared in the House, and although Adderley took the oppor-tunity to complain that the fifteen minute rule had been enforced only against Butler and Hanna, there was speculation that their presence in the House indicated a split over tactics in the PLP. They were later joined by Turnquest, and on 2 September Adderley explained on behalf of the three that they believed their duty to the people who elected them required their presence in the House, but they still supported the PLP platform and principles.

Meanwhile, Pindling had led the other PLP MHAs to a session of the United Nations Committee on Colonialism in New York, where he declared that the local situation was explosive. The British representative pointed out that Pindling had accepted the 1963 constitutional proposals subject only to minor reservations and explained that the secretary of state had offered discussions in the Bahamas in October. Adderley stated that the three did not agree with the mace-throwing nor the appeal to the United Nations but would stay in the party. However, on 5 October the National General Council suspended the three for a period of two years unless they undertook never to go against the wishes of the party majority. The dissidents replied that the procedure for their suspension was unconstitutional and the party constitution gave no power to require a boycott of the House which was clearly an illegal attempt to interfere with members of the House. They then proceeded to form a new party, the National Democratic Party (NDP). Adderley was to be parliamentary leader, Holland Smith chairman, Bethel first vice-chairman, Purkiss secretary-general, and Turnquest treasurer. By November the mace was back from London, where it had been repaired, but the remaining PLP members continued their boycott of the House until February 1966, by which time they had been absent for nine months.

In a public statement explaining the party's action, Wallace-Whitfield and Thompson, as chairman and secretary-general respectively, declared that the party was committed to majority rule operating through a National General Council on which all elements were represented, and suggested that the dissidents were elitists:

> The Party rejects the proposition that the progressive and liberal forces in the country have "a comparatively small number of people qualified for leadership". On the contrary, for a country the size of the Bahamas, there are many, many persons qualified for leadership. It is the system here alone which obstructs them in taking their rightful place in public affairs. The Party further believes that the people should be the judges of their leaders and not just these three men.[26]

They pointed to the fact that Adderley had stood against the party at the 1956 election and made the revealing comment: "The Party is completely satisfied that the three members knew of the action with regard to the mace, and if any of them did not know they had every opportunity to know." If that statement was anything more than a bit of clumsy pleading by Wallace-Whitfield, it would confirm claims that Pindling's action was deliberate and premeditated, though not necessarily that the crowd was expected to erupt into violence when the mace came through the window.

The dissidents called the mace incident "a violent act of useless destruction", and saw the culmination of unfair dealing with early party stalwarts Taylor, Stevenson, C. A. Dorsett and Livingston Johnson (who had contested the 1962 election but were not subsequently given seats on the National General Council), and Purkiss in their treatment at the 1964 party convention:

> A major turning point came at the 1964 Convention when the group [i.e., "the small group of men who now control the P.L.P."] tried to change the name of the Party. It was obvious then that after 10 years of existence as the P.L.P. there were men in control of the Party who wished to destroy it from its very foundations. Since the 1964 Convention the group has taken more deliberate steps towards advocating physical violence as a means of achieving the Party's political objectives. The change of the Government by force and "the shedding of blood" has been openly advocated by some members of the group.[27]

The schism did present a dilemma: Would the PLP, which appeared to be shedding its right wing member by member, now adopt more radical tactics? Having failed at the ballot box despite the operation of adult suffrage, and having lost half the small number of seats won at the 1962 election, would Pindling or perhaps some new leader within the PLP turn to the streets with strikes and mass intimidation? The answer came in February 1966 when the four remaining PLP parliamentarians returned to the House. Their immediate explanation was the encouragement given to the cause at the United Nations meeting, but this was minimal. A more realistic explanation was that they could not afford to lose the forum that the House provided and the new issue that was emerging — the place of organized gambling in the Bahamas.

For some time reports from the United States had warned of underworld involvement in the Freeport casino operation. Although such reports were denied by Bahamian authorities, including the commissioner of police, who held that existing controls were adequate to prevent any such thing, the government's decision late in 1965 to grant a new casino licence, this time at Paradise Island (formerly named Hog Island) just across the harbour from Nassau, deepened public concern. Church groups, led by the Bahamas Christian Council, attacked the the decision and were not mollified by warnings that Freeport tourism, reinforced by gambling, was likely to pull ahead of Nassau's. In the House, PLP and NDP members attacked both gambling and the very existence of Freeport. Its population had now grown to 8,500 and that of Grand Bahama as a whole to 21,000; Adderley warned that in twenty years Freeport could control the Bahamas, "a monster in this

PLP demonstration on Bay Street, Arthur Hanna being carried (Courtesy of *Tribune*)

Lynden Pindling and Carlton Francis campaigning (Courtesy of *Tribune*)

country which can only devour the Bahamas, unless the Bahamas controls it now".[28] Hanna, who on 17 March was again removed from the House together with Butler, complained that the population of Freeport was "made up primarily of gangsters".[29] The government refused to make any inquiry into casino profits or to set up a gambling commission; the PLP and NDP pressed for both on a number of occasions. The conflict-of-interest theme was interwoven with the Freeport issue: Pindling claimed that as chairman of the Development Board and later minister, Sands had been paid $1.1 million. At the end of July the government issued a vague set of guidelines for ministerial conduct: no minister should permit his private interests to influence the discharge of his public duties.[30] However, a number of specific allegations continued to float about: interests in land which might close a popular public beach, in mail-boat contracts, supply of goods to government departments.

Despite such suspicions about public morality, there was some solid evidence of economic growth. The number of tourists continued to increase. The number arriving directly at an Out Island rose from just over a hundred thousand to a quarter of a million, and there were even signs of the long-awaited economic diversification. An American company, Owens-Illinois, which had a timber cutting concession at Abaco,

Table 7. Growth in tourism, 1963-66.

	Number of Tourists	Percentage Increase over Previous Year
1963	546,404	22.8
1964	605,171	10.8
1965	720,420	19.0
1966	822,317	14.1

disclosed that they would start sugar growing with a quota for the United States market of ten thousand tonnes per annum. Sands was publicly sceptical of the success of such a venture and defended his first love, tourism, as a more stable source of income than industry which must always be handicapped by the Bahamas' lack of raw material, skilled labour, and cheap power. The American underwater base at Andros was completed at a cost of $17 million, and plans were announced for an oil refinery at Freeport to produce fifty thousand barrels a day at a cost of $10 million. Even more promising for employment prospects was the growth in hotel construction at Freeport and on Paradise Island. Against this the opposition could merely claim that the cost of living was going up: 7.1 per cent since 1963, the TUC claimed; only 3.1 per cent according to Ministry of Labour figures. A protest march on the cost of living led to three TUC officials being charged with marching without a permit, but they were discharged by the magistrate before whom they appeared.

Early in 1966 the compilation of the new electoral rolls began, and at first went very slowly, reflecting, some thought, a growing dissatisfaction with the UBP government. By mid-February, when half the expected Out Island voters had been enrolled, only a quarter of the expected New Providence voters were on the books, and the government acted on an NDP suggestion for a national registration week, which added another two thousand to the rolls. The PLP submitted a petition to the Queen complaining about the "undemocratic allocation of seats in the House of Assembly and the unfair delimitation of electoral boundaries", the conflict of interest involving ministers, and the admission of "the worst criminal elements of this hemisphere thus endangering our ancient heritage as a God-fearing Christian community".[31] The Queen visited the Bahamas later that month, but the offending policies stood. Another political grievance was the erection of barricades around the House of Assembly building during sittings; the PLP sought their removal without success.

In June 1966 an Afro-Bahamian Club was formed. It approached the Ministry of Education for more teaching of African and black history: "As the great majority of Bahamians are of African origin, we feel that it is absolutely essential to teach African and black man's history and culture which has up to now been very largely neglected".[32] The *Tribune* replied that proper Bahamian history should be taught first: "Let us teach our children to be Bahamians — first, last and all the time. This visionary association with Africa will get us nowhere, for the simple reason that Africa doesn't want us."[33] The chairman of the club's education committee explained that the existing curriculum was designed to make black men feel inferior:

> Our children are compelled to study about the European brightmen (the conquerors so to speak) and nothing about themselves. After 300 years our schools do not have a proper history of the Bahamas. Why? I will tell you why. It is impossible to write a proper history of the Bahamas without mentioning Africa and a proper and true history of the Bahamas might begin with the great men of Africa and lead up to the achievements of our own black people.[34]

A correspondent answered him:

> Most countries teach their own histories and that of a historically democratic people such as Britain and the U.S. However, the Bahamas does not have an appreciable history than can be taught

alone in schools and since we are a British colony it follows that
British history should be the main requirement of our schools, but
African history, Holy smoke man, what culture or civilization does
Africa have anyway? None, unless you call ignorance, savagery and
deep superstitition culture.[35]

There were more in the same vein, to the point that one might wonder
how many PLP *agents provocateurs* infiltrated the *Guardian*'s columns.

In September Fawkes moved for a select committee to consider "the
advisability of inviting the Government of the United Kingdom to
convene a constitutional conference with a view to establishing the
independence of the Bahama Islands". The proposal was promptly
rejected, Stevenson claiming that "our wealth is here because the Union
Jack is flying over these islands".[36] The *Guardian* commended the
decision to reject such a committee which might be "misinterpreted";
the Bahamas could not afford independence, and there was no reason
for it. The PLP and NDP supported Fawkes, and Braynen, who was
drifting once more out of the UBP, commented that he could see no
harm in the proposal; subsequently Fawkes and a PLP delegation
appeared before the United Nations Committee on Colonialism, Fawkes
arguing for independence and the PLP for constitutional reform. The
PLP also took the opportunity to solicit technical and financial assistance for the Bahamas and to repeat stories about a link between the
UBP and American gambling interests that had appeared in British
newspapers, but they differed from Fawkes on the question of independence, arguing that the lack of preparation by the administering power
and the UBP government's opposition to majority rule would make
independence now "an incitement to open and violent rebellion
because there would be no democratic means to obtain a change of
Government".[37] They were in favour of independence when the proper
preparations were completed. But before Bahamians could address
their attention to the independence question, political debate was transformed by an article in an American newspaper.

On 5 October 1966 the *Wall Street Journal* published an article on
Bahamian affairs by two staff journalists, Monroe W. Karmin and
Stanley Penn, who subsequently received a Pulitzer Prize for investiga-
tive journalism for their work. It alleged that secret documents
provided insight into "how gambling came to Grand Bahama"; that the
"man in charge" of the casino at Freeport, Frank Ritter, was wanted in
the United States for tax evasion, as were two associates in the casino
management, Max Courtney and Charlie Brudner, and further that the
three had operated a nationwide bookmaking operation in New York;
and that a much more sinister figure, Meyer Lansky, was suspected of
having an interest in the casino. The article also charged that various

members of the Executive Council, which had agreed to grant the exemption from the criminal code under which the casino operated, benefited from arrangements with companies controlled by Wallace Groves, the principal figure in the development of Freeport, and that two other prominent figures, R. H. Symonette, now Speaker of the House of Assembly, and Sir Etienne Dupuch, editor of the *Tribune,* had had comparable arrangements, although Dupuch had already terminated his. It further claimed that the New York public relations firm that acted for the Ministry of Tourism had purchased the manuscript of a book entitled *The Ugly Bahamian,* and the book was being suppressed. It pointed to the rise of the PLP, although it doubted whether the party was yet strong enough to win the next election, and observed that Pindling's "most potent political weapon" was "the Grand Bahama gambling, with its potential benefits of Government tax revenue and its potential dangers of mobster infiltration".[38]

The *Guardian* immediately sprang to the government's defence, attacking the *Wall Street Journal* for "a tirade of unsubstantiated accusations about the Bahamas . . . The motive for the article is a mystery. It was probably prompted by some power-hungry person or someone who is jealous of the economic success of these islands." It went on to repeat the well-worn statements about conflict of interest:

> The conflict of interest issue is one which has always been with us and presumably will be with us for many, many years to come. This Colony needs its best men as legislators. And the best men here are also the highly successful businessmen who have, by their success in the commercial field, proved themselves capable of handling the affairs of this country.
>
> The Bahamas doesn't pay its legislators. Even if it did it is extremely unlikely that the pay would be high enough to attract the high calibre of people now serving in the House and Senate.[39]

Equally inevitably the PLP and the NDP fell on the story gleefully. Writing in his party's paper, Pindling said, "We opposed but no one paid any attention. We exposed but no one believed. Like a thief in the night our Government had foisted upon a trusting and unsuspecting people a nightmare. The people did not listen to the call 'to watch' and they were conned — yes conned — by their own Government."[40] If the allegations were true then the governor should "immediately fire the whole lot". The PLP approached Braynen as deputy Speaker to recall the House to discuss the article; he refused as the matter was not of sufficient urgency. Both Pindling and Adderley demanded a royal commission into the matter. While the *Guardian* continued to abuse the *Wall Street Journal* for an article "as deliberately distorted and scurrilous a piece of writing as we have seen published about the Bahamas"[41] and wondered whether Florida and Puerto Rico interests affected by

Bahamian competition were behind it, the opposition parties pressed
for an investigation.

The governor, on a visit to the United States, told a club luncheon
in Memphis that it was his duty to see that the charge that gambling in
the Bahamas was linked to organized crime in the United States was
not true: "Most of that criticism is the result of sensational journalism,
long on rumour and short on fact . . . I would respectfully suppose that
greater judgement would be needed to succeed in Wall Street than was
evidenced in this article — but perhaps it was intended to entertain
rather than inform."[42] Pindling, said the governor, had forfeited the
confidence of the Bahamian people and should resign. Back in the
Bahamas, the governor spoke at Freeport to warn, "More bad publicity
may be in store", and suggested there was malice in the criticism of
Freeport.[43]

Adderley led an NDP delegation to London to pursue demands for
a royal commission and seek a number of constitutional changes before
any election could be held: revision of the New Providence–Out Islands
ratio to reflect the distribution of population and new boundaries; a
limit on the size of cabinet, with more safeguards over conflict of
interest; an increase in the government-nominated bloc in the Senate.
The NDP also warned that an election should not be held while half
the population of New Providence was not yet enrolled (when the rolls
closed there were still five thousand fewer electors than in 1962), but
by 11 November both PLP and NDP were agreed that a snap election
would be called to catch the opposition off-balance, and the PLP added
that the UBP would seek independence after the election. Adderley
cabled the secretary of state to stop a dissolution. After the dissolution
was announced, he was told that he should have sent his communication through the governor; the governor explained to him that his cable
had said that government could be carried on without a dissolution but
added: "When the advice to dissolve was tendered to me by the
Premier, no alternative to the present Government was in sight, and the
present Government had made it clear to me that they would not carry
on without a dissolution."[44] In fact the 1963 Constitutional Conference had agreed:

> The Governor, in deciding whether or not to dissolve the House of
> Assembly, will act generally in accordance with the advice of the
> Premier. He may in his discretion, however, also dissolve the House
> if a majority of all the members of the House of Assembly pass a
> resolution of no confidence in the Government or if the office of
> Premier is vacant and he considers there is no prospect of his being
> able to appoint a person who can command a majority. He may dis-
> regard the Premier's advice if he considers that a dissolution is un-
> necessary and would not be in the interests of the Bahama Islands.[45]

On 1 December Sir Roland Symonette announced that a general election would be held on 10 January 1967. He stated that decisions about constituency boundaries, conflict of interest, and gambling had all been made within the Constitution. The government was ready to stand on its record of full employment, a rising standard of living and peaceful prosperity, of long-range projects and improved services, of international investment encouraged by "confidence in the stability and integrity of this Government".[46] He went on to attack the opposition for hindering the progress of good government, debating irrelevancies, and disregarding the rules of the House and for disgraceful acts like throwing out the mace. To this last point Pindling replied, "The Premier has complained that throwing the mace out of the window of the House of Assembly was a disgraceful act. I say this: how much more disgraceful an act was it to throw a man, a human being, a representative of the people, out of the door of the House of Assembly."[47] For the PLP the three biggest issues would be the electoral boundaries, gambling, and conflict of interest.

In a memorandum to the secretary of state, the PLP repeated its call for a royal commission and attacked the distribution of electorates, the lack of limits on electoral expenses, and the almost total control of the media by the "present political structure". Declaring, "It is our view that the Colonial Office helped to get us in the present mess and it is our view that the Colonial Office must help get us out", the memorandum alleged that there had been a deliberate withholding of information at the constitutional conference. The exemption certificate had already been granted; the governor knew this, so did the Colonial Office, and the UBP delegates as well. Had it been general knowledge, there would have been more discussion of controls of the police and internal security and of conflict of interest. The memorandum referred to R. M. Solomon's attack on the previous commissioner of police and his eventual replacement by the present commissioner. Had this been part of a plan, and had the payment of special inducement pay to the new commissioner been to secure his loyalty to the cabinet? Had it affected his decision to admit the three gamblers named in the *Wall Street Journal* article?[48] The commissioner promptly sued the *Bahamian Times* and its editor, and Pindling and Butler for libel contained in the memorandum, whereupon a group of "church leaders" — actually PLP stalwarts — protested to the governor about the commissioner having charge of the elections while he was suing leaders of one party; the governor replied that he had every confidence in the commissioner. Subsequently Government House issued a statement replying to the PLP memorandum to the secretary of state pointing out that the commissioner's inducement pay had been a temporary arrangement until salaries were reviewed, after which the sum was much reduced, and that the grant of the certificate of exemption had been released on 11 April 1963, a month before the constitutional conference.

On 19 December the governor flew to London, and on 21 December the secretary of state told the House of Commons that the premier would welcome an inquiry into allegations about gambling – to which the general manger of Bahamas Amusements Ltd added its agreement. However, as questions of conflict of interest were now *sub judice,* presumably because Sands was suing the *Economist,* which had called for an inquiry into the allegations, the secretary of state declined to comment on that subject. Pindling, too, made a quick trip abroad: to London to protest against the British governments' caution and at the same time to encourage the continuing flow of capital, and then to the United States, where he told a meeting held at the Overseas Press Club of New York that the PLP did not want to ban gambling but would clean it up.

The election campaign extended over the Christmas holidays – Pindling condemned this as greedy, selfish, and unChristian – and was marred by some hooliganism, especially attacks on UBP meetings and premises and some NDP meetings. Building workers had a short strike, as did employees of the Electricity Corporation; following sabotage of some electrical installations, a frigate arrived ostensibly to provide support for the utilities should this be required. As Symonette had fore-shadowed, the UBP stood on its record, encouraged no doubt by figures for tourism in 1966 available just before the poll which showed a good rise over the previous record of 1965. Sands himself published a full-page advertisement answering the conflict of interest charges: he had complied with the rules and had not been paid the fees alleged in the PLP's memorandum to the secretary of state (which copied the *Wall Street Journal* article), although he had had a consultant's agreement with the company; his charges were in line with those charged by American lawyers for similar work.[49]

Given the circumstances in which the election had come about, there was little occasion to refer to race. The UBP election platform began with a pledge for equal opportunity and "the continued fostering of full co-operation and goodwill between all classes and races within the Colony, so that all Bahamians, regardless of creed and colour, will continue to have equal opportunity for the enjoyment of the economic and social advantages offered by our way of life".[50] The PLP made immigration control a central feature of its policies, and this always had a racial flavour, but its election platform looked to higher things:

> Over the last four years our beloved Bahama Islands have been steered far off course. The Ship of State is now caught in the Sea of

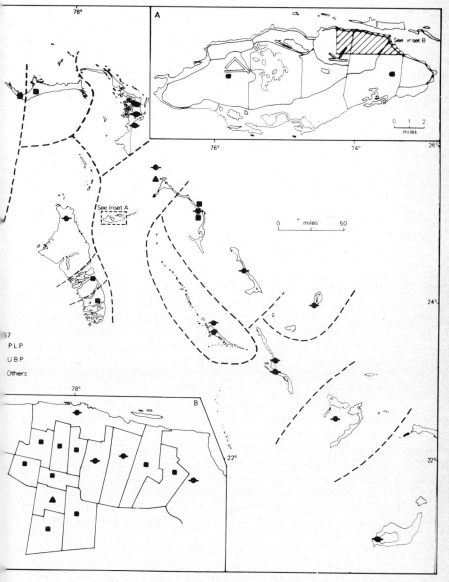

Map 4. Results of the 1967 general election

Shame and Corruption. The Ship of the Bahamas has been steered by men who have put personal gain before country, who have placed tourist figures before God. We believe it is time for a change. Time for the Ship to be steered back into more peaceful waters. We believe it is time that we put God first.[51]

The UBP secured two Out Island seats unopposed: San Salvador and Crooked Island, where the NDP candidate was disqualified by the returning officer — that decision was later overturned in the courts, but the UBP retained the seat at the ensuing by-election. At Grand Bahama Harold De Gregory, the former UBP member who had been elected as an independent at the previous general election, did not stand again, and the two new seats were won by the PLP. The PLP retained the two seats at Andros they had originally won in 1962, Pindling recapturing one of these from Stevenson, though they lost the third seat created for this election to the UBP. Most surprisingly the PLP won two of the three seats at Eleuthera, with George Baker for the UBP sandwiched between the two PLP candidates first and third. Alvin Braynen, who had left the UBP again, held his seat at Harbour Island, defeating one of the two sitting UBP members, the other having moved to a New Providence constituency and a new UBP candidate coming in instead. Thus the twenty-one Out Island seats went: UBP 14, PLP 6, independent 1.

In New Providence the pattern was reversed. Fawkes had been left alone by the PLP "in order to complete the unity of all sections of labour in the country",[52] but more probably because he was unbeatable in St Barnabas. The UBP won the two seats which were obviously safe, Nassau City and Fort Montagu, and two of the marginal seats, Centreville and Palmdale. Thus the seventeen New Providence seats were divided: UBP 4, PLP 12, Labour 1.

If votes from single-member and multi-member constituencies could legitimately be added together, then the figures would have been: UBP 19,418; PLP 18,548; Labour 1,292; NDP 826; and independents 2,858. A more realistic version of the figures would suggest that the PLP had the support of a thousand or so more voters than had backed the UBP, but either method of counting would show the two principal parties close together, the NDP wiped out, and other candidates nowhere — save for the two veteran mavericks, Fawkes and Braynen, who now held the balance of power.

NOTES

1. *Guardian,* 19 December 1962.
2. Set out in full in *Guardian,* 27–28 April 1963; for the PLP proposals see *Tribune,* 20 April 1963.

3. Report of the Bahamas Constitutional Conference Held in London May 1963. Cmnd. 2048 (1963), chap. III, para. 4. The text was printed in *Tribune* 23 May 1963.
4. The text of the Taylor-Stevenson statement to the Miami press and some elaboration on it is in the small journal Taylor was then publishing, *The Saturday Post and Mail,* 16 March 1963.
5. *Herald,* 13 April 1963.
6. *Tribune,* 11, 12, and 22 July 1963.
7. Ibid., 26 July 1963.
8. Ibid., 7 August 1963.
9. *Guardian,* 23 May 1963.
10. Ibid., 6–7 July 1963.
11. *Tribune,* 31 January 1966.
12. Ibid., 1 March 1963.
13. *Guardian,* 28–29 September 1963.
14. Ibid., 26 June 1964.
15. *Tribune,* 20 November 1964.
16. Ibid., 4 December 1964.
17. Ibid., 26 November 1964.
18. Ibid., 23 April 1965.
19. Ibid., 27 April 1965.
20. Ibid.
21. Ibid., 3 May 1965.
22. Ibid., 7 May 1965.
23. Ibid., 25 May 1965.
24. Ibid., 2 June 1965.
25. *Guardian,* 31 May 1965.
26. *Tribune,* 8 October 1965.
27. Ibid.
28. Ibid., 17 March 1966.
29. Ibid., 18 March 1966.
30. Ibid., 30 July 1966.
31. Ibid., 26 February 1966.
32. Ibid., 8 July 1966.
33. *Tribune,* 22 August 1966.
34. *Guardian,* 30 April 1966; *bright* in this context means light-complexioned.
35. Ibid., 9 September 1966.
36. Ibid., 6 September 1966.
37. *Bahamian Times,* 24 September 1966.
38. The article was reproduced in *Bahamas Observer,* 8 October 1966, and *Tribune,* 10 October 1966.
39. *Guardian,* 7 October 1966.
40. *Bahamian Times,* 8 October 1966.
41. *Guardian,* 26 October 1966.
42. *Tribune,* 3 November 1966.
43. Ibid., 23 November 1966.
44. *Guardian,* 3 December 1966.
45. Cmnd. 2048, para. 25.
46. *Guardian,* 2 December 1966.
47. *Bahamian Times,* 3 December 1966.
48. Ibid., 17 December 1966.
49. *Tribune,* 7 January 1967.
50. *Guardian,* 19 December 1966.
51. *Bahamian Times,* 24 December 1966.
52. *Tribune,* 3 December 1966.

6

Black Power: The First Phase, 1967-70

The stalemate was quickly resolved. Braynen and Fawkes were approached by Symonette and Pindling; both pledged their support to Pindling. Pindling saw the governor, said that he was ready to form a government, and was duly commissioned. On 16 January he announced his ministry, reduced from the UBP's fourteen to eleven in number: he would become premier and minister for tourism, Milo Butler minister for health and welfare, Arthur Hanna minister of education, Carlton Francis minister for finance, Cecil Wallace-Whitfield minister for works, Jeffrey Thompson minister for internal affairs, Curtis McMillan minister for communications, Warren Levarity minister for Out Island affairs, agriculture, and fisheries, Clement Maynard and Clarence Bain ministers without portfolio – and Fawkes minister for labour.[1] The ministry was youthful: the average age of under forty-two was brought to that figure by two older members, Butler aged sixty and Bain sixty-two. McMillan was only thirty-three, Thompson and Levarity thirty-four, Wallace-Whitfield and Pindling himself thirty-six.

The *Tribune*, still bitter over the part played by the American press in destroying the UBP government,[2] congratulated Pindling and declared that there was no need for panic; the Bahamas had experienced two major social revolutions in ten years, there was still a capable opposition, and the Senate had a heavy responsibility.[3] (A few days later, however, it was warning of a possible recession, and claiming that some investors were cutting back.) The *Guardian*, too, was restrained; it did not criticize the new ministry, and its interviews with men-in-the-street found a general willingness to give the new government a chance to prove itself.[4] The *Bahamian Times*, understandably elated, carried the headline "Bay Street Rule broken and the New Era begins", and also the news that Pindling had told a party victory rally that they should not expect miracles overnight "but you the people of this country can rest assured that when the loaf is shared your slice will be there".[5] The most prescient analysis came from the rejected NDP leader, Paul Adderley: the real question now was how long the PLP would allow the UBP to survive. The significant development had been

Paul Adderley (Courtesy of *Guardian*)

the break in UBP dominance of the Out Islands at Grand Bahama and Eleuthera, and there was no longer any reason to vote UBP on the Out Islands. Therefore the PLP should go for another quick election.[6]

Pindling's behaviour in the post-election days could not be faulted. He warned employers against victimization, and employees against any temptation to slack: "We need to work harder today than we have ever done before. My government has promised you a square deal, a better life. It will not drop out of the sky. Hard work, honesty and determination are the only things that will do."[7] He told a meeting of international bankers at Lyford Cay that his government would honour the financial commitments of the previous government and not impose personal or corporate income tax. The government would "foster the climate of free enterprise" and be a good neighbour to the United States. Interviewed on Miami television, he denied that gamblers had helped the PLP; the party had no commitments to anyone, though it had had the loan of a boat and an airplane during the campaign. By the end of the month he, Carlton Francis, and the party whip, James Shepherd, were in Washington to finalize the loan for harbour works.

Relations with the United States occasioned one minor flurry of excitement. The American baseball player Jackie Robinson, who had broken Jim Crow practices in major league baseball and was now on the staff of Governor Nelson Rockefeller of New York, arrived to talk with the new government. Robinson announced that he was registering as the Bahamian government's representative in the United States, but his complaint to the United States vice-president that no congratulatory message had been sent to Pindling led to charges that Rockefeller was dabbling in Bahamian politics to win votes at home.[8] On his arrival in Nassau Robinson was suitably discreet: "The United States has an opportunity to better relations between the races through an interest in the first Negro government established in the Bahamas."[9] But whatever the wisdom of dallying with a Rockefeller aide, the endorsement of prominent American Negroes gave the new government an extra fillip of prestige: on the day the new legislature opened, a reception at Government House was entertained by Miriam Makeba, Harry Belafonte, Bill Cosby, and Sidney Poitier, a Bahamian who had already publicly associated himself with the PLP and had flown to Andros to congratulate Pindling as soon as the election results were known.

The defeated UBP attributed its defeat to lack of organization and poor communications in New Providence, and to the fact that MHAs and ministers had too much to do in the campaign – the day of the amateur in politics was over.[10] There were some recriminations about the party's failure at Eleuthera, and when the party nominated Eugene Dupuch and a young Negro, Barrie Farrington, to its two places in the Senate, a former minister, Trevor Kelly, who had lost his Eleuthera seat in the debacle, quit the party in protest. G. A. D. Johnstone stood down as party chairman, and a new executive was elected by a predominantly Negro conference.[11] Again Adderley provided the soundest comment: the UBP would be unlikely to benefit from PLP mistakes for a long time, Symonette would not make an effective leader of the opposition, and Sands, the man who could lead them, was now a millstone around their necks.[12] There was now a convergence of the two parties, the UBP becoming more liberal in pursuit of votes, the PLP becoming more conservative in pursuit of business support. The UBP did not need to broaden its base, which was broad enough, but needed to change its top, which was now composed of the Young Turks of 1949.[13]

When the legislature met on 9 February a crowd of twenty-five thousand swarmed around the city centre. Some booed the UBP members as they went in. Braynen was elected Speaker on the nomination of Pindling, seconded by the former Speaker, R. H. Symonette. A PLP member, Clifford Darling, was elected deputy Speaker in Braynen's place. In the Senate, where the PLP still had only four places (Rhodriquez again, Dr Doris Johnson, Simeon Bowe, and Edgar Bain), the same independent president and deputy president, Leonard Knowles and Godfrey Higgs, were re-elected.

Dr Doris Johnson (Courtesy of Oscar Johnson and *Bahama Life*)

Given the brief period in which the PLP had been in office, the governor's speech was understandably vague:

My Government intends to prepare and to invite you to adopt a comprehensive development plan designed to expand the economy and to develop social services so as to bring the maximum benefit to all sections of the community. Closely related to this my Government recognises the need to re-examine the whole basis of the economy with a view to determining whether there is any scope for diversification and, if so, in what direction. The tourist industry has served the economy with outstanding success in recent years and the promotion of this trade must continue to be the main direction of my Government's efforts, but prudence demands that secondary industries be encouraged.

Education would be developed, and there was mention of engaging overseas teachers. Existing clinics would be expanded into health centres to relieve pressure on the hospital.

On the sensitive subject of Bahamianization and immigration, the speech promised:

> It is the intention of my Government to consider measures to accelerate the recruitment and training of Bahamians for senior posts in the public service, with emphasis on training in Public Administration, both locally and at overseas centres. The aim of an all-Bahamian public service, however, is not to be achieved at the expense of efficiency and my Government acknowledges that contract officers from overseas may continue to be required for some time, to tide over the interim period, and to train Bahamians.
>
> My Ministers intend to ensure that the lead in training and in the advancement of suitably qualified Bahamians in the public service will be followed by employers in commerce and industry.
>
> Consideration will be given to amending the Immigration Act to provide more stringent immigration control, with particular reference to the taking up of employment by immigrants, illegal entry and employment without permission.

There would be a review of labour legislation and special effort to keep the cost of living "within reasonable bounds". There would be an investigation of gambling and establishment of a statutory commission to control gambling.[14]

The first few months of the new order resembled comparable times in most countries. The former ministers complained that their policies had been stolen and defended their records in office; the new ministers complained of past neglect and the shocking state of affairs they found. Allegations of intimidation and corruption at the previous election were tossed back and forth across the House and outside it. There were complaints of heavy-handed intervention in departmental affairs by new ministers, most notably Butler in medical matters, and of the Speaker's undue sensitivity in shifting the *Guardian*'s parliamentary reporter to the public gallery for claiming the Speaker had said "subduedly" after which the paper's editorial observed that the word was new to the English language. The two most important developments took place outside the legislature: on 13 March the Gambling Commission opened under the chairmanship of Sir Ranulph Bacon, who had been appointed by the previous government; and the new electoral boundaries commission was appointed.

The PLP's first budget in March pushed the Ministry for Tourism

($5.5 million) down to third place in departmental spending, behind Education ($7.2 million) and Health ($6.3 million). There had been a surplus of $3.5 million in 1966 instead of the $1.5 million budgeted, and Francis was critical of the UBP's financial record. For the first time parliamentary and ministerial salaries would be paid, and back-dated to 16 January when members were elected. The rates set were generous by Bahamian public service standards: for the premier, $27,142 plus $11,428 entertainment allowance, the same total as the governor received; ministers, $24,000 plus $2,857 entertainment; ministers without portfolio, $18,500 plus $2,857 entertainment; MHAs, $10,200; plus a 17½ per cent housing and cost-of-living allowance for ministers and a 20 per cent housing and cost-of-living allowance for members. The Speaker should receive $18,500, and the deputy Speaker and leader of the opposition $11,400, senators an honorarium of $5,000 each, with an extra $2,000 for the president and $1,000 for the deputy president. The UBP abstained from the vote to introduce salaries, and one of their members declared that his salary would be paid to charity.

The government's first electoral test came when an election court voided the no-contest result at Crooked Island where the NDP candidate had been disqualified. The government immediately adjourned the House for seven weeks to fight the campaign, but despite a massive and expensive concentration of PLP forces on the remote electorate, the UBP former MHA and new party chairman, Basil Kelly, won narrowly by 337 votes to 290. Many of the old charges of electoral malpractice were now laid at the PLP's door: that rumours had been spread that it was "illegal" to vote UBP, that the old age pension would be stopped, and that pro-UBP public servants would be transferred; and that the local commissioner had hoisted PLP banners on public buildings.[15] Whatever the truth of such claims, it was certainly obvious that the PLP at last had access to campaign resources to match the UBP's; its friends could provide airplanes and helicopters to move supporters around a remote and scattered constituency. The uncertainty was how many of the PLP's 290 voters were an accretion of strength since the general election.

One traditional political device was given another run. The *Guardian* published a letter dated 5 May 1967 beginning "Dear Lester", which purported to be shorthand notes taken by a young PLP supporter at a meeting at which a minister outlined the government's financial plans. A national bank and a national insurance company would be started, funded by compulsory levies on the private banks and insurance companies. There would be compulsory investment of 60 per cent of insurance premiums in government securities or housing mortgages. Taxes and licences would be raised substantially, and there would be a business tax of 10 per cent on profits and personal income tax of 4 to

5 per cent on earned income and 10 per cent on unearned income, a real estate sales tax and an inheritance tax of 25 per cent. Clubs and private schools would be taxed until they either integrated or closed down. The immigration of Negroes from the United States, the West Indies, and Haiti would be encouraged, and the immigration of whites discouraged unless they were investors. Most imaginatively, parliamentarians would be exempted from public utility charges. A basic wage of a dollar an hour, with time and half for weekends and holidays, would be set for domestics. Subsidies to Out Island mail-boats would be stopped, and if the owners refused to continue the service, their boats would be compulsorily purchased for a national freight service which would charge double the rates.

It was a comprehensive bundle designed to frighten every conceivable interest in the country, and the *Guardian* commented coyly, "Most, if not all, the innovations will strike thoughtful people as too outrageous to be taken seriously. But people are believing that this document does, in fact, reflect the thinking and the planning of the radical elements in the new government."[16] It demanded that Pindling reply. Not surprisingly Pindling declared that the letter was a complete fabrication. For that the *Guardian* thanked him: "We can feel reassured that the present government's legislative innovations will bear no resemblance to the measures projected in this controversial document."[17] A couple of days later it returned to the subject of the national insurance company to claim that a private company with the word *national* in its name had just been incorporated with two of its directors "said to be" PLP parliamentarians, and its telephone number established by a series of telephone calls that led first to the Cabinet Office, then to the private number of a parliamentarian with an office in the building occupied by the Cabinet Office, and finally to the government's local public relations firm which supplied the number.[18]

One sign of the changing times came in June when the UBP's ablest leader, Sir Stafford Sands, disposed of his law practice and indicated that he would spend his summers abroad. In the short run this was taken as proof of reluctance to testify before the Gambling Commission, which had been frequently on the front pages with evidence of, *inter alia*, contributions paid by the Grand Bahama Port Authority to UBP funds through Sands.[19] In the long run it was a realistic recognition of the irreversibility of the political change that had taken place. As Adderley wrote at the time, no other single person had as much effect on the political and economic life of the Bahamas over the previous twenty years, yet "the effective leader of the U.B.P. silently stole away, and put an end to the end of an era. Nobody seemed to be sorry, nobody seemed to care, least of all the U.B.P."[20] His impending retirement from the House was justified as refusal to be "a paid professional politician".[21] When his letter of resignation was read to the House, he was bitterly attacked: one PLP member said he should be pushed into a barrel of tar and rolled downhill into a burning pit; Fawkes with antiquarian enthusiasm called for the letter to be given to the public hangman and burned publicly; and Milo Butler called him a "wicked devil" and went on to criticize the Queen for giving honours only to those who had done injury to the people of her colonies while frowning on those who did good. His former colleagues sat silent through the storm.

The UBP displayed its adaptation to the changing times by choosing a Negro electrician, Cleophas Adderley, to contest the City constituency Sands vacated. On the eve of the by-election Sands returned to the Bahamas to testify before the Gambling Commission. He refused to answer questions about a cheque for $515,000 from a New York trust company on grounds that it might incriminate him and refused to give details of his bank accounts because they involved clients' affairs, but denied one payment of $576,000 which had been alleged, and insisted that his $10,000 a month consultancy fee from the Port Authority had been paid to UBP funds together with other sums given to him for the party. He also stated that in 1960 or 1961 he had refused an offer of $2 million from Meyer Lansky, who was seeking a casino licence for New Providence. Despite such a damaging performance, the UBP held the seat comfortably: Adderley 590, Milo Butler, junior, for the PLP 311, and the former MHA, Bert Cambridge, who had quit the UBP when he failed to secure selection, a derisory 4. As the City electorate comprised probably no more than 40 per cent whites, it showed that the UBP could still win Negro votes — but for the first time the PLP carried one polling booth narrowly and came close at a second. The by-election led to one sharp exchange when Cleophas Adderley, challenged about his marital affairs, turned the attack back on certain leading PLP figures who had English wives: "I have got two wives — yes. But they are both the same colour."[22] UBP supporters hailed the by-election as proof of the success of "the new image" of the UBP and "a major breakthrough in the political development of the country" because a candidate's racial origins now meant nothing.[23] But it also showed some erosion in the UBP's electoral support in a safe seat. The contest was sufficiently tame for Pindling to fly off to the United States half-way through the campaign.

The Detroit race riots in the United States at the end of July led Bahamians to consider the question of Black Power. Thus the Negro prior of St Augustine's monastery and headmaster of the school of the same name, Father Bonaventure Dean, said at a Teachers Union banquet:

In the Bahamas we do not have Black Power because this implies a "power", within a country which lacks the legitimate power to achieve its goals. In the Bahamas we have black men in power. Whether or not their exercise of power will develop in this country a black nation as opposed to a Bahamian nation depends on how well we teach a lesson in the correct meaning of *justice* and *equality for all*.

That black men have been treated unjustly by white men is an *uncontestable fact*. It would be wise for white men to admit this. They may have done so in ignorance but they have done so none the less. I believe that an admission that they have acted wrongly will help to blunt the edge that could too easily become a sharp instrument of revenge in the black man.

Black men must teach a lesson of the correct exercise of authority and the real meaning of justice because not to do so is to repeat the evil of the past and impede the progress of the country. The correct system of education can pave the way to this because it will be based on the *individual personal worth of each human being* regardless of color, race or creed.[24]

Probably most UBP-voting whites were not yet ready for such an admission. The *Guardian* was critical of the idea of Black Power, the essence of which was that Negroes must be supreme and whites must go: "But, although the whites are a minority, they will always retain a large measure of economic control, and the community must, therefore, continue as a multi-racial society in which both the non-white and the white groups have got to work together. The weakness of the P.L.P. government is the fact that it IS an all-Negro government and one which makes no pretence at having the interests of the white population at heart."[25] Only the UBP could prevent political anarchy and economic destruction, although the Black Power wing of the PLP was controlled by Pindling for the present.

Some evidence of a harder line within the PLP was provided by a Fanonist article in the *Bahamian Times* a few weeks later.[26] For the moment one area in which Black Power might display itself was immigration control. At the end of March the government indicated that it wanted more Bahamianization by the hotels; they should undertake a vigorous training programme for Bahamians, and government would discourage employment of casual visitors to the Bahamas in the hotels.[27] In May a flood of Haitians landing illegally brought mass arrests, over three hundred in three weeks, and a statement by Doris Johnson that they should be integrated into the Bahamian community was attacked with the argument that Bahamians should be looked after first.[28] In July the minister for internal affairs claimed that issuing of work permits was proceeding smoothly: since the general election 2,707 had sought permits and 2,313 had received them, 125 had been refused, and 269 deferred. The successful applicants included 1,113 Haitians and 105 Jamaicans, compared with 469 Americans (some of whom would have been Negroes), 247 English, 134 Canadians, 31 Cubans, 28 Italians, and 19 Germans.[29] He outlined the government's immigration policy, of which the critical part read:

Permission to work:
(a) Government's sacred trust to ensure that immigrants do not create unfair competition for employment.
(b) No expatriate may be offered employment in a post for which a suitably qualified Bahamian is available.
(c) Applications to employ persons already in the Colony as visitors will not be entertained.
(d) Employer may recruit from abroad after
    (i) advertising locally,
    (ii) consulting Bahamas Employment Exchange,
    (iii) submitting replies to advertisements and certificate from Bahamas Employment Exchange . . .
(g) Permission is normally granted for one year . . . Temporary permission is normally granted for a period of one month.[30]

During the City by-election campaign the PLP candidate sought to reassure expatriates and affirmed that the country needed talents and skills. Pindling made a special appeal to the Greek community; both expatriates and Greeks were particularly numerous in the constituency. At the end of the year the government announced that a manpower survey would be conducted by a firm of consultants, Clapp and Mayne, with the assistance of the United States Department of Labor and the University of Puerto Rico. For the present, prosperity continued on an even keel and there were still more jobs than Bahamians to fill them.

Concerning Freeport, the PLP government proceeded with equal caution. On taking office, Pindling remarked that his government would look at the agreement but it would be unfair to say anything further at that stage. In April he indicated that steps would be taken to tighten up government controls over Freeport and improve communication between the government's office at Freeport and the premier's department in Nassau. In June the House unanimously passed a bill to levy a tax of a million dollars a year on each casino, and despite some grumbling about its retroactive operation the Senate passed it 10–4. One of the two casinos operating at Freeport promptly closed, but it was emphasized that this was not in reprisal for the tax, merely that the tax was too much to carry at that stage of development.[31] In July the *New York Times* quoted Pindling as saying that he intended to re-establish the government as the principal authority at Freeport,[32] but the next month he assured a meeting of several hundred at Freeport that the government was not about to kill the goose that laid the golden eggs. He denied that the government was going to repeal the Hawksbill Creek Act, under which Freeport had been established, or to put Freeport out of business, but repeated that he was bound to ensure that the government was paramount in all parts of the Bahamas. With some justification he chided Freeporters as being prone to panic over rumours.[33] In November a PLP minister, Clement Maynard, referred to the immigration loophole at Freeport and implied that it would soon be plugged.

The PLP sought to enfranchise eighteen-year-olds but were blocked by an 8–7 vote in the Senate. At the end of November the new electoral boundaries were announced, and immediately denounced by the UBP as allowing the PLP seventeen seats in New Providence and the UBP only three. Writing in the *Guardian,* which was absorbing his *Bahamas Observer,* Paul Adderley commented that if an election were held the following week the UBP would secure only ten to twelve seats:

> The Negro population outnumbers the white by 10 to one. That's not our fault. That's a fact of life. And it's also fair to have 10 times as many Negroes represent us as whites. No white-dominated party will ever run this country again. What white people don't understand is that they can be governed successfully by black people. They have to get used to the idea that they are going to be ruled by black men and these black men are not out to wreck the country.[34]

Amid rumours that one PLP MHA, Uriah McPhee, was seriously ill, the government got the new boundaries through the House on the Speaker's vote. The UBP attacked Braynen for dropping all pretence at independent status (he had previously been criticized for pro-PLP speeches outside the House), but he ruled a motion of no confidence in himself out of order. A few days later Braynen challenged a UBP member who was reported to have said at a party meeting that the Speaker was "undemocratic" for voting like that. He named the member, and when his suspension was carried, 17–14, all UBP members walked out of the House. Two days later another UBP member was named for criticizing the Speaker at a party meeting and led from the House by police; again the UBP walked out.

A month before, the Gambling Commission had reported and was highly critical of certain UBP ministers. Sands had presented the application for Bahamas Amusements' exemption from the Penal Code "in conditions of great secrecy", and the matter was dealt with with "unusual expedition"; at the time it was presented, "five of the six non-official members had received or were about to receive some financial benefit either from the Port Authority or the Development Company, as also were a Member of the Senate, the Speaker of the House of Assembly, and a Member of the House of Assembly". It was also critical of the commissioner of police, who had accepted an advantageous conveyance of land; he promptly resigned. The commission concluded that Sands's fee of £200,000 for obtaining the exemption certificate was "even by Bahamian standards, out of all proportion to the legal services he had rendered . . . The enormity of the fee demanded and the speed and manner with which payment was effected, coupled with every circumstance of his handling of this application, leave us in no doubt that he was selling his services primarily as an influential Member of the Executive Council and not as a lawyer." The five consultancy agreements with three other members of the Executive Council, the Speaker, and the MHA were motivated solely by the company's wish "to smooth the passage and ensure the success of the application", and the commission could not accept that they "could not have received these consultancy agreements in complete ignorance of the intention behind them".

Although the *Guardian* claimed that the commission had failed to find any evidence of the allegations made in the American press which had triggered the inquiry, further damage was done to the UBP's reputation. Pindling gave notice that he would move for the retirement from public service of those named as consultants — the three UBP MHAs and Etienne Dupuch in the Senate; the other two former ministers, Sands and Raymond Sawyer, had already retired. The grounds Pindling gave were that they were "guilty of a grave crime against the people of the Bahamas".[35] When the debate took place on 24 January 1968 the motion read: "Resolved that having regard to the Report of the Commission of Inquiry on Gambling, this House is of the opinion that the Members of the Legislature found therein to have received consultant fees and other questionable payments were guilty of a crime against the people of the Bahamas, and ought to be and are hereby condemned."[36] On 26 January the House passed the resolution.

One other item of parliamentary business requires mention. In December the PLP whip moved for a committee to investigate discrimination. Some PLP MHAs called for legislation with gaol sentences for discriminatory acts: Milo Butler suggested a fine of a hundred thousand dollars. The UBP indicated that it supported the idea of a committee but thought it should also inquire into political discrimination. The motion was debated on several days, generated more heat than light, and was passed.

Early in January 1968 Pindling told a reporter from the *New York Times* that the PLP planned to move towards full internal self-government while remaining a British territory with British citizenship. Specific changes mentioned in the story were depriving the governor of power to nominate a majority in the Senate, and ministerial control over police and internal security.[37] R. H. Symonette criticized the suggestions as ill-advised and premature because Bahamians, whatever their political persuasion, had not controlled government long enough to establish confidence in their reliability. He cited the United Kingdom, where the Labour Party had a huge majority but still had to devalue the currency because of a lack of international confidence.[38]

The report of the constitutional committee indicated that all members were agreed on cabinet assuming responsibility for the prerogative of mercy and the introduction of single-member constituencies, and on the proposal that in matters of Bahamian defence and foreign affairs the Bahamian government should be consulted in advance by Britain, but otherwise were divided on party lines. The majority, PLP and Fawkes, wanted a Senate in which ten would be nominated on the advice of the premier and five on the advice of the leader of the opposition, transfer of police and internal security to a responsible minister, and rendering the public service and judicial and police commissions fully executive – that is, their recommendations would have to be accepted by the governor. The UBP minority were opposed to sudden changes which might affect confidence, but conceded that many of the changes could be achieved *de facto* over a period of time.[39]

When the proposals came before the House for endorsement there was a protracted debate along predictable lines, though there were some new elements such as the charge by Francis that Britain held the Bahamas in an "economic stranglehold", that Bahamian reserves in London were used for the benefit of other Commonwealth territories and the British economy, and that the colonial system of education had been geared so that only now were colonial peoples beginning to understand the power of the economy.[40] One UBP Member, Basil Kelly, offered the opinion: "I don't believe in our lifetime we will have a man whether he is black, pink or white who will have the capabilities of running this country",[41] and was rebuked as "the voice of Neanderthal Man":

> The UBP and the cloistered minority which they represent have consistently acted with the assumption that that other section of the Bahamian people, which constitutes a majority in this country, were totally incapable of governing the Bahamas. This assumption, which has been stressed and re-stressed with intensity and frequency, in itself denotes contempt by the UBP and the formerly privileged merchant princes for the mass of the Bahamian people. And in that contemptuous attitude is contained the destruction of the UBP.[42]

The minister of state, Lord Shepherd, who was in the Bahamas for informal discussions lasting four days, explained that so long as the Bahamas was a dependent territory, ultimate responsibility for internal security had to remain with the British government. That government would not force nor delay independence for the Bahamas, for which the sole criterion was the will of the people. He personally was against a referendum to test feelings about independence and constitutional advances.[43]

Generally on racial questions PLP spokesmen took a restrained line. When, at the start of a debate to continue the committee on discrimination, a UBP member asked both sides to refrain from making contentious remarks about colour, an editorial in the *Bahamian Times* pointed out that while it was fine for him to say that he had never practised discrimination himself, he still had to purge himself of not having condemned it and for patronizing places where discrimination was practised. Even so, the need was to lead whites closer to the black majority, not to make showpieces of a few unthinking blacks who still supported white influences.[44] Still more significant was an article in the same paper by "Roger de Coverley" warning against excessive adoption of the style of American Negroes. The achievements of American Negroes in their fight for equality was a matter of pride for Bahamians, but the temptation to regard all whites as enemies should be resisted. The government was conducting a courtesy campaign: the American Negro could afford to be discourteous because if he lost his job the Great Society provided a welfare cheque, but in the Bahamas loss of a job meant tragedy.

> When men of little insight ascend the dais and speak to a crowd of "new Bahamians" with the tongues of the Stokeley Carmichaels and Rap Browns, there is trouble abrewing; for while there are many admirable aspects possessed by these two dixie perpetrators of Black Power, there is absolutely not a single one of those aspects which can serve to further the cause of our national goal at this point . . . the Bahamian Negro has won his fight for equality, and is now engaged in the business of building a nation. This business engages the efforts of all Bahamians — those in Long Island as well as those in the Grove.[45]

There were few expressions of conciliation from the other side. So, when Arthur Foulkes in the House referred to the heritage of exploitation the British left behind, a letter by "San Fairy Ann" pointed out that the British were needed in the Bahamas to run the country: "As for the exploitation of Africa, Mr Foulkes has clearly not heard of the Zulu King Dingaan and his periodic slaughter of his own people, but doubtless Mr Foulkes has heard of Nkrumah and other black dictators who to-day are making life a misery for the black man in Africa where poverty, slavery and cannibalism are as much in evidence as ever from about the equator and north."[46] An only slightly less offensive statement came from a *Guardian* writer:

Apart from a few reactionaries who may still be among us, I do not
believe that white Bahamian classes have ever consciously subscribed
the principles of White Supremacy. But I will certainly agree that
there has been, historically, a definite area of economic disadvantage
which the Negro population has largely brought upon itself. It takes
a very fair-minded Negro to admit that. It is much easier to tell the
masses, and have them believe, that they have been deprived (and
many of them have been) of economic opportunities and advantages
because of the colour of their skin. No Negro politician who has any
serious hope of being elected could afford to tell his prospective
constituents that their own unrealistic and unhealthy rate of population increase is the basic cause of their condition.[47]

On 16 February 1968 Uriah McPhee died in Boston. A Baptist
deacon, on his deathbed he handed a note to a parliamentary colleague:
"I do not want my wife and my colleagues to mourn after me because
my death was something predestined and it was done for a very wise
purpose."[48] On 21 February the new session of the legislature began
with a speech from the throne promising top priority for education
and pledging that there would be no income tax or moves for independence. On 23 February McPhee was given a huge state funeral, and on
27 February a general election was called for 10 April. The rush of
voters to enrol which had begun on the news of McPhee's death
accelerated. Sir Roland Symonette was quoted as saying that the
UBP was considering offering as many Negro candidates as possible,
but for the biblically minded the 10 January 1967 election had been
the flight from Egypt (*sic*) and that on 10 April 1968 was to be the
crossing of the Red Sea.[49] Carlton Francis reassured those unhappy at
an Easter campaign: "We are fighting a holy war and we are in the
midst of a holy season."[50]

In some respects the new election was a rerun of its predecessor.
However, now it was the PLP that could run on its record already set
out in a government booklet, *Progress Report to January 1968,* which
like the UBP's earlier documents showed all graphs rising steadily —
education, tourism, provision of utilities — with a photograph of
"over the hill" at night showing the provision of street lighting as
dramatic evidence of the new look, government revenue and expenditure. There were complaints about rowdiness, and in one incident at
Fox Hill on 14 March a UBP meeting was broken up. Several other of
their meetings were stoned. However, the UBP's quest for new candidates gained them some liabilities; an article by Foulkes claimed that
five or six had previous convictions, and four or five had served time in
jail. Certainly one had an alarmingly long record involving convictions
for stealing, car stealing, possession of narcotics, indecent assault,
assault, damage to property, and running a lottery.[51] R. H. Symonette,

who was the UBP's campaign co-ordinator, denied that the party had a
two-million-dollar campaign chest and observed that votes could no
longer be bought; the *Bahamian Times* printed a photograph of a novel
scene, a candidate at Cat Island *receiving* donations from voters. The
National Democratic Party decided not to contest the elections, stating
that the people should be given a chance to give the government a clear
mandate if they wished. Fawkes, after some rumours that he had joined
the PLP once more, was not opposed officially, but when a prominent
PLP member stood against him, ostensibly as an independent, Fawkes
claimed that the PLP was working for his opponent. Braynen, who
chose the predominantly Negro part of his old constituency, was not
opposed by the PLP and was given some tacit support. Apart from one
other candidate who stood against Milo Butler and received eighteen
votes (the UBP candidate managed only twenty-seven), they were the
only independents offering. The polarization of the Bahamian electorate which had been under way at the last two elections, 1962 and 1967,
was now complete.

The total enrolment was 55,000 compared with 45,000 in 1962 and
38,000 in 1967. The electorate divided strongly in favour of the PLP:
21,908 to the UBP's 5,842 in New Providence, 10,183 to the UBP's
6,455 in the Out Islands. Something like 20 per cent of the electorate
had swung from the UBP to the PLP in the fifteen months since the last
election. As the *Guardian* conceded on the eve of the election, "The
performance of the P.L.P. Government since it came to power has con-
founded many of its critics and shown great promise. It has not made
many mistakes."[52] After the election it was even more despondent: "It
is the consensus today that the UBP has ceased to exist as an effective
opposition organisation, although it is hoped that its seven parliamentary members will function, with Mr Fawkes, as the official Opposition
in the House . . . Certainly, the UBP will never again be able to enter a
full slate of candidates in the general election."[53]

Paul Adderley commented that it was apparent that the UBP could
elect candidates only where there was a clear majority of white voters.
Not one of their Negro candidates had run well in a Negro district. But,
he added, no doubt correctly, the result would have been the same had
the party run nothing but "old guard" candidates or nothing but
Negroes.[54] In future two Negro parties would compete on personalities
and issues.[55]

Pindling's new cabinet had only two new faces. Milo Butler moved
to Labour in place of Fawkes, Curtis McMillan followed him at Health,
and Arthur Foulkes entered the ministry at Communications. Arthur
Hanna took a new portfolio of Trade and Industry, and was succeeded
at Education by Cecil Wallace-Whitfield, whose portfolio of Works went
to Clement Maynard. The other new member of the ministry was Doris

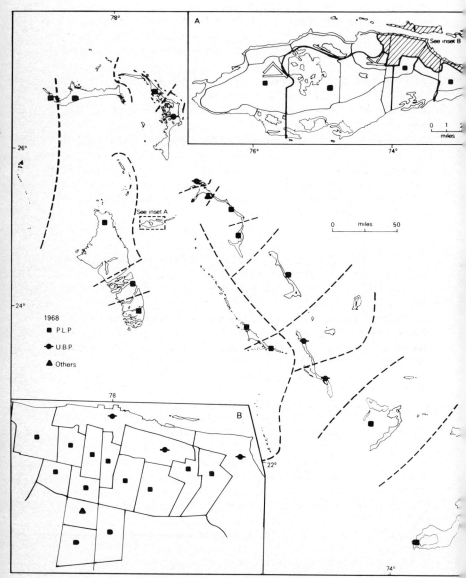

Map 5.   Results of the 1968 general election

Johnson as minister without portfolio and government leader in the Senate. Braynen was re-elected Speaker. The PLP chose two new senators, Cadwell Armbrister and Henry Bowen; the UBP named its former minister for education, Godfrey Kelly, who had been defeated at Cat Island, and C. A. Dorsett, an ex-PLP member and 1967 NDP candidate.

The new speech from the throne reiterated that delivered before the dissolution: first priority to education, no income tax — though the real property tax and licence fees would be reviewed, and no independence yet:

> Despite what was said to the contrary in some quarters, independence was not an election issue so far as my Government was concerned. On the other hand, it is unrealistic to overlook the policy of the British Government that the individual countries of the Commonwealth should govern themselves. My ministers therefore intend to take such steps as may be advisable, particularly in the training of Civil Servants, in readiness for the future.[56]

The balanced budget on 8 May reflected the government's priorities: of the total of $66 million, $10.7 million went to education, followed by health, works, and tourism — now dropped to fourth place.

For the PLP at this stage it must have seemed that the promised land was indeed in sight. With an overwhelming majority in the House of Assembly, the government could secure constitutional changes from Britain without difficulty. In August Pindling disclosed his proposals. The Senate would be reformed to give the government firm control there as well: ten members nominated by the premier (who in 1970 assumed the courtesy title of prime minister) against four nominated by the leader of the opposition and three others, still chosen by the governor. To symbolize the new status, the colony would be known as "the Commonwealth of the Bahama Islands". To meet two PLP grievances, the "belonger status" given to non-Bahamians would be replaced, and an investigation would be made into whether the government could regain the authority over Freeport it had lost under the Hawksbill Creek Act. To meet a complaint made against both the previous and the present government, provision would be made that a member of the legislature would forfeit his seat if he entered into a contract with government without informing his presiding officer and securing a resolution from the chamber exempting him from the provision.

The constitutional conference opened in London on 19 September with the UBP resisting any change, but their objections were soon swept aside. The one point that presented some difficulty, control over the police, was compromised: the governor would retain ultimate responsibility but would delegate immediate responsibility to a minister. This arrangement, it was explained, would leave the commissioner to carry out his professional duties without political interference, while the minister would be responsible for the general organization and well-being of the force. The new constitutional instruments came into force in May 1969; the PLP named five new senators, including one woman, Mrs Bertha Isaacs, and the UBP two; none of the seven had sat in the legislature previously. The "independent" bloc was reduced to three: the president, Leonard Knowles, former House member Gerald Cash, and the former attorney-general, Kendal Isaacs.

At the end of 1968 a bill to extend parliamentary privileges was introduced, seemingly aimed at the hostile daily newspapers. Publication of "false or misleading" accounts of parliamentary proceedings would be contempt, and the aggrieved chamber's determination could not be challenged in the courts. The Speaker's jurisdiction was extended to enable him to deal with any remarks made outside the House which reflected on his conduct as Speaker. With a certain irony in the light of the fate of the mace and the hour-glasses in 1962, a new offence of wilfully damaging or attempting to damage parliamentary property was created; the penalty would be a fine of six hundred dollars or six months imprisonment. The same penalty was imposed for interfering with parliament or creating a disturbance in its vicinity. After referral to a select committee it was further strengthened: anyone connected with a newspaper which had published a false or misleading report of proceedings could be banned from the chamber for a year. Despite the objections of the local press and the International Press Association, and the resistance of the opposition, the bill became law.

With the government in firm control of both houses, the only remaining constitutional step was independence. In February 1970 Pindling predicted that would come within three years. Some of the pitfalls of independence were illustrated three months later when a Cuban exile group in Florida claimed to have sunk two Cuban fishing boats and taken their crews hostage for the safety of nine exile commandos who had mistakenly sought to celebrate the ninth anniversary of the Bay of Pigs invasion with a raid on Cuba. Castro asked the British government to investigate whether they were being held at a secret base in the Bahamas, and the Cuban radio warned that if the British and American governments did not prevent their territory being used for hostile acts, Cuba would have to take the necessary steps itself. The PLP paper demanded to know where the British Navy had been, and declared that the incident showed that it was necessary for the Bahamian people to stand on their own feet and provide their own protection. The government had previously ordered four armed patrol boats — the first two arrived at the end of the year — and the *Bahamian*

Times condemned those who had been ridiculing the local navy. Bahamians would sleep more soundly "knowing that four Bahamian boats with crews dedicated to the security of country were on hand, than we can now, living with the myth of British protection and responsibility".[57]

A few months later a new marine hazard appeared on the northern flank when the United States dumped nerve gas in the ocean 240 kilometres off Abaco. Hanna complained that Britain had not given adequate support to Bahamian protests and spoke of the need for independence. The following month he announced a contest to provide a national anthem and a national flag, and the talk of independence produced a flurry of concern ranging from modest concerns about the costs to the *Tribune*'s fear that a future local government could invite the Russians to establish a naval base.[58] But Pindling, quite possibly concerned that some recent Black Power enthusiasms were causing alarm (see above), pledged that independence would not be rushed.

Following the rout of the UBP at the April 1968 election, the debate over racial discrimination had been largely transformed into questions of immigration policy, and here the PLP and the Negro majority believed that they had the upper hand. When the select committee on discrimination cited five hotels and clubs and one bank in February 1969, a *Bahamian Times* editorial called for remedial action:

> The day is long past when we had to go cap-in-hand to an investor or an employer and gratefully accept whatever conditions he proposed regarding the staffing of his hotel or business. We are now the centre of a thriving tourist business, and it is the man with money to invest here who should be anxious to please us by conforming to the very sensible regulations which govern the employment of non-Bahamians.[59]

But as the employment of non-Bahamians might equally mean Jamaicans or Haitians, the racial implications were muted. Indeed the first big drive against illegal immigrants, in June 1968, was begun with a reference to a supposed three thousand Jamaicans who had entered the Bahamas in the previous ten months, and their rough handling led to a pı test by the Jamaican government. The specific mention of Jamaica s was played down, and tribute was paid to the contribution expatriates of all nationalities were making to the development of the Bahamas.

The report on the national workforce by Clapp and Mayne in March 1969 showed how substantial the immigration problem could be. In 1968, 17 per cent of the workforce of 65,500 were expatriates; in administrative, executive, and managerial positions the figure was 42 per cent, and for professional and technical staff 35 per cent. At Freeport there was no sector of employment in which the Bahamians constituted more than 50 per cent. Yet to meet the projected doubling of the workforce between 1968 and 1973, the expatriate share of the total would have to rise to 30 per cent.[60] Relatively little use had been made of "belonger" status. Replying to a parliamentary question in November, Doris Johnson provided annual figures:[61] Fewer than five hundred persons had been granted the status, and many of these were dependants. The overwhelming proportions of non-Bahamians in the

Table 8. Immigration applications, 1964-69.

	Applications	Granted
1964	160	4
1965	71	170
1966	94	119
1967	181	136
1968	177	66
1969	132	Not available

workforce were there under work permits under the Immigration Act 1963, and the government set about tightening its control over these. In February 1969 the flat annual fee of $30 was replaced by a scale of annual payments ranging from $25 for unskilled workers and domestics to $250 for professionals and senior managers, plus a $20 residence fee for dependants. In November a new work permit system was introduced: permits valid for three years would be available for senior and skilled personnel, but the applications for such permits would have to show details of the employer's training programmes and timetable for the phasing out of non-Bahamians or else show the creation of additional positions to be filled wherever possible by Bahamians.

Employers complained that many applications were rejected and most took far too long in processing. The government argued that fourteen to twenty-one days was the average time for processing, but many took longer because the employer applicant failed to provide adequate details at first, and claimed that very few had been rejected. In 1967 there had been 1,678 approvals granted for New Providence and only 55 rejections, and for the three Out Islands where most development was taking place (Grand Bahama, Abaco, and Eleuthera) 36 granted and 6 rejected. In 1968, 2,645 were approved for New Providence and 135 rejected; for the three Out Islands 652 were granted and 65 rejected. Employers remained unconvinced, partly no doubt because things had been easier when the UBP was in power, while PLP stalwarts were unhappy at the light sentences awarded in the courts when employers in breach of the permit system were prosecuted, and the immigration authorities were sometimes criticized from the bench by expatriate magistrates for their tardiness in deciding particular applications. In August 1969 the magistrate at Freeport, after dismissing a charge of illegal work for lack of evidence, added as *obiter dicta* that undue delay in granting work permits for "key personnel" might contravene the Hawksbill Creek agreement.[62]

As Pindling conceded in a broadcast to mark the end of three years of PLP government, there was a scarcity of trained Bahamians. The government saw it as a social problem, the employers as an immigration problem. Either way it boiled down to

> how best to protect the interests of Bahamians in the Bahamas so that they are not swamped and become strangers in their own country. We have to devise a means whereby the Bahamian can exercise a political, social and economic role in his country, and this progress has to be related to immigration. The problem is, can we convince the non-Bahamian employer that he has an obligation to the Bahamas and the Bahamian to upgrade his employees. If he can't be convinced of that then we have an immigration problem.[63]

The government's own difficulties with the public service illustrate the dilemma. The report of the Public Salaries Review Committee discussed the shortage of suitable young recruits. In 1969 of 4,500 school-leavers only 8.5 per cent had the basic requirement of five junior certificate passes suitable for clerical employment. (Only 5 per cent had three or more O-levels and only 1 per cent had one or more A-levels.) If these 390 with five junior certificate passes were reinforced with 100 who had been educated abroad to a comparable level, there was a pool of some 500 — but the public service, which was expanding at a rate of 15 per cent per annum, needed 500 to 600 for its own staffing, apparently leaving none for the private sector. In practice the government found it hard to compete with the private sector, and as a result each year it had to recruit some 200 expatriates and take on 300 to 400 Bahamians whose lack of training laid by future problems unless their deficiencies were remedied while in service. At the beginning of 1970, against a public service establishment of 7,938 (it had been only 4,318 in 1966), there were 1,970 vacancies and 870 expatriates employed. Only two-thirds of the public service's needs had been met by Bahamians, and many of these were under-qualified.[64]

Lying behind the scarcity of trained personnel were the gross inadequacies of the education system, dating back to the days of the UBP government and beyond. Yet remedying those inadequacies in the short run meant running counter to the government's pledge of

Bahamianization and the related wish to promote a national culture. At the beginning of the school year 1968/69 the minister of education, Cecil Wallace-Whitfield, faced with a shortage of 150 teachers, sought to recruit them in Britain. Salaries would not allow recruitment in the United States or Canada, and Caribbean countries were loath to part with their own trained teachers, so Britain was the only possibility. Yet it left him open to charges such as Fawkes's: "Will English teachers who come to the Bahamas at this time understand the true constitutional position here? The fact is that at this stage of our development we are establishing a Bahamian tradition and our children should be education-ally led back to Africa and not taught by representatives of a colonial power."[65] The same point was made by the prior of St Augustine's, Father Bonaventure Dean, who argued that British education was a disservice to the Bahamas, not least because expression in the local idiom was necessary to promote a national identity and external examiners were unsympathetic to dialect.[66]

In July 1969 Wallace-Whitfield explained his problems to the Chamber of Commerce. Capital expenditure of $45 million was required for education, but only $5 million a year was available. The teaching service was only two-thirds of its proper strength, and of the teachers it had, almost half were unqualified. In primary and Out Island all-age schools well over half were untrained. Given such inputs it was not surprising that academic performance was so poor. In 1967 of 700 students attempting O-levels, 345 failed to pass a single subject and only 48 passed in five or more.[67] Moreover, the independent schools were also under pressure – Catholic schools accounted for a quarter of the student population in New Providence and one-tenth in the Out Islands – and some were having to borrow money to pay salaries, yet the government could do little to increase its aid. High priority had to be given to reducing the number of unqualified teachers, yet they were not eligible for training overseas. To meet their needs a second teachers' training college was opened at an abandoned missile-tracking station at San Salvador.

The PLP government assigned a steadily growing proportion of the budget to education, but how sound were the sources of revenue to underpin the drive for education? Presenting the 1969 budget, the minister of finance, Carlton Francis, warned that the rising cost of living could wreck the economy and explained that the growing sophis-tication of the Bahamian economy and its involvement with the economies of major powers left it vulnerable to policies over which it had no control. As a world banking centre it was sensitive to disorders in the international monetary system; as an importer of most goods consumed in the Bahamas it was affected by price increases in its suppliers, mainly the United States; dependent on tourism as the mainstay of its economy, it was exposed "to the uncertainties of a notoriously fickle industry".[68]

Skilfully encouraged by the previous government, and by Stafford Sands in particular, Nassau had blossomed as a base for international banks, trust companies, and off-shore funds. At the end of 1966 there were 78 banks and trust companies operating. By the end of 1969 there were 120 banks and trust companies and another 140 financial institutions engaged in limited banking operations, and at the end of 1970 the figures were 164 and 118 respectively. The 1969 bank and trust company workforce was estimated at 2,300, of which 80 per cent was Bahamian, and their expenditure at $25 million, but only $500,000 went directly into the government's hands as licence fees. When in July 1970 Francis wondered whether there was any acceptable means by which some local advantage could be derived from the large volume of funds passing through Nassau, he was warned that any rise in banking costs would drive away the Eurodollar business and reminded that banks were already hampered by poor communications and such service inadequacies as frequent power cuts.

The main thrust for economic growth still had to come from the tourist industry. At the end of 1968 there were 9,500 hotel rooms in the Bahamas, and for the first time the annual intake of tourists passed the million mark. In November 1969 a start was made on the first major hotel in New Providence for some years, development having shifted to Freeport and to Paradise Island in the meantime under the stimulation of casinos in the vicinity.

Table 9. Growth in tourism, 1967-70.

	Number of Tourists	Percentage Increase over Previous Year
1967	915,273	11.1
1968	1,072,273	17.1
1969	1,332,396	24.3
1970	1,298,344	−2.6

In 1969 the growth of 24.3 per cent was a record; in 1970 a negative growth was a record also. Over the preceding period 1960−65 United States tourists had spent $227 million in the Bahamas − but the Bahamas had spent $383 million in the United States, mainly paying for imports. The shortfall of $155 million had been covered by the inflow of capital plus some income from Bahamian-owned investments in the United States; reliance on capital flow on that scale was dangerous. A report by Checchi and Company on government finances pointed to the other danger, the Bahamas' dependence on tourism, which accounted for 71 per cent of gross national product, two-thirds of employment, and nearly 60 per cent of government revenue. Yet if revenue was to be increased in the coming years, tourism would have to pay more; the report suggested a hotel room tax and an increase in the departure tax.[69]

The government acted the following year: an annual room tax of three dollars a room imposed on the larger hotels, and a nightly head tax of seventeen cents rising to twenty-five cents for the busiest four and a half winter months. But the hotels were already complaining about their high operating costs, claiming that it now cost twice as much to service a hotel room in the Bahamas as in Puerto Rico, and three times as much as in Florida. Increasingly the local press and the opposition warned that the attitude of Bahamian hotel staff and other locals who came into contact with the tourists was discouraging their staying or coming back. In March 1970 Pindling launched a Friendship Campaign stressing the importance of tourism to the economy, but some of his supporters rejected the proposition that any decline in tourist growth was attributable to surliness or poor service by Bahamian employees:

> The fact is simply that a very large percentage of the visitors to the Bahamas come from Florida and other areas south of the Mason-Dixie line, where a black man is considered by many whites to be an upstart and a rude person if he dares to make it clear that he refuses to be treated as an inferior being. Put another way, some visitors refuse to treat service people as people and then they cannot understand why they are treated coldly in return.[70]

The reduction in air fares from North America to Europe also hurt the Bahamas — in 1969 87.5 per cent of tourists came from the United States and a further 5.1 per cent from Canada. Efforts to bring European tourists in the opposite direction never altered the North American dominance significantly.

Few Bahamians dared consider the damaging effect that tourism was having on the economy. For example, national food demand of $43 million (1968), which was met by local production for only one-third of its value, was swollen by feeding the tourists on imported foodstuffs. (By contrast, Jamaica, for example, produced almost three-quarters of its food.) The government declared 1969 to be the year for stimulating agriculture and began a survey of the country's land resources, but the revival of Bahamian agriculture was little more than party rhetoric. At the party's 1970 convention one PLP minister observed that in office he had learned that "Bahamians were not prepared to go back to the days of the fishing village and have no use for the 'back to the bush' philosophy". He was answered by the minister of finance in the no confidence debate (see below) a few weeks later: "There has been some talk about going back to being a fishing village. If however we are going to protect our country for our children then we will have to call in outsiders, but on our terms, even if it means going back to a fishing village."[71]

A few experiments in commercial agriculture had been tried in the Bahamas in recent years. One, a dairy-farm at Hatchet Bay on Eleuthera founded by a wealthy American in the 1930s, had survived; others, situated on Andros and Grand Bahama and producing for the near-by American market a few specialized crops by taking advantage of the early growing season, had enjoyed short-lived successes. The most ambitious scheme, to produce ten thousand tonnes of sugar a year on Abaco by a company previously harvesting timber in the area, closed in 1970 after losing over ten million dollars in two years. There were a few ventures in other directions. A salt plant opened at Long Island in 1969; another had operated at Inagua since the 1930s. In 1970 a project for the underwater mining of aragonite near Bimini began. In August 1968 plans were announced to build a sixty-million-dollar refinery at Freeport to process low sulphur fuel oil. But such instances of economic diversification were few and far between and were capital intensive rather than providing much scope for the employment of Bahamians save in the construction phase.

The government sought to encourage large investors who would create employment rather than small investors who would compete with the emerging Bahamian capitalists — employing their own money or bank credit, or sometimes fronting for American investors. In 1970 Pindling spelled out the government's strategy in a lecture to an American university audience. They would seek direct investment in government bonds, reinvestment of a proportion of profits locally, establishment of a local research and development programme, offering of some equity on the local stock market, and extension of share options to local employees. Justifying the Development Corporation, which was set up to make government a partner in resort, residential, recreational, and commercial projects, matching its land resources to the investor's capital and technical knowledge, the minister introducing the legislation explained that local savings in the commercial banks totalled perhaps ten to twelve million dollars, while foreign investment in the Bahamas was worth two thousand million. Certainly local capitalists had some access to imported savings through the banks (too easily in some cases, it appeared later), but any substantial capital growth had to tap the foreign investor. But what the investor was to invest in was never clear.

Not all Bahamians were benefiting from the continued growth in the economy. In 1970 the Community Action Committee, set up by a PLP back-bencher, investigated conditions in Bain's Town, one of the poorer areas "over the hill". The average weekly income was fifty-six dollars, of which 85 per cent was spent on food and rent. The average household comprised five persons living in three rooms; fewer than 40 per cent owned the land they lived on — a high proportion owned moveable wooden houses resting on land they rented or squatted upon. More than one quarter had a weekly income less than forty-five dollars; only 12 per cent had over a hundred dollars a week. A quarter of the homes were without electricity, over three-quarters lacked running water, yet 20 per cent owned a motor car and 30 per cent a television set.[72] But the interest rates on government housing loans had crept up to 10 per cent — and of course few in such an area would have had the income to qualify them for government loans — and there were reports that government access to loan money was drying up. The public debt rose steadily: $25 million in 1967, $37 million in 1968, $66 million in 1969, and the cost to the budget of servicing public debts increased correspondingly. By 1969 it was a third of the amount being spent on education, a development that caused more concern in the Bahamas than in most countries, for until the mid-1960s there had been no public debt payments to be met. Government's initial commitment to education and health left little scope for other forms of welfare such as housing and income support, and when the minister of finance indicated that the government was investigating a general social security scheme to cover old age, illness, and unemployment, he had to admit that the existing age pension of thirteen dollars a month was mere tokenism.

Another dimension of the unevenness of growth was shown in the 1970 census. Although the population of the Bahamas as a whole had risen by almost forty thousand since 1963, almost all the increase was concentrated on two islands, New Providence and Grand Bahama. Their proportion of the total population rose from 69.7 per cent to 76.2 per cent over the inter-censal period. In the islands adjacent to New Providence and receiving some overspill of the benefits of tourism — Abaco, Andros, Harbour Island and Spanish Wells, Eleuthera, and Exuma — there was a slight increase of just over two thousand, but even so, their proportion of the total population fell from 20.5 per cent to 17.2 per cent. In the remaining islands to the south-east, there was a decline in every island (except for tiny Rum Cay and Long Cay, each with fewer than a hundred inhabitants), for a total loss of over fifteen hundred. Their share of total population fell from 9.7 per cent to 6.5 per cent. Always disadvantaged by remoteness from Nassau and inadequate communications, they slipped further back as prosperity spread out from Nassau.

In the second half of 1970 bits of gilt began to come off the gingerbread of economic growth that had been plentiful for nearly twenty years. Gramco, a trust fund operating a large real estate fund in the United States, the U.S. International Fund, had to suspend sales and redemptions. The Wellington Bank closed its doors. The oldest Out Island resort, French Leave at Eleuthera, went into receivership. In October the minister of finance predicted that there would be a short-fall of $13 million in government revenue, down to $84 million from a projected $97 million, and the Monetary Authority had to deny rumours of an impending devaluation of the Bahamian dollar.

Perhaps the most startling development was the suspension of operations by the principal domestic air-carrier and one of the major carriers of tourists to and from the Bahamas, Bahamas Airways Limited (BAL). The company had a long history, mainly of ownership by BOAC, which had taken it over again in 1961, and after a period of steady losses had sold 85 per cent of its shares in 1968 to the Swire group. In October 1970, without any prior warning to the public, the company cancelled its flights, flew its aircraft out of the country, and threw 750 employees out of work. Over the next few days a tangled story emerged from charge and counter-charge. It appeared that for some time the company had been pressing the government for financial assistance, offering half its shares for government acquisition. The government was cautious or dilatory, depending on the point of view, and asked for time to consider the financial situation – there was talk of liabilities of $35 million. The government's critics blamed the company's decision to throw in the towel on the Licensing Authority's award of certain overseas routes to a local company which had not yet started operations, Bahamas World Transport. That company was owned by American interests who already owned a medium-sized hotel in Nassau. The company had been formed by Pindling's old law firm, and his former partner, Kendal Nottage, was an officer of the company – but it was quite a usual arrangement for Bahamian law firms to supply officers to maintain company structures for overseas owners. BAL had recently appointed two of the independent senators, Cash and Isaacs, both lawyers, to its board, and Isaacs claimed that the government had reneged on an undertaking given in 1968 that there would be no encroachment on BAL's routes. Arthur Hanna criticized the wisdom of the company in appointing "two people who have no affiliation with the present government" to its board when it needed men who wanted to see the government survive and would have kept the government informed on what was happening. To the outsider it appeared that the government had been less than well-disposed to BAL but had been surprised when it folded up so suddenly and left 750 unemployed.

If that was the most dramatic example of things starting to go wrong in the economy, the most important was the slow deflation of the Freeport balloon. Following his government's triumphal re-election, Pindling disclosed that the Hawksbill Creek Act, which had established the *imperium in imperio* which was Freeport, was being considered to see whether the principles of the Bahamian Constitution were violated and warned that the more successful Freeport became the greater would be the social problems it created. Certainly its demands were already straining public service resources as more and more officials, immigration, customs, police, post-office staff, etc., had to be posted to Freeport. One dimension of its burgeoning growth was shown at the 1970 census: from 1963 to 1970 the population of Grand Bahama increased from 8,230 to 26,043; two-thirds of that growth occurred in Freeport, which grew from 3,012 to 15,298, and much of the rest was in the West End area near by. There was nearly as much growth in absolute numbers in Grand Bahama as in New Providence, which went from 80,907 to 101,182. Given such heady growth rates – 216 per cent in seven years for Grand Bahama, 408 per cent for Freeport – even allowing for the low base, the boosters' speculation of 150,000 by 1980 did not seem too fantastic.

The first problem for the PLP government was the impending sale of the shares of the Port Authority to a Philippine mining company, Benguet. After much humming and hawing, the government approved the sale and took the occasion to exercise its option to acquire 7.5 per cent of the Port Authority's shares for just under a million dollars – not the full third that it could have claimed. It used the occasion to ask as a condition for the sale that the Port Authority agree to transfer its licensing function to the government and to the standardization of immigration and customs controls with what operated elsewhere in the Bahamas. The Port Authority pointed out that the change required the consent of 80 per cent of the licensees, but they would use their best endeavours to get it. The government observed that they were aware of that requirement, and the Port Authority replied that it accepted "the procedural arrangements", and on that ambiguity the situation rested without the licensees' consent being obtained – or the negotiations being made public.

Thereupon the government set about asserting its authority over the operation of Freeport and in particular the entitlement of companies and individuals who held licences to operate businesses there, licences sold by the Port Authority, to import "key personnel" outside the usual immigration controls which operated for the rest of the Bahamas. The covenant in the agreement read:

> That during the continuance of this Agreement the Port Authority or a licensee shall have the right to bring into the Colony and to employ within the Port Area such key, trained and/or skilled personnel as in the opinion of the Port Authority or of any licensee (as

the case may be) are necessary for the construction, operation, administration, and other purposes of the Port Project, the Port Development Area, for the Manufacturing Purposes, for the Administrative Purposes, and for the purposes of any and all other businesses, undertakings, and enterprises carried on within the Port Area by the Port Authority or by any licensee and that the Government will not withhold permission for the entry of such key, trained and/or skilled personnel into the Colony AND the terms "key, trained, and/or skilled personnel" used in this sub-clause of this clause shall be deemed to mean and include the family and dependants of any such key, trained, and/or skilled personnel AND PROVIDED ALWAYS that the Government reserve the right on grounds of personal undesirability (a) to withhold permission from an individual to enter the Colony, and (b) to compel any individual to leave the Colony.

A further section of the agreement provided that if the Port Authority or a licensee wished to recruit unskilled labour, they gave the government thirty days notice, and then if government could not supply the required workers they could be brought into Freeport for an initial maximum period of three years. At the beginning of 1969 new immigration regulations were announced. A work permit would now be required for Freeport, and it had to be obtained before the individual arrived. Importers were required to provide sureties for the payment of customs duties from which they had many exemptions under the Hawksbill Creek Act. When the government acquired its Port Authority shares a few months later, Pindling warned that administrative arrangements were being tightened up so that Freeport would no longer be a "privileged enclave", explaining that more had been read into the original agreement than was really there. This had been partly the fault of the government for not enforcing the law, and partly the fault of those "who [had] got away with so much for so long they [had] mistakenly concluded that they had a right to what had been winked at".[73]

A dispute with racial overtones over whether Bahamians were being discriminated against in renting housing at Freeport led to another warning in July. The government would not issue any further permits for the sale or leasing of houses or flats there and would encourage real estate agents from other parts of the Bahamas to take an interest in Freeport — where much of the housing had been built speculatively and sold to overseas owners as investments. On 25 July at the start of the refinery project Pindling delivered an ultimatum. After expressing concern at the lack of soul in Freeport, he declared, "In this city where, regretably, almost anything goes, where promisingly some economic opportunities have come to Bahamians, Bahamians are nevertheless still the victims of an unbending social order which, if it now refuses to bend, must now be broken."[74]

The speech caused an immediate panic in Freeport. Asked at a press conference whether it was government policy to slow down business expansion at Freeport, Pindling replied that the main trouble had been administrative delays in processing the work permits, but the concern now spread far beyond immigration controls. Bitter altercations broke out between some licensees and the Port Authority, which was accused of failing to stand up to the government. Licensees secured an opinion from leading counsel in London that work permits could not be required for "key" personnel under the Hawksbill Creek Act, but if the government changed the legislation there was little that could be done. Hanna replied that the right to import "key" personnel had to be read with the obligation to train Bahamians for responsible positions which Freeport had neglected to do, and the government insisted that permit applications show that an employer had used his best endeavours to employ Bahamians and train Bahamians. A sizeable bloc of licensees sought arbitration of their dispute with the Port Authority, and eventually a smaller number sued the company for breach of contract, retaining the ubiquitous Fawkes. The government pressed ahead with legislation, which received the royal assent in March 1970 despite a petition from the Port Authority to the governor against the breach of faith involved.

During the debate on the amending legislation a number of PLP back-benchers expressed anxieties about the economic effect of the changes, and the two Grand Bahama MHAs, Maurice Moore and Warren Levarity, were particularly agitated. They were warned by Hanna against giving assistance to the party's enemies, and when the UBP commended the dissidents, Francis commented, "This has always been one of the methods of the white man to try to spread disorder in the ranks of the Negro people."[75] Investment in Freeport had slowed down in 1969; by 1970 it was reduced to a trickle. Stories of the expulsion of residents who had established local businesses but could not secure permits to continue to operate them appeared regularly in the local press. The government remained adamant, and in September 1970 appointed a commission of inquiry with wide terms of reference to review the development of Freeport. Its chairman was Sir Hugh Wooding, formerly chief justice of Trinidad, and other members Sir Fred Phillips, formerly governor of St Kitts, M. L. Lindsay, retired commissioner of the Royal Canadian Mounted Police, and McAllister Lloyd, an American citizen who was chairman of the United Nations Investments Committee.

In addition to its economic worries, the PLP government was always at risk in the field of labour relations. One constant danger was that some minor industrial dispute would blow up into violence which would attract international attention and damage the tourist trade.

So in June 1968 a dispute over alleged discrimination in four of Freeport's hotels suddenly turned into a small riot in which tourists and white employees were roughly handled. In the end, fourteen men were acquitted by a Supreme Court jury 8–4 on a charge of rioting, and the only man who was convicted was a man who already had a criminal record. He was sentenced to three years imprisonment for causing grievous harm to a hotel security officer. A protracted strike at the Bank of London and Montreal (Bolam) in Nassau from December 1968 to February 1969 produced a series of court cases for obstruction, trespass, and the like, but the firm handling by the police – who incurred the hostility of the strikers – allowed it to peter out.

Equally serious was the failure of a stable and effective leadership to emerge in the majority of trade unions and in the federal body, the Bahamas Federation of Trade Unions (BFTU). The BFTU's affairs were complicated by its involvement with an American trade union, the Service Employees International Union (SEIU) which represented hotel workers in the United States and Canada, and by the political roles of its president, Senator Cadwell Armbrister, and secretary, Simeon Bowe, who had moved from the Senate to a seat in the House at the general election. The charitable might have supposed that the SEIU wished to help Bahamian unionism onto its feet, the realists that as Bahamian hotels were mainly owned by American chains their organization by the same union would make for greater bargaining power, the suspicious that American involvement in trade union affairs abroad was often a cover for something else – and noted in this case that the SEIU's permanent representative in Nassau had previously been AFL-CIO representative in Africa. In the first instance the SEIU put up fifty thousand dollars to help the BFTU set up an office and six thousand dollars a month for some time to help it get going. In due course it sought to obtain affiliation dues back from the BFTU's supposed six thousand members, and there the trouble started. The BFTU attempted to fix a two-dollar-a-month levy, of which 80 per cent would go to the SEIU. Armbrister and Bowe survived one attempt to depose them within the BFTU on grounds of a conflict of interest with their political careers, triggered partly by Bowe's attacks in the House on the wage claims of Fawkes's garbage collectors' union, and because they were suspected of seeking a one-big-union structure. At various times Armbrister was involved in a number of attempts to merge various unions, and the BFTU was seriously weakened by an attempt to write into its constitution power to compel its member unions to amalgamate.

Whatever the reasons, the Bahamian trade union movement remained weak and divided, prone to squabbles, and with its membership more nominal than real. When in 1970 Dudley Williams, president of the Fuel, Engineering and Allied Workers, which stood outside the BFTU umbrella, ridiculed it for representing only three of the country's seventeen trade unions, Armbrister answered that of the seventeen unions formally registered only seven functioned at all, and only four of these were really active and all four were in the BFTU. He may well have been right.

However, even if the union movement was almost useless, the government had a responsibility for industrial relations and an interest in the welfare and political support of Bahamian workers. In mid-1969 it circulated a draft bill to revise the existing labour legislation, left over from UBP days, to assist unions by compulsory recognition, collective bargaining, and a voluntary check-off (i.e., deduction of union dues by management), and to replace the existing Labour Board with an Industrial Relations Board with substantial arbitral powers. It also forbade expatriates from holding office in unions or employers' associations, which was part of the government's general policy, and required the minister's approval for international affiliations, which was presumably to keep an eye on the SEIU. But it also extended the cooling-off period before a strike could legally take place, and it did not require the closed shop as some union leaders, particularly Armbrister, sought. Armbrister warned the PLP convention that unless the labour movement got "a fair shake" from the government in the form of both closed shop and compulsory check-off, the workers would take things into their own hands and there would be anarchy; and when the legislation finally came to the Senate in July 1970 he criticized the government for letting the unions down and then voted for the bill. As Pindling had told him at a BFTU seminar held to discuss the legislation six months earlier, the union movement failed to make its objectives known to the government, but it was doubtful whether the union movement had enough firmness of organization to formulate its objectives apart from an instinctive pressure for wage rises.

The other organizations that could have had considerable influence in the Bahamas at this time were the churches. Like the unions, their internal difficulties filled the front pages and the letters-to-the-editor sections of all Nassau newspapers. Many of their troubles revolved around finding a meaning for Black Power and were aggravated by the radicalizing tendencies at work among young clergymen around the world in the 1960s. Particular attention was given to the opinions of two Bahamian Negro Catholic priests, Father Bonaventure Dean and Father Prosper Burrows, and one expatriate Methodist clergyman, the Reverend Neville Stewart, who was also headmaster of the formerly racially exclusive Queen's College, now well integrated but still middle class. The first issue was whether it was right for a cleric to refer to past racial injustices, for if he did, this inevitably meant criticizing the UBP and by implication welcoming the PLP's accession to power. Given the ingrained traditionalism of many older Bahamians of both races and all faiths, it was perhaps not surprising that all hell broke loose when young Father Burrows observed in a sermon in the Catholic cathedral that if Christ returned today he would not recognize his church and queried the celibacy of the clergy.

What had greater significance, and originality, was the suggestion by youthful radicals that existing church structures were identified with colonialism and racism and their doubts about the relevance of traditional Christianity to contemporary Bahamian life. As usual, the senior shepherds were wiser and more patient than many of their flock; thus the Catholic bishops of the region meeting at Montego Bay in September 1969 gave a qualified endorsement to the idea of Black Power:

> Seen through the eyes of some thoughtful advocates, black power is a force meant to lead towards eradication of racism and all its social, cultural and economic adjuncts. It is a cultural force devised to awaken in all men a sense of their universal brotherhood. There are still too many areas where the God-given dignity of the black man is not being recognized. We share the anxiety about the full and authentic freedom and complete emancipation and the progress of our various countries.[76]

However, the bishops added, that did not entitle some to use the label of Black Power for a call to inverse racism and separation, or to preach hatred and violence.

The PLP government, too, tried to avoid slipping over into racial extremism. It was prepared to manipulate the symbols of race pride, as in the proposal for a statue of "Afro-Bahamian woman" in Rawson Square sought by a back-bencher, Oscar Johnson. But when Bahamian students at Florida Memorial College in May 1970 complained that they had been beaten and tear-gassed in a college riot over demands for black history teaching, Pindling told Fawkes, who was seeking a select committee to investigate the affair, that as none of the students were in Florida on government scholarships and none of them faced criminal charges, it was a private matter — unlike the recent disturbance at Sir George Williams University in Canada. In June, at a charity concert, the visiting soul singer Nina Simone rounded on Negroes in her audience whom she considered lukewarm to the Black Power songs she had been singing and told them to take back the land the English had taken from them and stop being frightened of expressing themselves. The government was embarrassed.

A few days later, a group of members of Unicomm, a youth body which had split off from the PLP's original youth organization, the National Committee for Positive Action, burned a paper Union Jack in

a quiet corner of the Queen's Birthday celebrations at Clifford Park,
handed out leaflets calling for a local honours system, and later
picketed the levee at Government House. The PLP chairman, George
Mackey, criticized the flag-burning as "premature and unwarranted",
for the British were not refusing independence for the Bahamas, and
went on to decry the excessive quoting of Nkrumah at political
meetings: "They should be sensible enough to pattern themselves after
someone who had made a success of his affairs".[77] Shortly afterwards,
Dr Trevor Munroe, a lecturer at the University of the West Indies who
had been recently banned from Trinidad following the Black Power
mutiny there, addressed a Unicomm meeting on the politics of development. He called for a revolutionary rather than a reformist ideology,
and observed that a black premier did not ensure black government.
Pindling, very much the reformist, suggested that Unicomm's motives
should be looked at: "When an organization provides a forum for the
novel proposal that the way to achieve a new economy is to destroy the
one we have, I believe it is time for its objectives to be re-examined by
more serious and sober students of the Bahamian scene."[78] He at least
remained confident that the country's problems could be solved within
the existing democratic system and under the rule of law.

But some of the PLP's opponents were claiming that there were
flaws apparent in the way the democratic system was being worked.
Fawkes, and to a lesser, certainly less energetic, extent the UBP,
brought forward a series of charges of conflict of interest or down-
right malpractice by PLP ministers and back-benchers. Fawkes's efforts
frequently brought him into conflict with Speaker Braynen, who struck
down a series of questions and motions relating to ministers' share
holdings, contractual interests, and interests in legal practices as not
relating to public affairs. Two government contracts in particular came
under fire. One to service Health Department vehicles was awarded to
a company owned by the PLP's first vice-chairman, who was also a
minister's brother, and there were charges that little service was
received for the large payments made. The other, for construction at
the prison, went to a company of which a back-bencher was president.
The minister defended the decision by pointing out that there was
nothing to prevent a back-bencher from tendering for government
contracts, but his second point, that the contract had actually been
signed by the company's vice-president, backfired when it was revealed
that the vice-president had only recently been released from the
premises where his company was to carry out the contract. Another
instance of undue influence, in a hostile form, was alleged to be the
award of the contract for the new Post Office which did not go to a
well-known British company whose Bahamian associate was Sir Roland
Symonette of the UBP, but to an American company which had no

previous local experience — and later came to grief with the job. It was indiscreet to award the contract to produce the government gazette (for which privilege the publisher pays to secure the legal advertising it brings) to the *Bahamian Times* without calling for tenders, but not surprising considering the bitter hostility of both *Guardian* and *Tribune* to the government. There had been similar byplay in taking the contract from the *Tribune* to give it to the *Guardian* a few years earlier. But after allowance is made for the odium that attached to the UBP at its fall and in the subsequent disclosure, it is doubtful whether the PLP lost much electoral support over the allegations that were bandied about.

To the outside observer, party ranks were firm. A handful of back-benchers appeared a little difficult; two sought select committees into matters within a minister's responsibilities, and the minister protested against their discourtesy. When the Commonwealth Parliamentary Association met in Nassau, one delivered a classic back-bencher's lament: public servants had too much influence, bills were prepared before back-benchers knew what was in them, ministers had to be watched "because they tend[ed] to move away from the people by moving away from the people's representatives".[79] Within the party there was dissatisfaction with the performance of some ministers and even a campaign to have two removed. At the PLP convention in 1968 Pindling confronted Wallace-Whitfield and said that he was prepared to accept the minister's resignation; the matter was quickly smoothed over as a misunderstanding. The following January there was a minor reshuffle of ministerial responsibilities, including the abolition of the Out Islands portfolio as a step to breaking down the division between New Providence and the other islands. Warren Levarity was moved to Transport, but in September he was dismissed, the ostensible reason being his drinking problem and his handling of an airlines licence application.[80] The post as minister of transport was given to Doris Johnson, previously without departmental responsibilities, and the choice of a woman and a senator gave offence to the back-benchers. A meeting of the parliamentary party was called at a club at Small Hope Bay in the prime minister's constituency at Andros, but before it began a further minister resigned, Arthur Foulkes from Tourism and Telecommunications. Pindling moved swiftly to contain the difficulties: two new ministers were named, Livingstone Coakley and Clifford Darling; two back-benchers were appointed chairmen of public utility corporations, and four were made parliamentary secretaries — the idea of having such junior posts had been about for some time — and the possibility of creating a fifth parliamentary secretaryship was left dangling.

The unexpected stimulus of schism within the PLP failed to get the

UBP back on its feet. It had not bothered to appoint a shadow cabinet until August 1969 — all eleven parliamentary members were then assigned duties — and at its annual convention the three leading members were absent overseas. A demand that Sir Roland Symonette stand down as leader fell flat, but he sent a message that he would retire at the end of the year and did so. G. A. D. Johnstone became leader of the opposition in his place. One of the parliamentary members who was at the convention, Basil Kelly, suggested that the party should consider winding up, and a later meeting authorized talks with Adderley's NDP for that purpose. These dragged on through the first quarter of 1970 without reaching agreement; the UBP later claimed that the NDP had demanded dissolution of the UBP and admission of its members to the NDP and resignation of four UBP MHAs to provide safe seats for NDP leaders.

Given the unrest in the PLP, decay of the UBP, and near disappearance of the NDP, it was not surprising that there were rumours of new parties being started. In October 1969 a "Socialist Democratic Party" composed of political unknowns flashed through the newspapers and was never heard of again. In April 1970 an ostensibly multiracial, actually all-Negro, People's Advancement League was formed, and in June 1970 the Commonwealth People's Party claimed to have been in existence for more than a year.

At first Pindling sought to deny that indiscipline was a problem in the PLP and tried to make a virtue of the recent upheavals: "I think that we have to be very careful in a party structure not to stifle individual thought within the party framework. The P.L.P. has always been a live party and to stay alive it has to be receptive to new ideas and new thoughts and has to be able to accommodate these thoughts."[81] But on the eve of the next PLP convention in October 1970, a Pindling supporter, Senator Henry Bowen, told a hotel workers' meeting that there was a plot under way to oust Pindling. In his opening speech to the convention, whose theme was supposed to be nation-building, Pindling warned, "Many of us in our party have become overcome with envy and consumed with jealousy; and some of us have been stung by the serpent of greed. We have become too concerned with who make ministers and who make prime ministers and have become too unconcerned with who make representatives. Let us not fool ourselves as to where the ultimate power lies. It does not lie with me. It rests with the people."[82] As for his critics in the party: "If you can't cut bait, get the hell out of the boat."[83] He was backed strongly by Hanna, who suggested that those who thought another organization was better suited to them should leave the party. Foulkes insisted that Senator Bowen's allegations of a plot against Pindling were "vicious, filthy slander", and the two MHAs from Grand Bahama, Levarity and Moore, called on the accusers to come forward. Another suspect, the former chief whip, reported that political aspirants were at work in five constituencies seeking to oust the sitting members – and claiming Pindling's backing for what they were doing. When another MHA made a similar charge, Pindling denied that he had authorized use of his name: "It just happens that people want to use my name, and it has given me no end of trouble."[84]

On 23 October Wallace-Whitfield delivered the convention's keynote speech, which turned from the party's past achievements into an attack on creeping totalitarianism within the party with the question: "Does this party have room in it for the questioning youth or only for a few of the old timers and hordes of boot-lickers and yes men?" Wallace-Whitfield finished by announcing his resignation from the cabinet and quoted Martin Luther King's words, "Free, free at last, my soul is free at last." On 27 October Curtis McMillan followed him out of the ministry.

Pindling stopped the gaps with other ministers, and both factions began a series of party meetings and public rallies to test their support. The extra-parliamentary organization stepped back from the fray when the chairman and secretary issued a joint statement that the party was not responsible for the general direction and control of members of the government, which was in the hands of cabinet, and the *Bahamian Times* avoided apportioning blame, saying that the paper had been built by both factions and neither had approached the paper to try to influence it. The parliamentary party met once more, on 9–11 November at the Paradise Hotel in New Providence to determine who had the numbers, but was unable to achieve a reconciliation. On 15 November a meeting of the dissidents at Lewis Yard settlement at Grand Bahama was broken up; Wallace-Whitfield and Moore were both hit with chairs, and Wallace-Whitfield claimed that there had been an attempt to kill him. Five men were later fined and bound over to keep the peace, and both sides backed away from the danger of further violence.

In response to rumours that, when the House met, Hanna would move a motion of confidence in the government to force the rebels into line or else direct rebellion, Fawkes introduced his own motion of no confidence which listed nine matters ranging from the appointment of a senator to ministerial duties and the Bahamas Airways affair to some of the allegations of conflict he had pursued in the House in previous months. Fawkes himself was ejected from the House after one of his customary slanging matches with Speaker Braynen. After a debate lasting eleven and a half hours, his motion was defeated 19–15. Eight PLP rebels (ex-ministers Wallace-Whitfield, McMillan, Foulkes, and Levarity, and Moore, Elwood Donaldson, James Shepherd and George Thompson) voted with the seven UBP members. Two other PLP back-

benchers were absent. One, Loftus Roker, withdrew from the House
before the vote was taken. The other, Oscar Johnson, stayed in his
constituency at Cat Island. Early in December the National General
Council of the PLP suspended the eight who had voted against the
government for a period of two years, subject to their right of appeal
to the 1971 convention. The reason (given three days later) was that
they had acted contrary to the interests of the party.

Foulkes told one rebel meeting: "Even Moses was not permanent
and everlasting because he slipped up and displeased God . . . We will
select other leaders to take us to the Promised Land."[85] The PLP's
majority in the House had been slashed — though in the Senate, where
appointment had been on the prime minister's nomination and
ambition ran less strongly, or at least could be directed to seats in the
House that were now up for challenge, it remained solid. Any further
erosion of parliamentary support could bring the government down;
perhaps any further explosions within the party could bring its leader
down. But the UBP, as the only alternative represented in the legislature, had shown itself incapable of providing an effective opposition,
and the UBP and NDP had been unable to produce an anti-PLP alliance.
Now there was the possibility of a much broader united front to
capitalize on the signs of economic stagnation that were mounting.

Pindling warned the party: "It is slackness that got us in this situation now. I say we have got to pull the ropes tighter."[86] The 1971
budget painted a gloomy picture of the state of the sails: in 1970 there
had been a shortfall of revenue of over $12 million, yet the government
was budgeting for a growth in revenue in 1971 of 25 per cent and still
expecting a deficit of nearly $17 million. Carlton Francis explained
that the Bahamian economy was too healthy to qualify for World Bank
soft loans; when he had approached the British government to make the
application he had been told to raise taxes or borrow. Tax increases in
1971 were included in the budget, but they had to be set against
declining customs revenues which resulted from the ebb in the
tourist tide.

NOTES

1. *Tribune*, 16 January 1967; detailed responsibilities were announced a few
   days later, *Guardian*, 21 January 1967.
2. The exposés continued after the fall of the UBP government — e.g., Bill
   Davidson, "The Mafia: Shadow of Evil on an Island in the Sun", *Saturday
   Evening Post*, 25 February 1967; and Richard Oulahan and William Lambert,
   "The Scandal in the Bahamas: Lax Laws and a Powerful Clique Invite the
   High-Rollers to Swarm In", *Life*, 3 February 1967.
3. *Tribune*, 16 January 1967.
4. *Guardian*, 17 and 18 January 1967.

5. *Bahamian Times,* 14 January 1967.
6. *Bahamas Observer,* 28 January 1967.
7. *Tribune,* 18 January 1967.
8. Ibid., 2 February 1967.
9. Ibid., 3 February 1967.
10. *Guardian,* 28 January 1967.
11. *Tribune,* 23 February 1967.
12. *Bahamas Observer,* 4 February 1967.
13. Ibid., 25 February 1967.
14. *Tribune,* 9 February 1967.
15. Ibid., 27 April and 3 May 1967.
16. *Guardian,* 3 June 1967.
17. Ibid., 20 June 1967.
18. Ibid., 23 June 1967; see also *Tribune,* 25 July 1967, for a parliamentary question on the subject.
19. *Guardian,* 29 March 1967.
20. *Bahamas Observer,* 17 June 1967.
21. *Tribune,* 2 July 1967.
22. *Guardian,* 23 August 1967.
23. Ibid., 29 and 30 August 1967.
24. *Bahamian Times,* 5 April 1967; emphasis in original.
25. *Guardian,* 3 August 1967; see also *Tribune,* 1 August 1967, for another editorial on Detroit riots.
26. *Bahamian Times,* 26 August 1967.
27. *Guardian,* 1 April 1967.
28. *Tribune,* 3 June 1967.
29. Ibid., 22 July 1967.
30. Ibid., 25 July 1967.
31. *Guardian,* 24 June 1967.
32. *Tribune,* 15 July 1967.
33. Ibid., 8 April 1967.
34. *Guardian,* 1 December 1967.
35. *Tribune,* 19 December 1967.
36. *Guardian,* 25 January 1968; from 1 January the *Guardian* had become formally the *Guardian and Bahamas Observer,* but will still be cited by its earlier, shorter and more familiar title.
37. Ibid., 8 January 1968.
38. Ibid., 10 January 1968.
39. Ibid., 12 January 1968.
40. *Tribune,* 17 January 1968.
41. Ibid., 24 January 1968.
42. *Bahamian Times,* 24 January 1968.
43. *Guardian,* 20 January 1968.
44. *Bahamian Times,* 13 January 1968.
45. Ibid., 31 January 1968.
46. *Guardian,* 29 January 1968; see also the *Guardian* of 25 January 1968 for a similar letter by "One who knows".
47. Ibid., 13 February 1968.
48. Ibid., 21 February 1968.
49. Ibid., 23 March 1968.
50. Ibid., 25 March 1968.
51. *Bahamian Times,* 12 March 1968.
52. *Guardian,* 9 April 1968.
53. Ibid., 19 April 1968.

54. Ibid., 13 April 1968.
55. Ibid., 20 April 1968.
56. Ibid., 25 April 1968.
57. *Bahamian Times,* 20 May 1970.
58. *Tribune,* 22 August 1970.
59. *Bahamian Times,* 22 February 1969.
60. Ibid., 19 March 1969.
61. *Guardian,* 28 November 1969.
62. *Tribune,* 18 August 1969.
63. Ibid., 13 January 1970.
64. Ibid., 2 May 1970.
65. *Guardian,* 22 August 1968.
66. Ibid., 19 October 1968.
67. Ibid., 17 July 1969.
68. *Bahamian Times,* 18 January 1969.
69. *Guardian,* 5 November 1969.
70. *Bahamian Times,* 1 April 1970.
71. *Tribune,* 20 November 1970.
72. *Guardian,* 1 August 1970.
73. Ibid., 18 March 1969.
74. *Tribune,* 26 July 1969.
75. *Guardian,* 20 February 1970.
76. Ibid., 8 September 1969.
77. *Tribune,* 7 July 1970.
78. *Guardian,* 30 July 1970.
79. *Tribune,* 5 November 1968.
80. *Guardian,* 8 September 1969.
81. *Bahamian Times,* 31 December 1969.
82. *Tribune,* 19 October 1970.
83. *Guardian,* 20 October 1970.
84. *Tribune,* 20 October 1970.
85. *Guardian,* 7 November 1970.
86. Ibid., 3 November 1970.

7

Black Power: The Second Phase, 1971-77

If the PLP government was to survive, the state of the Bahamian economy could be of critical importance. In the early 1970s the evidence was not encouraging. The number of tourists declined in 1970 for the first time since the post-war boom got under way, falling 2.6 per cent over 1969. New Providence held its own, and even managed minimal growth of 0.7 per cent, but at Freeport the tourist numbers fell by 7.8 per cent. Although the tide turned in 1971 and the national total was almost 10 per cent above the previous record year, 1969, there were still well-publicized cases of hotels closing for the summer months, and one at Coral Harbour in New Providence closed permanently. The finance industry continued to be relatively stable in its contribution to the local economy, but in September 1971 the government trebled licensing fees to a rate of $30,000 per annum for commercial banks, $15,000 for trust companies, and $6,000 for other (restricted) banking institutions. The drift of such businesses to the newest tax haven in the Cayman Islands accelerated amid complaints that there were difficulties with the Bahamian immigration authorities over the entry of skilled staff. Even though the commercial banks had held $2,000 million in foreign currency on deposit at 30 June 1971, there were rumours that the Bahamian government was unable to raise a $15 million loan and had to resort to an advance of the casinos' gambling fees to keep afloat. In a little over a year some fifteen hundred companies were struck off the register for failure to pay licence fees or to lodge annual returns; thereafter fewer new companies were formed than were struck off. A later amendment to the Companies Act required disclosure whether or not a company was at least 60 per cent Bahamian-owned; those which did not have the required proportion of local ownership were subjected to an annual fee of a thousand dollars, again encouraging the flight of brass-plate companies. Steps were taken to weed out the more doubtful financial operations which were giving the Bahamas a bad name abroad. An Insurance Act in 1970 reduced the number of registered insurance companies from 345 to 90; in 1971 a Securities Act gave the minister of finance power to deal with other companies. The third major sector of economic activity, construction, suffered most, as the PLP's opponents had predicted would be the case. At Freeport it came to an almost complete halt.

The government, learning quickly, attributed its economic difficulties to external factors. Pindling told a bankers' luncheon that the cheap money policies that had prevailed in the period 1967–69 were at fault. Following the 1967 devaluation of sterling, some $80 million had been repatriated to the Bahamas and loaned extensively, but very little had gone to Bahamians for productive investment. Instead, consumer spending had shot up, and there had been a consequent drain on foreign exchange.[1] To his analysis, one could add the harmful effects of the mid-1969 recession in the United States, the 1971 devaluation of the American dollar, and the future effect of British restrictions on investment in the sterling area by United Kingdom residents. The Bahamian monetary authority warned that there had been a substantial outflow of capital and decided to treat sterling as a foreign currency for exchange control purposes. However, a report of the United States Department of Commerce, which provided some support for the government's explanations by linking Bahamian economic trends to the slowdown in the American economy as the principal influence, also mentioned Bahamian government policies as a factor contributing to the loss of momentum.[2]

The government was beset on three economic fronts. One was stagnation and recession in the principal sectors of economic activity just mentioned. The second was domestic inflation. The retail price index had shown a steady, but in most years unspectacular, trend upwards: 6.9 per cent in 1966, 3.7 per cent in 1967, 5.2 per cent in 1968, 10.5 per cent in 1969, 4.7 per cent in 1970. To guard against a sudden surge in food prices, in March 1971 the government introduced, but did not immediately implement, price controls. The legislation was passed despite the objections of the UBP, the Chamber of Commerce, and the Bahamas Business League, a spokesman for small Negro businesses. In the House of Assembly the PLP rebels, by then known as the Free PLP, cautiously abstained from voting, but Wallace-Whitfield condemned the move as a first step towards communism. The government's third difficulty was the growing need for massive spending on public utilities and welfare. By 1971 the swollen population of New Providence and limited natural supplies produced a water shortage of millions of litres per day. The sewerage system had been a problem for fifteen years, and it was estimated that modernization and extension would now require between $30 million and $50 million for an acceptable standard of service. The British government provided a grant of $120,000 to study the problem. In the welfare field, the opposition introduced a motion calling for an increase in the old age pension which was then being paid to 3,600 persons in New Providence and 2,500 in the Out Islands. The motion was amended by the government to give authority to the minister of finance to apply a price freeze to food-stuffs when he thought necessary, and passed.

The most pressing economic problems were at Freeport. The commission of inquiry reported in March 1971, and its report was tabled in the House of Assembly in June.[3] The commission upheld the government's actions, although it was criticized for poor public relations, an inefficient Immigration Department, and lack of commu-nications with the private sector. As to the charges of bad faith that had been levelled at the PLP government, the commission confirmed that at the 1968 constitutional conference all parties had agreed to empower the government to abrogate the agreement in any respect relating to immigration, and had done so knowing that the government intended to take, and maintain, firm control over immigration into Freeport. The report provided further documentation of the extent to which past activities at Freeport had created a non-Bahamian enclave in business, employment, and property ownership. At the time negotia-tions began for the sale of the Port Authority to Benguet, there had been 1,400 current licences to conduct a business or carry on a profession at Freeport; only 155 of these licences were held by Bahamians. Only 34 per cent of the total workforce was Bahamian. An even lower proportion of Bahamians were in the better-paid jobs: 11 per cent in professional and technical jobs, 14 per cent in administra-tive, executive, and managerial posts, 22 per cent in clerical work. There had been about five thousand individual sales of real property – building blocks, condominium units, or houses – of which approxi-mately 99 per cent had been to non-Bahamians.[4]

The 1970 census exposed the wider Bahamian demographic problem. Natural increase amounted to three thousand annually. In 1969 birth and death rates had been 26.9 and 6.8 per thousand respectively, and substantial fluctuations in the reported birth rates, for example 31.4 per thousand in the previous year, 1969, and down to 22.4 per thousand in 1973, suggested that the published figures often under-estimated the real rate of growth. Of the total population, 43 per cent was under the age of fourteen, the school-leaving age in the Bahamas, and of course a higher proportion of the Bahamian-born were below that age. The census counted twenty-seven thousand non-Bahamians who had entered the country in the period 1950–70: 24.6 per cent from the United States, 19.8 per cent from Haiti, 14.9 per cent from Britain, 12.2 per cent from Jamaica, 8.9 per cent from Canada, and 6.3 per cent from the Turks and Caicos Islands.

In July 1971 the government introduced a new scale of work-permit fees. "Belongers" were required to pay $500 unless they had been continuously resident for twenty years before 1967 – that is, before the start of the post-war boom. Other non-Bahamians had to pay an initial fee of $250 and a further sum annually, ranging from $25 for labourers and domestic servants, to $200–300 for skilled workers, $400 for middle managers and higher technical staff, and $500 for professionals and top managers. The government promised that application of the work-permit rules would be eased, even though it also claimed that 90 per cent of new applications and 99 per cent of renewals were granted;[5] however, henceforth a maximum work-period of five years would be normal. In August the permanent secretary responsible for immigration warned that there were a number of non-Bahamians without special skills who would now be phased out; their employers should not seek renewal of their work permits unless special circumstances applied. In November he explained that the government's policy was to prevent large numbers of expatriate personnel settling permanently because they could "exert considerable change which would be alien to the traditional social and political norms of the population".[6]

When the opposition proposed legislation to give non-Bahamian husbands of Bahamian women the same rights of residence that non-Bahamian wives of Bahamian men already enjoyed, the government rejected it on the ground that only British husbands would benefit. An approach by the Turks and Caicos government in February 1972 to secure a preferred status for its people were also rebuffed, even though 191 Turks Islanders had constituted a large proportion of the 484 expatriates given "belonger" status in 1969–71.

When arguing for a local hotel-training school, the director of tourism provided some useful statistics on employment in that industry. Of the 12,500 Bahamians employed in hotels, some 6,500 were unskilled and 5,500 skilled. Only 435 Bahamians held supervisory posts and 145 managerial posts. However there were 2,000 expatriates employed, mainly in the upper levels.[7] The executive director of the Hotels Association subsequently claimed that the proportion of expatriate staff had fallen from 19 per cent in 1967 to 3–4 per cent in 1972,[8] but whatever the exact figures might have been it was clear that only a small minority of Bahamians working in hotels had risen above the maid, waiter, or kitchen-hand level and very few indeed had been trained for any higher responsibilities. The attitudes of Bahamians to tourists also engendered some controversy. The Ministry of Tourism conducted a survey of six thousand in 1971 and found that a quarter complained of service "below standard" or "inferior", even though two-thirds found the Bahamian people generally more friendly than average "compared with other vacation places . . . visited".[9] When a letter from an irate tourist, complaining about the hostile attitude of the great majority of Bahamians he had encountered, was printed on the front page of the *Guardian,* he was answered in political terms: "Perhaps he is part of a plan to return the Bahamas to the old days when freedom and justice, democracy and pride was only for the whites and, as we call them, Conchy Joes. Possibly he expects to meet here like some of the Southern States of America."[10]

Despite its economic problems, the PLP government routed the new party formed by a combination of PLP rebels and former UBP supporters at the 1972 election (see below) and restored its comfortable majority in the House of Assembly. But, despite its political successes, its economic problems continued. Freeport's tourist economy remained depressed, although Grand Bahama provided one of the new bits of good news and evidence that some economic diversification away from reliance on tourism and finance was possible. The first petroleum refinery continued, and a second was started. It was expected that by the late 1970s the two refineries would employ between fifteen hundred and two thousand workers, the majority Bahamians, and, the government hoped, could provide the basis for a petro-chemical industry. A few warned of the threat oil spillages would present to the fishing industry and to tourist beaches, but the government was re-assured by the refineries' expensive anti-pollution arrangements. It displayed awareness of the costs of becoming a "dirt haven" when a proposal to boost the declining fortunes of Cat Island with a sewage-sludge processing plant — the raw material would have been shipped from Philadelphia for conversion to fertilizer — was rejected out of hand. Although legislation to encourage light industry in New Providence had been on the statute book for years, and an industrial estate designated, given the scarcity of trained labour and its high cost, and the appalling state of public utilities on the island at the time, the prospects for industrialization were bleak. In 1972/73 only 2,200 members of the workforce were engaged in manufacturing, compared with 1,400 employed by the water and electricity utilities and 400 in mining and quarrying.

The disproportionate weight given to Out Island electorates made doing something for agriculture and fishing good politics, just as the country's reliance on imported foodstuffs should have made it good economics. Some 5 to 10 per cent of the population still depended on farming, at least on a part-time basis, for their living, but their produce worth only $8 million a year equalled less than a fifth of the local consumption of foodstuffs. One handicap was the small size of most farms; at Exuma, one of the best farming areas, four-fifths of the farms — that is, land actually cultivated — measured less than a hectare.[11] Another difficulty was the quality of what was grown. The Ministry of Agriculture complained that of the $1.5 million worth of local foodstuffs bought by government in 1973, one-fifth had to be fed to pigs as sub-standard. Inefficient transport to, and distribution in, the New Providence market increased the local farmer's problems, but probably the greatest obstacle to his success was the ingrained preference for imported foods which made local consumers strongly resistant to price rises of local produce.

In 1972 American development aid provided $10 million for a scheme to raise livestock at northern Andros, and at its inauguration Pindling declared that Andros alone could make the Bahamas self-sufficient in foodstuffs. After the Bahamas had secured independence and adhered to the Lomé Convention, the government indicated that it was investigating reacquiring the sugar lands on Abaco to resume production, but then it discovered that the agreement negotiated by the UBP government had alienated ten thousand hectares of crown land and given an option over a further ten thousand hectares without making provision for reversion should the company terminate operations. To prevent it closing, the government had to spend $2.3 million to purchase the country's one successful agricultural venture, the poultry and dairy farm at Hatchet Bay on Eleuthera. It was placed under a new public corporation, but the new management failed dismally. Eventually the government announced a target of self-sufficiency in fruit and vegetables by 1980, in the hope that at least the import bill for feeding Bahamians (by then $18 million a year) could be eliminated, leaving only the $33 million bill for feeding tourists. But, as the minister for agriculture pointed out, it was really impossible to feed 205,000 Bahamians and 1.5 million tourists by "pothole farming and sailboat fishing".[12]

Tourism remained the mainstay of the Bahamian economy — 70 per cent of the gross national product was the commonly stated figure for

Table 10. Tourist-derived income, 1968-76.

	$m
1968	180.4
1969	235.5
1970	232.8
1971	277.5
1972	285.4
1973	n.a.
1974	328.0
1975	317.5
1976	368.0

its contribution — but the rising curve of tourist numbers had levelled off. The gross contribution of tourists in current dollars continued to show a slow increase in most years, though when allowance was made for inflation running at 5—10 per cent per annum the picture was rather less encouraging. A breakdown of tourist expenditure in 1972 showed that 44 per cent went on hotel accommodation and meals and beverages, and a further 16 per cent for meals and beverages outside hotels; 12 per cent was spent at the casinos; 16 per cent on shopping; 6 per cent on local transport; and 6 per cent on tipping.[13]

In the late 1960s it had been estimated that by the early 1970s the total number of tourists would be close to the 2.5 million mark, but it had settled just below 1.5 million. Unfortunately, room capacity had over-expanded in anticipation of rising demand. In 1966 there had been six thousand rooms; an additional three thousand were built in 1967 and a further three thousand between 1968 and 1972. But, reflecting the fact that tourism in the Caribbean region was not keeping pace with its growth in the rest of the world, the number of tourists arriving by air, those who would "stop over" to fill the new rooms, had risen by only 226,000 in 1968—72, barely 60 per cent of the number required to use the new capacity effectively. In New Providence and adjacent Paradise Island the number of rooms was up almost seventeen hundred, but the number of stop-overs rose only 100,000 or less than 50 per cent of the required number.[14] Hotels on Paradise Island at least had the attraction of the casino on the island and had an occupancy rate of 80 per cent in 1972; those on New Providence, without a casino close to hand, could manage only 60 per cent. Over the two years 1971—72 the eight largest hotels on New Providence accumulated losses of $8 million.

The casinos saved the tourist slump from being worse than it might have been. In 1972 there were 600,000 admissions to the casino on

Table 11. Growth of tourism, 1970-76.

	Number of Tourists	Percentage Increase over Previous Year
1970	1,298,344	−2.6
1971	1,463,591	12.7
1972	1,511,858	3.3
1973	1,520,010	0.5
1974	1,388,040	−8.7
1975	1,380,860	−0.5
1976	1,403,640	1.6

Paradise Island, 315,000 to the Freeport casino. Moreover, in a period of eight years they contributed $29 million directly to government revenue in the form of licence fees. On 28 November 1973 Arthur Hanna announced that from 1976 the government would take over the operation of the casinos; in the meantime the licence for the Freeport casino would be extended so that it would lapse at the same time as the Paradise Island casino's. This timetable proved to be mistaken; the licence for Paradise Island would not lapse until the end of 1977, so only the Freeport casino could be operated by government from 1976. The move was attacked, first from the PLP's back benches because of lack of consultation, to which Pindling replied that secrecy had been necessary to prevent lobbying and disruption of the stock-market; then by the opposition, which argued that the step would be seen as nationalization and so have a serious effect on foreign confidence, and the casinos could not be run as efficiently as under private mangement with hotel growth inhibited as a consequence; and finally by the churches, which objected to the government becoming further involved in gambling. Pindling stated his personal view: "I have no conscience position on casino gambling at all. I said this before taking office and I have made this clear many times since then. Casino gambling is a tourist amenity and we want it to stay an amenity. But government would prefer that decision taken relative to it be taken in Nassau, rather than Timbuctoo, because it affects the lives of the Bahamian people."[15]

When the opposition moved a resolution condemning the take-over, the minister for development, Carlton Francis, announced that he would abstain on the vote. Hanna scoffed at the churches, which objected to casinos but conducted raffles to raise their own funds. Francis retorted that his church was not one of those; he and two back benchers did abstain, and Francis subsequently resigned from cabinet. Equally embarrassing for the government was a resolution of the Baptist convention which condemned all forms of gambling and said that Baptists would "find it difficult to support any government that utilizes gambling as a source of national income".[16]

The government's next step to further involvement in the tourist industry came in July 1974 when the president of the Hotels Association warned that many of its members were considering reverting to closing down during the summer months. Two days later the newest, and one of the largest in New Providence, Sonesta Beach Lodge, announced that it would close in a fortnight's time and lay off four hundred staff. On 31 July Pindling asked the House of Assembly to approve a loan of $20 million to purchase three hotels with a total capacity of almost a thousand rooms, one of which was the Sonesta Beach Lodge. On the face of it, the deal had some attractions; for example, the Sonesta Beach Lodge had cost $15.5 million to build in 1971 and could now be had for $10.6 million. (There had been a maxim in the hotel trade that the first three owners of a new hotel fail, and only after a sufficient proportion of the capital cost has been written off can an owner show a profit on his investment.) Pindling defended the decision on the ground that public ownership would keep hotel profits in the country and be consistent with the government's philosophy to Bahamianize through ownership and participation, but the hastiness of the move was inconsistent with the government's earlier reluctance to move into Bahamian Airways, and undoubtedly the threat of closures and the subsequent increase in unemployment forced the government's hand at this time.

In January 1975 the composition of the board of the new Hotel Corporation was announced. Four of the appointments were unexceptional: Pindling as chairman and Hanna as deputy chairman (though one might wonder how much time the two most senior members of the government could give to the day-to-day affairs of the corporation), plus the deputy director of tourism and a finance executive with a local management company. The fifth appointment was more controversial: the former UBP speaker of the House of Assembly, R. H. Symonette, who had earlier been anathema to the PLP, although he had by then withdrawn from political life. His inclusion on the board led to rumours that both he and Roy Solomon had been invited to join the PLP. The rumours were quickly denied, but there were still protests from the party's back benches to which Pindling replied that there were very few Bahamians with experience of hotel management; this Symonette had. When the hotels started making money, Pindling promised, shares in the corporation would be offered to the public.

Another element of the tourist industry that continued to worry the government was air transport. The world-wide energy crisis at the end of 1973 increased travelling costs, in addition to inhibiting the North American economy and inflating the prices of Bahamian imports. The airlines defended themselves against charges that reduction in the number of flights to the Bahamas was restricting the number of tourists by claiming that the number of seats available remained high; the case was that fewer were being occupied. However, Pan-American, the Bahamas' oldest international carrier, withdrew from the Miami–Freeport route in 1973 and then suspended its Miami–Nassau and New York–Freeport routes in 1974. The government's own Bahamasair had a protracted dispute with the airport workers' union in which the government became embroiled when it first overruled the management's agreement to a modest wage rise only to back down later. The company got into financial difficulties when it sought substantial new capital to equip for more profitable long-haul routes, and it was rumoured that the company required monthly assistance from the Bahamas Treasury to meet its payroll. Two privately owned airlines based on the Bahamas collapsed completely. Bahamas World Airways, which had been financed by Robert Vesco's Bahamas Commonwealth Bank, failed to convince the United States Civil Aeronautics Board that it was owned and effectively controlled by Bahamians in order to obtain licences to fly United States–Bahamas and United States–Europe routes. The second airline, Flamingo, was carried down in June 1973 by the closing of the Nassau Bank and Trust company, which had lent it funds.

The finance industry also had its fair share of bad news. At the end of 1972 Arawak Trust, one of the first trust companies to open in Nassau, closed and moved to the Cayman Islands. Two years earlier it had employed sixty-four people, including fifty Bahamians. By the time it moved, its staff was reduced to thirty-six, including thirty Bahamains; that decline probably corresponded to the reduction in the trust company sector as a whole. Moreover, some new investors in the Bahamas did little to enhance the country's reputation abroad. There were allegations that the fugitive financier Robert Vesco had invested $20 million in the Bahamas, including several millions dollars in Treasury Bills. The monetary authority denied that his Bahamas Commonwealth Bank had bought any Treasury Bills directly, but conceded that they could have been acquired from other banks. Rather more interest attached to rumours of his loans to prominent members of the PLP, including the prime minister.

Pindling made an extensive disclosure of his personal financial affairs as a result of the allegations. They are worth setting out in some detail, for they are probably fairly representative of the rise of a new and substantial Negro bourgeoisie in Nassau. The principal allegation had been that Vesco had lent Pindling a substantial sum to buy a large house at Skyline Drive, an exclusive area near the old official residences for the most senior expatriate officials. Pindling explained that since the late 1950s he had saved six thousand to eight thousand dollars a year, which was perfectly plausible for a moderately successful lawyer at the time. In the mid-1960s he had bought a building site near the centre of Nassau on which to erect an office block to house his own chambers together with additional space for rent, again a common enough arrangement. For the purpose he borrowed $200,000 from a local bank; that bank had been taken over by Vesco's Bahamas Commonwealth Bank and the mortgage assigned – hence the connection with Vesco. In 1973 he had sold the site for $400,000, and with the profit from the sale and the sale of his previous home and some securities, plus a new mortgage of $50,000 from a third bank, he had bought the new home for $450,000. It had been renovated with his savings and overdraft facilities from a fourth bank, and he owed nothing to Vesco or Vesco's bank.[17] The three ingredients in the story are high and rapidly rising incomes for Bahamian professionals and businessmen, easy bank credit, and rising land values. Many others, both white and Negro, made similar gains in net worth in ten or twenty years. As for Vesco, he survived an attempt by the United States government to extradite him from the Bahamas, moved on to Costa Rica for a time, and then returned to the Bahamas.

Another, more lurid, tale involving the PLP leader was provided by one Louis P. Mastriana, who told a United States Senate committee that he had been offered a hundred thousand dollars by Elliot Roosevelt, son of the former president of the United States, and Mike McLaney, who had been a supporter of the PLP in the 1960s, to assassinate Pindling. The motive, Mastriana alleged, was that McLaney had paid the PLP a million dollars to secure a casino licence; when it had not been forthcoming, he had commissioned the assassination. Both Roosevelt and McLaney, who was then managing a casino in Haiti, denied the allegation. Pindling stated that no promise of a casino concession had ever been made to McLaney, who had not provided a million dollars but only some campaign transport, for which he had subsequently been paid sixty thousand dollars in full settlement, the money being raised by a levy on PLP parliamentary salaries.

Despite such extraordinary stories, and the drift of business to new tax havens like the Caymans, banking business continued to expand in Nassau. In early 1973 there were 200 licensed commercial banks, and another 108 conducting restricted business. By then the Bahamas had as many branches of foreign banks as there were in London, although they held only a quarter of the assets lodged in London. Many had been formed by relatively small American banks to serve the needs of a few large clients with overseas interests, and their contribution to local employment was minimal. Even legitimate business had its political dangers: the Council of Churches asked Pindling to prevent Bahamian banks being used to transmit loans to the South African government: one had put through $200 million in a couple of years. Company incorporation, which with conveyancing had been the principal source of income for Bahamian lawyers who were now rapidly multiplying in number, fell off badly. By the mid-1970s there were fewer than two hundred incorporations a year, with as many companies leaving the register. Still, at the end of 1971 there had been almost fourteen thousand companies on the register with a nominal capital of $2,800 million.

Against the background of a stagnant economy, the government had to meet its steadily rising expenditures. Each year the budget provided for a substantial increase in government expenditure, predicated mainly on an increase in revenue but also entailing a substantial increase in the public debt, which in turn demanded a larger share of expenditure to service the debt. From a mere $47.6 million in 1967, the public debt grew to $135.6 million in 1974, with a huge jump of $35 million in 1973/74, which included the $20 million needed to purchase the three hotels. With Nassau banks awash with funds, the government's modest local loans were easily over-subscribed, but it found access to soft loans from abroad more difficult. The United States Export-Import Bank provided $11 million for education needs just before independence. This the cynics attributed, together with the Andros livestock project loan, to a wish to ensure the support of an independent Bahamas on the sensitive question of recognition of Cuba. Adherence to the Lomé Convention produced another $2 million from the European Development Fund in grants and soft loans. But, in the main, the government was restricted to such revenue as it could secure without breaching the frequently given commitments never to introduce income tax or a corporation tax, and to hard loans whose particulars it was usually loath to disclose. Almost every budget produced some new tightening of an existing screw. Licence fees rose. Those for Out Island businesses were brought into line with the higher New Providence rates. The 1973 budget abolished the two-hundred-dollar duty-free allowance which encouraged Bahamians to shop on their frequent business and pleasure trips to Florida. On that occasion Hanna warned: "And as the Finance Minister said a while ago, if it means scraping the barrel and razing this country to the ashes, we will raze it to the ashes and build it again so that we can live as men. That is my philosophy. And we will return to the fishing village rather than surrender our national dignity and pride."[18] Freeport's contribution to the Treasury, which had quadrupled between 1966 and 1972 to provide a sixth of total government revenue, rose no longer. The slowing down or decline in imports because of the general state of the economy meant shortfalls in anticipated customs duties, which still provided 60 per cent of receipts.

As poor planning and shortages of material and manpower frequently meant that estimated expenditure also fell short, the annual budget was a hit-and-miss affair which left the government vulnerable to criticism for mismanagement from the opposition and the daily newspapers, and occasionally from its own back benches. Real property taxes were increased to a flat 1.5 per cent on market value over $50,000, and 0.5 per cent on the first $20,000 and 1 per cent on the excess for properties valued between $20,000 and $50,000. The original intention had been to start taxing at $10,000 market value, but protests within the PLP had raised the figure to $20,000. As the latest scheme for low-income housing, funded by a loan of $10 million from the Chase-Manhattan Bank, provided for units costing $20,000 for a house and lot, with interest at 10 per cent and a maximum term of fifteen years, it will be seen that the scope of the real property tax was extensive — and also why so few "low-income" borrowers were able to avail themselves of such government assistance as was available.

The government's most ambitious welfare innovation, the scheme for national insurance, was funded outside ordinary revenue by a contribution of 11 per cent of insurable wages and income. It came into operation on 7 October 1974 for employees and 5 April 1975 for the self-employed. Other welfare schemes were much more modest. In 1973 the old age pension was doubled to twenty-six dollars a month, and in 1974 a belated start was made on an aged persons' home to cost a million dollars. The home had been delayed for two years because of lack of funds.

Two useful accounts of prevailing conditions were provided in 1974 by the interim report of a select committee of the House of Assembly on "the people's plight" as the mover of the resolution had called it, and by the first report of the National Household Survey taken in November 1973. The select committee found that the number of un-employed at the end of 1973 had been 6,700 and must have risen since then. For the next three years, eighteen hundred school leavers would join the workforce each year. The select committee's call for ten thousand new jobs immediately was utopian in the light of its own economic analysis. Hotels would provide no further jobs for the next three years because no new hotels were planned. There was no scope for increased employment in finance, and the construction industry was at an almost complete halt. The select committee's expectation that between eighteen hundred and two thousand new jobs could be found in light industry was, as already suggested, implausible. Its call for a rapid expansion of agriculture and fishing disregarded the universal experience that this requires capital rather than labour unless accompanied by radical social reform. Similarly its suggestion of a scattering of small hotels and guest hotels throughout the Out Islands by providing increased financial assistance for their construction, better local airstrips, and more promotion failed to compare capital investment to jobs created.[19]

The National Household Survey found that the proportion of the total population in the workforce had declined sharply from 41.3 per cent in 1970 to 37.3 per cent in 1973. In part this would have reflected the decline in the non-Bahamian proportion of the workforce from 24 per cent to 12 per cent over the same period, in part the increased number of children. In mid-1973 the workforce was estimated to number 78,400, of whom 8.6 per cent were unemployed; among those under the age of twenty the rate of unemployment was 28.8 per cent. Over the 1970–73 period, the average *per capita* income for Bahamians had increased in current dollars from $1,234 to $1,682; for non-

Bahamians it had fallen slightly from $4,134 to $4,065. The number of households in the $15,000–$20,000 bracket had increased by 75 per cent, some evidence of the rapid expansion of the upper middle-class.[20] Unfortunately, neither report provided any data on the distribution of incomes, save between all Bahamians and all non-Bahamians. The next National Household Survey, conducted in 1975, showed a drop in average *per capita* income for the whole population from $1,943 in 1973 to $1,544, and a remarkable closing of the income gap between Bahamians, who now averaged $1,523, and non-Bahamians with $1,632.[21]

One clue to income distribution was provided by a release from the Ministry of Development in 1974 (see table 12) which sought to

Table 12. Composition of workforce.

Category of Employment	Number Employed		
	Total	Expatriate	
			%
Casino	530	468	88
Communications-telephone	111	76	69
Accountants-professional	374	243	65
Doctors	76	49	65
Education-private	476	306	64
Directors-proprietors	1,061	561	53
Appliances-furniture	468	235	50
Engineers	458	230	50
Accounting-audit	252	126	50
Surveyors	104	52	50
Directors-managers: Banks	564	276	49
” ” Transportation	302	148	49
” ” Service industry	800	368	46
Service and sports workers	743	317	43
Marine construction	186	80	43
Cement-clay	594	253	42
Banks (trust)	397	141	36
Land development	929	324	35
Steno-typists	1,760	553	31
Teachers	1,795	544	30
Banks (commercial)	1,074	318	30
Bookkeepers-cashiers	1,539	426	28
Hotels with restaurants	9,372	1,708	18
Ministry of Education	1,776	314	18

disprove complaints that it was not issuing enough work permits.[22] There are considerable problems in interpreting these figures, e.g. how to reconcile the 18 per cent for hotels with restaurants with the claims by the Hotels Association that such a figure in 1968 had been reduced to less than 3 per cent in 1975, and the categories are crude and unusual to say the least. But from them one might hazard a very tentative guesstimate that between eight thousand and ten thousand Bahamians were employees or self-employed in occupations that yielded the sort of income that characterized the white part of the non-Bahamian community. In other words, the top sector of the occupational pyramid was split roughly two-thirds Bahamians and the small group of expatriates with "belonger" status, one-third expatriates under the work permit system.

Any hopes of improving that ratio in favour of the Bahamian-born rested on government policy in two fields, immigration and education. For immigration it would entail rounding up and expelling illegal immigrants, and tightening up still further the system of work permits. In mid-1974 another drive was launched against those illegally in the country. Over thirteen thousand registered for repatriation, eight thousand in New Providence and five thousand at Freeport, while hundreds left voluntarily during an amnesty period.[23]

In education the translation of policy into achievement would be slower and more difficult. One element of policy was the Bahamianization of the teaching service; by February 1973 it was claimed that this was complete in the primary schools.[24] However, the quality of Bahamian recruits left room for concern. The principal of the teachers' college on New Providence reported that as the number of entrants increased the proportion with the desirable qualification of five O-levels steadily declined. In 1961, when twenty-seven had been admitted to the college, 90 per cent had five O-levels; by 1967, when the number was up to fifty-three, the proportion was down to 12 per cent; in 1973, when 157 were admitted, only 6 per cent had five O-levels. Moreover, he added, the college itself had been gravely handicapped by rapid turnover of staff. In ten years it had had four principals, three vice-principals, and sixty-nine different staff.[25] In mid-1975 the San Salvador teachers' college closed when its cost and the difficulties of keeping staff on a remote Out Island proved too much.

Debate over the content of a Bahamian education system continued to be heated. It was not surprising that the Vanguard Nationalist and Socialist Party (see below) attacked the government for maintaining a system that supported colonialism by giving poor quality education.[26] But even within the service there was fundamental criticism. The ministry issued a White Paper which called the existing system "alien and irrelevant", and the teachers' union warned against "elaborate curricula frills which permeate modern foreign education" before the basic skills were imparted.[27] An investigation proposed revision of the Bahamas Junior Certificate and the GCE O-levels to make them more relevant, and incidentally disclosed that recent performance on both was still very poor. In 1973, of 1,937 candidates for the Junior Certificate, 40 per cent had passed no subject at all. Of the 1,057 who sat for more than four subjects, only 66 had passed in more than four; of the 786 who sat for more than five subjects, only 27 had passed in more than five. In the O-level examinations, of 746 candidates 29 per cent had passed no subject at all; only 73 had passed in more than four subjects. Yet, as the teachers' union warned, if relevance meant more scientific and technical subjects and courses, the costs would shoot up – and, something the union did not mention, the need for expatriate teachers would also increase.

Wisely the government rejected proposals for a local university, and chose instead to establish the College of the Bahamas by amalgamating the two teachers' colleges (subsequently reduced to one), the technical college, the evening institute, and the sixth form at the Government High School in Nassau. Even that modest development, which was decided upon in 1972, did not secure the necessary legislation until late in 1974, and then was further delayed by the reluctance of teachers to transfer to a new public corporation until their terms of employment were settled. Of course, education undertaken within the Bahamas does not tell the whole story. By 1971 there were some 250 Bahamians studying abroad on government scholarships, and, as there had been for many years, several hundred others studying privately overseas. But, given the grave deficiencies of upper secondary education in the Bahamas, it was difficult to increase the number who could enter post-secondary training abroad. Although the PLP government could justifiably point to the neglect of education by its predecessors, their own unwillingness to grasp the nettle by replacing an excessively academic curriculum and their political commitment to premature Bahamianization of the teaching service left them with little credit for willingness to pump ever larger sums of money into a hopeless system. The advent of independence would find most Bahamians ill-prepared for new responsibilities.

Closely connected with criticism of the educational system was the quest for a Bahamian national culture. In May 1971 the parliamentary secretary for community development, Edmund Moxey, put forward a scheme to build "Jumbey Village" to display traditional village life and to act as a crafts market. And, as a tourist inducement, the Ministry of Tourism started a "Goombay Summer Festival", including a mini-junkanoo parade. Some of the flavour of successive "Goombay

Summers" was given in a press release marking the third year: "Goombay Summer is designed to expose the visitor to Bahamian culture and all facets of the Bahamian way of life — the religious heritage, the goombay music, the Bahamian cuisine and the folklore depicting the colourful past from the landfall of Columbus in 1492 to the present day. It is also designed to give the tourist value for money spent during his stay."[28] Providing something for the tourists to do once they had reached Nassau had always been a problem. At one time anything that distracted their attention from shopping along Bay Street had been suspect, but more recently the possibility had been admitted that sun and sea, hotels and nightclubs had their limitations. "Goombay Summer" remained more of an exercise in tourist promotion than a cultivation of national culture.

Indeed, as Richard Crawford of the Adult Study Centre told a Rotary meeting, there was little on which the much-desired national culture could be built. There was no national literature. Local painting was sentimental and derivative. The traditional junkanoo parade early on New Year's Day morning, whose antecedents were attributed to West Africa though some claimed it owed more to Mardi Gras, was becoming commercial as business houses sponsored teams and the art of designing individual paper costumes declined. Goombay songs were being infused with pop music. According to Crawford, the only genuine, untouched thing remaining genuinely Bahamian was the jumping dance.[29] However, there is one serious omission from his list — folklore, for there have been several extensive collections of Bahamian folk tales.[30] In Jamaica the West African influence expressed in folk tales about Annancy, the trickster spider, was one of the earliest contributions to a Jamaican national culture to be recognized, and the Bahamian equivalents warrant more attention than they have received.

A matter of widespread concern was the extent to which Bahamian youths were mimicking American ways, especially the new tough, criminal blacks of the cinema. A local psychiatrist, Dr Timothy McCartney, warned:

> The Bahamas is a third world nation which means that we identify more closely with the bloc of developing countries of Africa, Asia, the Caribbean and South America, but we seem to be so Americanized. I believe that we are probably the greatest exponents of Americanism anywhere in the world today . . . I am just as afraid of American black nationalism here as I am of white colonialism. This is happening because we are not secure as Bahamians in our own right.[31]

Dr John McCartney, a Bahamian political scientist teaching in the United States who helped organize the Vanguard Nationalist and Socialist Party, replied:

Many Bahamians love to say that Black Power is an American import, and besides we are the majority in the Bahamas. I have always found that such people refuse to use their minds and look at the facts objectively. To begin with, all of the slaves in the U.S. and Caribbean came from basically the same cultural area and underwent the same type of slave experience. Another similarity is that in the same way that the black American was effectively shut from power, the Bahamian was more effectively shut out. Why? We could always fool ourselves that blacks were the majority . . . You may argue that we are the majority in this country, but when you see us closely linked to a country of 200 million people like the U.S. of which 180 million are white, majority talk is foolish."[32]

Within the churches, too, the debate over Bahamianization continued. An Anglican priest, the Reverend Murillo Bonaby, warned that his church's ritual was out of touch with the people: "The Anglican hangover of colonialism fits more easily into the English pattern. There is too much organisation in religious expression to suit the Bahamian and the church is almost afraid to allow people to express themselves in their worship."[33] However, when a mime dance was performed in the Anglican cathedral under the sponsorship of the Christian Council as part of "Goombay Summer" festivities, a leading Baptist minister, the Reverend H. W. Brown, attacked the council for becoming involved in secular affairs.[34]

The central issue of the Bahamian identity crisis, for the time being at least, was political independence rather than national culture. In January 1971 the minister of state at the Commonwealth Relations Office visited Nassau for talks. On one occasion Arthur Hanna referred to the suspension of the British Guiana Constitution in 1953 as an example of what could happen to a colony before it gained independence if it was in the interests of Britain;[35] but apart from that, anti-British sentiments played a small part in the debate because it had been made obvious that so soon as Bahamian wishes were known Britain would comply. PLP policy was that independence should follow the next election, at which the issue would be put to the people. As Pindling told a rally called to discuss independence: "It will be impolitic and uneconomic for the Bahamas to immediately proceed directly to independence. There is still much for us to do. I have no doubt, however, that we could be fully ready in two years time."[36] The Free PLP condemned the "undue haste" of such a timetable, and former UBP supporters attacked the idea of independence at any time, but the matter was out of their hands.

In June 1971, following a visit to London by Pindling, the governor's speech from the throne made it official: independence would follow the next election.[37] In March 1972, as he prepared to retire, the governor explained that if the present government was returned with a working majority at the election, the British government would take that as evidence that the Bahamian people had approved its proposals for independence.[38] A few days later Pindling tabled a Green Paper which set out those proposals in some detail and set the likely cost at $839,000. Thereupon the government campaign to educate the people for independence moved into high gear. A three-day public conference was held in April, attended by fifteen hundred and timed, rather suspiciously, to coincide with the first convention of the Free National Movement (FNM). The conference proceedings were enlivened by the appearance of Speaker Braynen, in full robes and tricorn and accompanied by the mace, to lead the crowd in singing "For He's a Jolly Good Fellow" to the prime minister. Braynen came in for further criticism when he told a two-day independence seminar for schoolteachers that he would welcome independence because it would get rid of "obnoxious Englishmen".

One of the concomitants of political independence would be new national symbols. In July 1971 a new coat of arms had been produced, with a new motto: "Forward, upward, onward together". Senator Doris Johnson, who frequently identified herself with the biblical heroine Esther, one of the few women in the Bible with a political role, announced that she had been given the design of the new national flag in a dream: a white Maltese cross on a black spheroid on a field of green. The Free PLP attacked her vision as "a blasphemy, a farce, and an insult to the Bahamian people to hear Dr Johnson talking about visions and personal messages from God being whispered in her ear",[39] and one of the anti-independence leaflets dropped from the air on a PLP rally warned of the straitened diet which would follow independence: "Cassava bread and dry conch gives Esther nightmares."

In April 1971 a petition was circulated at Abaco, asking the Queen to detach the island from the Bahamas and give it a separate status like the Cayman Islands. When, after some confusion whether the petition had already been sent directly to London, it turned up in Nassau bearing two thousand signatures, the accompanying deputation was denounced by the government information services for "uttering explicit threats to take treasonable action unless their demands are met".[40] This referred to a fiery letter, purporting to be from a prominent Abaconian, saying that Abaco would be another Anguilla and would use force if necessary to protect itself. The letter was subsequently repudiated as a forgery.[41] At Government House the Abaco deputation was told that the British government would refuse to accept the petition unless it was forwarded by the Bahamian government.

Two steps were taken to maintain Bahamian territorial integrity. One was an amendment to the Penal Code to make it an offense, punishable by twenty years imprisonment, for a person to engage in military operations "in circumstances giving rise to the presumption that his purpose is to coerce any Commonwealth or friendly foreign government or to facilitate attack upon neighbouring territories".[42] The other was the opening of negotiations with Cuba over fishing rights; in February 1969 the Bahamas had claimed an exclusive fisheries zone of twenty kilometres, whereupon both the United States and Cuba lodged objections. One prophet of impending doom was Earl T. Smith, who had been American ambassador to Cuba in the last days of the Batista regime, who predicted that an independent Bahamas would be likely to become another Cuba either by establishment of a leftist dictatorship or by a direct Cuban takeover and warned that in the latter event Washington would give no assistance.[43]

A neutral observer, however, would have been hard put to find any sign of a swing to the left in Bahamian politics. Pindling kept his options open by not filling the two vacant places in the ministry, but defections from the party continued. In February 1971 the party suspended its only full-time paid official, the party secretary Oswald Pyfrom, and replaced him with Kendal Nottage, formerly assistant secretary. Pyfrom denied that the National General Council had power to suspend him, as he had been appointed by the party convention; when the council did suspend him, he left the party and joined the rebels. In March the party's treasurer, Cyril Tynes, resigned. In April the party paper, the *Bahamian Times,* declared for the rebels; the government promptly transferred its printing contract to the *Guardian,* and the *Bahamian Times,* already in debt, ceased publication.

Despite the PLP's difficulties, its various opponents found themselves unable to organize a united front. The first casualty of the new situation was the NDP. When one group of its members, led by Orville Turnquest, began negotiations with the rebels, they were repudiated by the majority. In the meantime the party's leader, Paul Adderley, had resigned because of his own objections to the negotiations. In the end some members, including Turnquest, joined the rebels in the Free PLP, while Adderley went his own way and began a new monthly journal, *The Democrat.* The rump of the NDP reorganized their party without its ablest and most experienced members.

On 19 April 1971 the Free PLP announced formation of a central council of twenty-five members including the original eight PLP rebels, two former PLP MHAs, Turnquest and Spurgeon Bethel, Senator Kendal Isaacs, and Oswald Pyfrom who became a full-time administrative officer for the party. The party would have its own newspaper, *The Torch.* For its officers the new party elected Cecil Wallace-Whitfield as parliamentary leader, Elwood Donaldson chairman and Turnquest vice-chairman, Curtis McMillan secretary, Isaacs treasurer, and Bazel Nichols

Orville Turnquest (Courtesy of
Tribune)

Kendal Isaacs (Courtesy of
Tribune)

assistant treasurer. One consequence of the realignment was that the UBP had become the smaller of the two groups opposing the government in the House of Assembly, and accordingly Wallace-Whitfield replaced Johnstone as leader of the opposition. A columnist in the *Guardian* saw that change as historic, "a symbol of the fact that the simmering war between the Bahamian races had come to an end":

> So long as Mr Johnstone remained as Leader of the Opposition in the House, his presence there reminded the Bahamian people that the whites still opposed the blacks, and regardless of how sincere we believe Mr Johnstone to be each time he stood and criticized the Government, the groundlings in the gallery always viewed it simply as a white man once more telling a black man that the latter did not know what the hell he was doing.[44]

Another consequence of the realignment was that although the UBP had ceased to be the official opposition it still held the opposition places in the Senate, or rather three of the four, for Reginald Lobosky had already left the party after unsuccessfully disputing selection for the Shirlea constituency with Sir Roland Symonette. The Free PLP called on all four senators to resign because they no longer represented the opposition; the PLP called on Lobosky and Isaacs to resign because they were no longer what they had been, UBP and independent respectively, when appointed. No one did resign, and it was learned that one consequence of the 1969 alterations to the Constitution had been that there was no longer any power to compel senators to resign.[45] Isaacs, however, did stand down as vice-president of the Senate and was replaced by a PLP Senator, Milo Butler, junior.

The PLP experienced one more secession, this time to the left and more of a nuisance than a threat. Some members of the Unicomm, which it will be remembered had grown out of the party's youth organization, formed the Vanguard Nationalist and Socialist Party: "We call ourselves vanguard because we are the first party in the country that will address itself to a complete reconstruction of society. We call ourselves socialist because we believe that the wealth of the country belongs to the community and that there should be broader ownership of the means of production. We call ourselves nationalist because we believe that all principal institutions should be geared to suit the Bahamian people."[46]

Unicomm expelled five members for their part in forming the VNSP, but at least one PLP back bencher publicly welcomed its appearance. Its monthly journal, *Vanguard,* advanced a mixture of Black Power and New Left ideas, in large part aimed at the PLP for its backsliding:

> The lack of a basic and coherent political philosophy in the P.L.P. has been a major factor in its failure to do much to correct the

abuses of Bahamian society by the wealthy few, or to create genuine political and economic opportunity for the majority of the people. In effect, the P.L.P. since taking over the Government has resorted to a more subtle process of corrupt methods and practices employed by the U.B.P. in its day of power. There has been almost no improvement in the general lot of the people and the Government is dominated more than ever by foreign capital.[47]

Some evidence that not all critics had left the party appeared when a speech by the president of the Bahamas Federation of Youth, the PLP's latest youth body, was deleted from the agenda of the 1971 convention. Its text appeared later as a letter to the *Guardian* and attacked many aspects of contemporary Bahamian life.[48]

The first test of the new political situation came with the death of Clarence Bain in July 1971. The subsequent by-election for the Mangrove Cay electorate at Andros on 10 September was a disaster for the Free PLP, whose candidate polled only 66 votes to the PLP's 618 and the UBP's 199. Although there had been a swing from the PLP of almost 15 per cent, the loss of a popular MHA who had represented the area since 1956, together with the party's recent internal troubles, might have been expected to produce an even greater swing. Some UBP stalwarts argued that the result was due to the intimidation of voters, and there appeared to have been some, but a more realistic view was that the PLP could have won easily without intimidation. Shortly afterwards Oswald Pyfrom left the Free PLP with the complaint that none of its members were prepared to do any work, and that those in the House were resigned to losing their seats.[49] The only chance for the PLP's opponents was a merger and better communication with the voters.

In October the Free PLP changed its name to the Free National Movement (FNM) and issued an invitation to all to join it. The following months its executive began negotiations with the UBP, and now a merger was quickly arranged. One consequence was that Kendal Isaacs replaced Godfrey Kelly as leader of the opposition in the Senate, completing the removal of white leaders in the legislature. In December the FNM issued a high-flown manifesto which called for an atmosphere of stability and warned that independence within two years would be too soon because the people were not properly prepared. Harking back to the history of personal quarrels many of their leading members had had with Pindling, the FNM proposed more consultation between the prime minister and his other ministers, and between ministers and local members when constituency interests were involved. Foreign capital inflow was still essential, and the government should avoid nationalization or entering into commercial banking. It should not impose an income tax, and should abolish the real property tax for low and middle income families, relying on greater efficiency to match revenue with expenditure. Immigration policy should be administered so as to prevent unauthorized entries, but allowing "new knowledge, skills and other resources to enter the country". Expatriates should be dealt with fairly, and once in the country should not be harassed.[50]

In February 1972 the FNM announced thirty-six candidates for the next election. Only five were whites, including two of the sitting MHAs, Sir Roland Symonette and Norman Solomon. Johnstone agreed to stand down at Fort Montagu to enable Kendal Isaacs to move from the Senate, and Basil Kelly withdrew as candidate for Crooked Island in favour of Cyril Tynes, explaining his decision: "The U.B.P. way of life is finished forever in this country. Face facts, we are living in a black man's country and they are going to run it their way, not ours. I accept this and so should we all."[51] Subsequently the FNM endorsed another two whites for the remaining constituencies, making a total of seven out of thirty-eight.

Heartened by its strong showing at the Mangrove Cay by-election, the PLP convention, by a unanimous vote, formally expelled the rebels and chose a new party secretary, Earl Thompson. After the convention, Pindling filled the vacancies in the ministry by appointing Simeon Bowe and Loftus Roker, and at the same time he transferred the sensitive Labour and Welfare portfolio to Clifford Darling, head of the taxi-drivers' union. He was still unable to pick a new minister of education, however, and the portfolio remained in the overloaded hands of the minister of finance, Carlton Francis. One sign of the party's success and the dangers that success could bring was the celebration of the fifth anniversary of its accession to power: prayers and reminiscences of the heroic early days for the masses at the Southern Recreation Ground, a banquet for the party elite at the Paradise Island Hotel.

If a general election were not held by the end of 1972, there would have to be a redistribution. The Constitution required one every five years, and the last had been approved in February 1968.[52] On 10 August an election was called for 19 September, but the campaign was already well under way with both parties having selected a full slate of candidates. Two explosions at PLP rallies in a predominantly white settlement at Abaco led Pindling to warn that the country was entering an era of the "politics of desperation". He called on Bahamians "to choose between the philosophy of peace, love and progress, and one of dynamite, death and destruction . . . between our Bahamas, preserved and developed for present and future generations of Bahamians, as opposed to a Bahamas owned lock, stock and barrel by foreigners".[53] He had told the previous PLP convention that a White Paper on independence would be provided in 1972, but there would be no referendum on the question, as anti-PLP speakers now demanded, because Britain did not require one. He now promised that the White Paper would be tabled immediately after the election; the postponement was made an election issue by the FNM, who warned that the people were buying a pig in a poke.

During the campaign the PLP attacked FNM "terrorism" and emphasized national unity. Its posters showed white and black Bahamians standing side by side with the slogan "Peace, Love, Prosperity". The FNM countered with economic issues, one being that the government's proposals for a social security system — what subsequently became the national insurance scheme — was the first step towards income tax, and with the dangers of independence. One FNM advertisement showed a huge red shark chasing a tiny Bahamian fish with the caption "Will it be Red China, will it be Russia or Cuba that will swallow us after independence? No one knows what is in the White Paper."[54] As in previous elections there were some violent incidents. Constituency offices of both parties were attacked and meetings were disrupted. One FNM supporter was found murdered at Perpalls Tract to the west of Nassau, and two other FNM members were subsequently convicted and executed for the crime. It appeared from their trial that politics had provided the motive. A Canadian investor at Crooked Island was suddenly deported for becoming involved in local politics because he transported FNM supporters in his private airplane, but non-Bahamians were less apparent in the 1972 election campaign than in the three previous.

The enrolment was the highest ever recorded at 57,071, of which 35,957 were in New Providence constituencies and 21,114 on the Out Islands — or "Family Islands" as they were now known officially to emphasize their importance in the new order. The number of candidates was also a record; the FNM nominated in all thirty-eight electorates, the PLP in thirty-seven, while Fawkes's Commonwealth Labour Party (CLP) offered eight,[55] and there were nine independents. Women, however, still failed to secure recognition; only two of the ninety-three candidates were women, one each from the PLP and the CLP. The election result was another landslide for the PLP, which lost only one seat to the FNM (Crooked Island), regained the eight seats the rebels had occupied, and finally ejected Fawkes from the House. The FNM won six of the seven old UBP seats, picked up Crooked Island from the PLP, and defeated Braynen. The seventh former UBP constituency, North End Long Island, Rum Cay, and San Salvador, produced a dead heat; the UBP retained it eventually (see below). In terms of votes, the PLP lost a few thousand, and the FNM won a few thousand more than the UBP had polled in 1968, but the electoral pattern remained unchanged. Only where white voters were in the majority could an anti-PLP candidate survive; the exception was

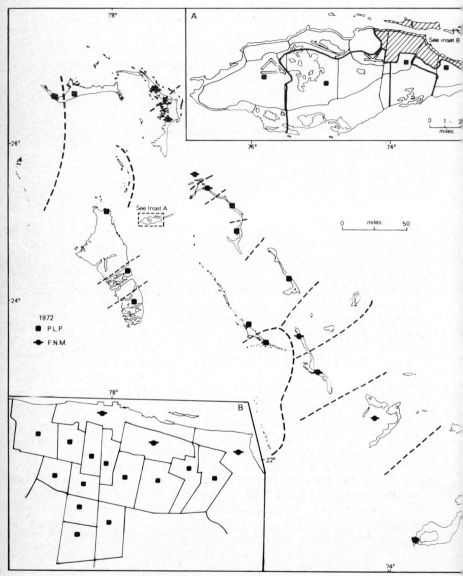

Map 6. Results of the 1972 general election

St John's, where a white FNM candidate, Noel Roberts, defeated Braynen, who ran as an independent with tacit PLP support.

The PLP's latest newspaper, the *People*, had the right explanation for what had happened:

> The past behaviour of the Bahamian electorate gave us a clue to what was symbolically important to the Bahamian people, and we found three things. Firstly in the minds of the Bahamian electorate the U.B.P. has always been and always will be equated with violence and victimisation. Secondly, the Bahamian people do not trust politicians who change sides at the first hint of trouble. They consider them traitors. Thirdly, the Progressive Liberal Party is considered the party which gave hope and freedom to the majority of Bahamians. Once these three symbolic attitudes were grasped, it was difficult to see how the eight dissidents could survive politically once they had merged with the United Bahamian Party. They, to all intents and purposes as far as Bahamians were concerned, had become U.B.P.[56]

Perhaps the party's greatest triumph was in recapturing the two Grand Bahama seats with the loss of only a few hundred votes. If the FNM's attack on the government's economic failure had any bite, it should have been at Grand Bahama.

Preparations for the constitutional change to independence resumed. The government's White Paper presented to the new legislature was an unexceptional document which nevertheless managed to split the small opposition. Kendall Isaacs accepted the verdict of the people, while continuing to deplore the timetable as premature, but a new FNM MHA Errington Watkins, followed the old UBP line of total resistance to the idea of independence. When constitutional talks were called in London, Watkins proceeded there separately from the opposition delegation to lobby against independence as the spokesman for Abaco, where he had won a seat. Extravagant claims, such as the threat that twenty thousand British subjects would be expelled from the Bahamas after independence, further annoyed the FNM leadership, who warned him to comply with party policy. Watkins's martial manner did attract support from one or two right-wing Conservatives, who warmed to an appeal from the Abaconian descendants of Loyalists who had fled the American Revolution and were now to be denied their connection with the Crown once more. He was accompanied to London by Leonard Thompson, a former UBP MHA who had contested the other Abaco seat for the FNM; Thompson eventually left the party in protest over its neglect of its anti-independence members and abandoned an appeal against the result in that constituency which just might have given the FNM another seat in the House and made Abaco's solidarity more convincing. One local body, the Greater Abaco Council, abandoned

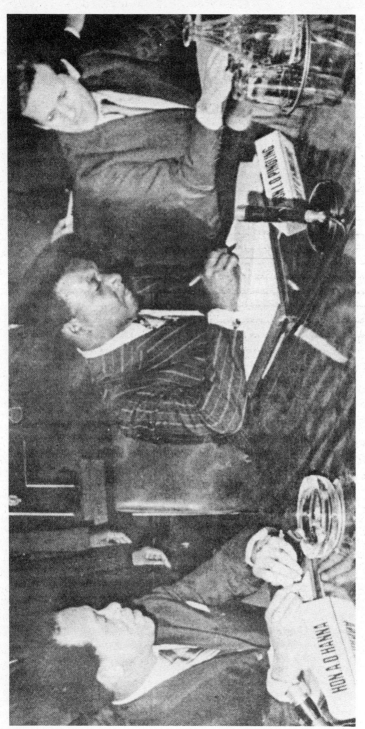

London constitutional conference; Arthur Hanna and Lynden Pindling (Courtesy of *Tribune*)

hopes of a separate status for the island, but another, the Abaco Independence Movement, stepped in to conduct a strident campaign which became inflamed by reports of American arms dealers, mercenaries, and the interest of a group of libertarian philosophers from California who proposed setting up a free market Utopia at Abaco. That last group subsequently sought to establish themselves on a reef in the Pacific near Tonga, and when they were thwarted by the Tongan government annexing the reef, became embroiled in a secessionist movement in the New Hebrides when that group neared independence. Much more significant in its long-term consequence was Watkins's motion in the House of Assembly for a referendum before independence. It split the FNM down the middle, with four members voting for it (Watkins, Sir Roland Symonette, Cleophas Adderley, and Michael Lightbourn) and four against (Isaacs, Cyril Tynes, Cyril Fountain, and Noel Roberts). The ninth member, who was then absent, Norman Solomon, subsequently declared his support for the Isaacs position.

The government had an easier time. The symbols of nationhood were speadily assembled. "March on, Bahamaland" by a local composer, Timothy Gibson, was adopted as the national anthem. A new flag was chosen, not that of Doris Johnson's vision, but comprising a black triangle in the left corner, with two aquamarine stripes separated by a gold stripe. The minister for home affairs explained the symbolism: "Black, a stronger colour, represents the vigour and force of a united people; the triangle, pointing towards the body of the flag, represents the enterprise and determination of the Bahamian people to develop and possess the rich resources of land and sea, symbolised by gold and aquamarine respectively."[57] The requisite legislation passed the British Parliament in May, despite some grumbling from a few Conservatives, and at midnight on 9 July 1973 independence was inaugurated before a crowd of fifty thousand.

The necessary changes in personnel also took place. After the general election Milo Butler became a minister without portfolio preliminary to becoming governor-general. He was knighted in June 1973, and was sworn in on 1 August wearing the traditional white dress-uniform which he promised never to put on again. In the new Senate Leonard Knowles stood down as president and in June 1973 was appointed chief justice. Gerald Cash became president, and as the House of Assembly elected Arlington Butler, one of the sons of the governor-general-designate and the former deputy Speaker, as Speaker, for the first time in Bahamian history both presiding officers were Negroes. Another independent senator, Livingston Johnson, was appointed Bahamian ambassador to the United States and the United Nations, and a PLP senator, Milo Butler, junior, was appointed consul-general in Miami. Upon independence the remaining independent senator, Cash, retired; later he became deputy governor-general. Doris Johnson became president of the Senate, and three PLP stalwarts were appointed to the vacant places to give the government a 13–4 majority in the upper chamber.

Following the 1972 election both parties had made substantial changes in the ranks of their senators. The FNM dropped all their incumbents and replaced them with two of the PLP rebels, Foulkes and Donaldson, Orville Turnquest, and another lawyer, Henry Bostwick, who had unsuccessfully contested a House seat. Turnquest was elected to lead for the party in the Senate, but within a few weeks one of his small band departed when Donaldson resigned both his Senate seat and the chairmanship of the FNM, saying that he had always opposed the merger with the UBP. Turnquest became party chairman in his place; the new FNM senator chosen was Garnet Levarity, father of the former MHA and minister, and for some years the government's principal official at Freeport. The PLP dropped four of its longest serving senators and replaced them with the defeated MHA for Crooked Island, a lawyer of Greek descent, A. P. Maillis, who had stood for the House as a PLP candidate on earlier occasions, Mizpah Tertullien, who replaced another woman senator, Bertha Isaacs, and Paul Adderley, who was promptly appointed minister of state and government leader in the Senate. So, ironically, Adderley and Turnquest, the two lawyers who had once joined the PLP together, been elected to the House together, left it together to form the NDP, and then parted company when the party broke up, became leaders of the two parties on opposite sides of the Senate. Apart from the addition of Adderley, other cabinet appointments were the promotion of Anthony Roberts, who had previously been parliamentary secretary, to Milo Butler's old portfolio of Agriculture and Fisheries, and the very rapid elevation of Darrel Rolle, winner of the previous year's by-election at Mangrove Cay, to Transport in place of Doris Johnson.

One bit of unfinished electoral business concerned the North End Long Island, Rum Cay, and San Salvador constituency. The government directed that a by-election be held with the same candidates. The FNM, who were seeking to win the seat through the election tribunal, boycotted the election, and the PLP candidate polled 573 votes to the reluctant FNM's 4. However, on 7 February 1973 the election tribunal examined the original ballot papers and found that Fountain had won for the FNM 475–471.

Following the disagreement over Watkins's campaign against independence, Isaacs suddenly resigned as FNM leader in the House of Assembly in June. Thereupon the FNM expelled Watkins and, after a hearing by a disciplinary tribunal, expelled the other three MHAs who had voted for his referendum motion, after which Isaacs returned to the leadership. There had already been stories that Symonette had been thinking of reviving the UBP, and once they were out of the FNM the four MHAs issued a statement attacking Isaacs for being more concerned to spare the government embarrassment than a vigorous opposition should. A year later a forlorn group of old UBP supporters, mainly Negroes, met to call for a restoration of the party; one of them expressed herself rather infelicitously when she said, "If Christ brought Lazarus back from the grave, he can also bring back the U.B.P."[58] Nothing came of the idea of reviving the UBP, and after a couple of months of independence Sir Roland Symonette rejoined the FNM, but with or without its ex-UBP component, the FNM remained a weak and divided opposition.

The first test of political strengths came soon after independence on a wicket very favourable to the PLP. Milo Butler's appointment to the governor-generalship produced a by-election at Bains Town on 19 July. Dr Norman Gay, who had stood for the party in the City constituency in 1972, won handsomely with 886 to 59 for the FNM's new secretary, Clifford Cooper, and a mere 18 for the Vanguard Nationalist and Socialist Party's candidate, Wesley Campbell; both Cooper and Campbell lost their deposits. A better test came a few months later when Sinclair Outten, the PLP victor in Fawkes's old constituency of St Barnabas, learned that he had been born at Turks Island and brought to the Bahamas when only a few weeks old. As a consequence he had been ineligible for election to the House. Outten applied for and was given citizenship, and was re-endorsed for the seat by the PLP. The VNSP had been weighed and found wanting in the Bains Town by-election; St Barnabas provided the occasion for another new force to the left of the PLP to try its popular appeal.

We have already seen how the BFTU disintegrated in the early 1970s; despite its collapse, however, it continued to supply two members to the PLP's National General Council. Following an unsuccessful attempt to revive the BFTU early in 1972, a new body had been set up, the Commonwealth of the Bahamas Trade Union Congress (usually abbreviated as the TUC). Seven unions, plus two Out Island branches of one of them, the hotel workers' union, attended its inaugural meeting, but like the BFTU, the TUC failed to establish itself as spokesman for the Bahamian working class or even for Bahamian trade unions. Instead, stepping into Fawkes's shoes as the PLP's principal critic came another union leader outside the TUC umbrella, Dudley Williams of the Bahamas Fuel, Engineering, Service and Allied Workers Union. Williams was already in dispute with the government over his attempts to organize the employees of certain public corporations. In 1972 his union extended its constitution to cover a wide range of occupations, but when a substantial proportion of the waterside workers tried to transfer their allegiance to his union, the Ministry of Labour intervened or, as Williams saw it, tried to break up his union.

Working under the label of the Bahamas Workers' Council, Williams put forward a more militant line than the TUC was prepared to give: "The only black people who have been able to move up are the upper-class blacks and the English educated blacks. The real 'grass-roots' demand a chance to move up also."[59] When the minister of labour, Clifford Darling, told the 1973 PLP convention that the best and most effective union was one confined to its own craft or industry, Williams replied that Darling's speech was reactionary and warned that the black poor might have to turn to a campaign of civil disobedience. Darling insisted that the government was not fighting the unions, merely protecting the interests of the people as a whole, but his government had become defensive in its dealings with the unions. So, when there was a sudden walk-out lasting only three hours at a number of hotels, the strike leaders were denounced for using the labour movement for their own political ambitions.

In an atmosphere of growing tension between the PLP government and at least some sections of the union movement, the by-election at St Barnabas, a solidly working-class constituency, took place in January 1974. By that time, it will be recalled, the government was also in hot water over its decision to acquire the casinos. The by-election result pointed in two apparently divergent directions. Outten for the PLP had lost more than half his votes in less than two years, down from 961 to 457. Yet the swing of a quarter of the total vote did not cost him the seat; he retained just over half the votes, and the remainder were fragmented between six other candidates. Foulkes for the FNM managed 194, Fawkes, who revived his Commonwealth Labour Party label for the day, polled 88, Dudley Williams 72, and three other candidates totalled 87 between them. Thus, if one adds Fawkes and Williams together as the joint claimants for the "labour" vote, in so far as that was the anti-PLP left-wing vote, it was still less than the FNM, to the right of the PLP, could muster.

The PLP had routed its external opponents, the FNM (split again into UBP and Free PLP factions) and those unionists who challenged the PLP's political leadership but proved unable either to form effective organizations or to win votes. It did, however, have trouble with internal critics, notably two back-benchers, Edmund Moxey and Oscar Johnson, whose enthusiasm for pet projects in their constituencies provided a regular source of irritation. Moxey, as parliamentary secretary for culture, had pressed for financial support for "Jumbey Village". When it failed to get assistance in the 1974 budget, he first picketed the House of Assembly and then entered the chamber still bearing his protesting placard. His resignation as a parliamentary secretary was demanded and obtained. In May 1974 he set up the People's Positive Action Committee to attack the next "Goombay Summer" programme because it ignored his "Jumbey Village" in particular and "over the hill" generally, in favour of a second artificial village to be constructed in the grounds of Fort Charlotte closer to the main tourist areas. Moxey also secured and chaired a select committee on "the social, cultural and economic plight of the people" whose interim report we have already noted. In the debate on its appointment, several other back-benchers joined him in criticizing the government. One was Oscar Johnson, who said, "The real power in this country is still being held by the white man just like it did before we came to power . . . The black man has been in office for seven years, but he has never been in power."[60]

In due course a group separated from the People's Positive Action Committee to form the People's Democratic Party (PDP), and though it is doubtful whether the PDP's members ever amounted to more than a handful, with the ready assistance of the daily newspapers, which reported anyone prepared to attack the government, it kept up a sniping fire on the PLP, alongside but separate from the VNSP and Dudley Williams's Workers Council. In October 1974, following allegations of a plot to kidnap the American ambassador, police questioned four men connected with the PDP and the VNSP, and in April 1975, following the death of a young man in an explosion, police found bomb-making equipment in two private homes. The original leader of the PDP, A. D. Butler, was succeeded by his brother Billy, who took it into a merger with the FNM in April 1976. When that party split (see below), Billy Butler moved to the new Bahamian Democratic Party, then after failing to win its endorsement, returned to the FNM. Even the minute VNSP experienced a breakaway, when a group led by Wesley Campbell formed the Bahamian Christian Social Democratic Party late in 1976.

But compared with the violent events of the early 1970s in Port-of-Spain or Kingston, or in many of the smaller islands of the West Indies, Bahamian politics remained parliamentary, relatively stable, and quite moderate. In March 1975 eleven of the PLP's back-benchers formed a caucus within the party. Within a few weeks three of the eleven had dropped out, but the remainder held a press conference to put forward a proposal for unemployment relief by spending $8 million on the construction of two thousand shower-and-toilet units in poor areas. A few weeks later one of the caucus, Edmund Moxey, called for an immediate change in the country's socio-economic structure, warning that the present system was alien to the masses' aspirations and contradicted the original philosophy of the PLP, but he was exceptional in the strength of his criticism of the leadership. His frequent public attacks on the party's lack of direction culminated in a rally called on 27 January 1976 to discuss unemployment, the state of the economy, and other "crisis issues". Only five of the original caucus members attended to join in a call to put the nation back to work. Shortly afterwards Moxey, who had also become involved in a campaign against capital punishment and been charged for taking part in a public procession without a permit, left the parliamentary party. He retained the support of two local organizations, the Kemp Road Youth for Action Club and the Coconut Grove Freedom and Justice Committee, and sitting now as an independent in the House of Assembly assumed Fawkes's mantle as the principal purveyor of allegations of corruption in the government. In April 1976 he managed to bring on a resolution on the subject, but despite support from the FNM it was defeated 13–4.

Another of the five caucus members who had attended Moxey's rally, Oscar Johnson, was also in trouble with the PLP. At the beginning of 1976 he was not reappointed chairman of the Electricity Corporation, and thereafter he waged a double-barrelled public campaign for better facilities for his Cat Island constituents and against his own removal from office. The latter culminated in a motion of no confidence he lodged against Loftus Roker, the minister who had not reappointed him, which the PLP National General Council unanimously rejected. Others of the remaining caucus members were more circumspect, but collectively they kept up a guerilla campaign in the House, seeking the appointment of select committees and the passing of resolutions on matters that embarrassed the party leadership.

Pindling himself was always ready to declare that the party must be prepared to move with the times. In that vein he had told the 1973 convention at Freeport: "To stay on top, this party must find new causes to champion and new social injustices to eradicate. And we must champion those causes and eradicate those injustices even if we discover them among ourselves."[61] He repeated the message at the 1974 convention. With two-thirds of the population under the age of thirty, there was need for a radical restructuring of Bahamian society. Already the country was on its way to a more just economic system, but it had done less to ensure a more just and equitable social order:

> We must not condemn the demand for equal justice and social equality as sheer nonsense, or as meaningless words, or even as words easily spoken but too difficult to turn into a reality. Because we belong to a different generation, we may honestly believe that there is equal justice and social equality now already but remember, we are dealing with a new generation whose starting point may well be where ours left off and whose horizons extend beyond our own.[62]

In 1973 he had warned that the danger to the Bahamas came not from Cuba or communism or Black Power, but from the disparity between the haves and the have-nots. But notwithstanding Pindling's view, some of the have-nots, and their advocates in the local intelligentsia, were dressing up their claims with the rhetoric of Black Power, even though communism remained unmentionable. By 1975 there was a serious crime wave, and some of the crimes had taken on a racial cast. Such incidents had occurred earlier — for example, an American girl in 1972 had been told she was being raped "because she was white"[63] — but now they were more common. A young man who fired a shotgun at two passers-by said he "only wanted to kill a white man"; he was sentenced to ten years and twelve strokes of the cat-o'-nine-tails, which had been brought back into use to deal with crimes of violence.[64] A select committee proposed increased penalties, including mandatory whipping for all drug offences and robbery.[65] The militant backbenchers objected, Moxey on the ground that the cat would only drive young offenders further into a life of crime, Johnson because more concern was being shown over the rape of white women than for the rape of black women. In fact, the first white was whipped in June 1975 for causing bodily harm to another white. The select committee had also included among its draconian proposals banning all movies that portrayed crimes and the prosecution of parents who failed to control their children, but it stopped short of Watkins's call of castration of sex offenders.

The head of the CID explained that 80 per cent of crimes were committed by those in the fourteen-to-twenty-one age group, but doubted whether unemployment had anything to do with the rapid increase in the number of crimes, up 57 per cent on the previous year.[66] There can be no doubt that high unemployment among juveniles was part of the explanation. So, too, was the poor state of the police force which had stopped recruiting in the West Indies as part of the Bahamianization policy, and at the beginning of 1974 was only two-thirds of established strength. The police also suffered from financial restrictions, and funds had to be raised by public subscription to purchase additional motor cars and radios for the force. Another aspect of the crime wave was the rapid growth of drug trafficking. In 1968, 3 Bahamians and 20 non-Bahamians had been charged with drug offences; in 1972 the numbers were 134 and 283 respectively. The Bahamas, with a million and more tourists and numerous small, uncontrolled airstrips and innumerable isolated rocks and cays became a staging-point on drug routes from Jamaica and Colombia to the United States. Huge caches were found at isolated places and smaller quantities seized from persons and aircraft in transit. Some drugs stayed for the local market, and some no doubt corrupted a few members of the police force.

The 1974 PLP convention resolved that a national youth programme should be started and, to meet the Bahamas' need for defence, the Home Defence Force of the Second World War should be reactivated. In March 1975 Pindling started regular "rap sessions" with youth groups, as well as a monthly press conference on radio. At the 1975 convention it was announced that the youth service programme would begin in March 1976, and the abandoned teachers training college at San Salvador would be reactivated for paramilitary and trade training. The 1976 budget provided $5.2 million for defence capital works, to be used for the purchase of the Coral Harbour development on New Providence as a military and naval base. At the 1975 convention the decision was also taken to establish a new party organization, the National Alliance, aimed at young voters. It did not secure the National General Council's endorsement, and after a few months disappeared from sight. After the 1977 election the explanation was offered that the National Alliance had not been proceeded with to avoid confusing the party with new issues, and certainly the party leadership had enough on their hands without a new, potentially radical, youth movement.

Presumably in response to the frequent charges of corruption brought against his government, Pindling sought new controls over conflicts of interest. One, amendment of the law of bribery, went through the House easily, but a bill to require disclosure of the private interests of members of the parliament, modelled on Jamaican legislation, produced a political crisis. After cabinet had considered a number of drafts, a final version was pushed through a poorly attended meeting of the parliamentary party and introduced on 28 July 1976. Just before the luncheon adjournment, Carlton Francis, who had the floor, moved that the bill be referred to a select committee. His motion was seconded by Moxey, and Speaker Butler, who had earlier been reported to have threatened to resign rather than submit to disclosure requirements, immediately put the question. The motion was carried by a combination of the three FNM members then in the chamber with four PLP back-benchers, all ministers being absent. The composition of the select committee suggested that major changes to the bill would be likely, and Pindling countered by proroguing the House to discharge the committee. One of the PLP four, Lionel Davis, was removed as a parliamentary secretary for his part in the affair, but when the party whip reported the matter to the National General Council he failed to request disciplinary action and nothing was done at the time.

It was reported that Pindling had warned the National General Council he would move a motion of no confidence in the Speaker unless Butler resigned first, and when the House reconvened Butler stated that he had been summoned to a meeting with Pindling and Hanna but had refused to attend on the ground that he had resigned the party whip upon his election to the speakership. The disclosure of interests bill was passed 27–8, with only the FNM and two independents voting against it, but Carlton Francis announced that he was voting under protest and Lionel Davis criticized Pindling's handling of the matter. Pindling then indicated that there was no question of action being taken against the Speaker, nor was it a personal matter between them. However, the National General Council subsequently resolved that all five, the four back-benchers and the Speaker, had not acted in the best interests of the party; the condemnation added the name of Senator E. J. Rolle, who on another occasion had absented himself from a vote on Bahamian membership of the Inter-American Development Bank because he thought the proposal useless but did not wish to vote against his party.

As was so often the case, the opposition proved unable to capitalize on dissension in the PLP's ranks. At the beginning of 1976 Kendal Isaacs stood down as leader of the opposition in the House because of ill-health. He had been effective in rallying the FNM after its failure at the 1972 election, but the more aggressive members of the party still complained that he was too ready to give the government its due when he thought appropriate. His successor, Cyril Tynes, was overshadowed by more experienced figures in the party. At the time of Isaacs's resignation, Cecil Wallace-Whitfield defeated Orville Turnquest 26–18 for the party's non-parliamentary leadership and was soon suspected of managing the selection of candidates for the impending general election to push his own supporters and eliminate his opponents. Wallace-Whitfield had already secured endorsement for one of the party's few safe seats, Marsh Harbour at Abaco; his critics sought to replace him as the official candidate with Basil Kelly, but instead Kelly was picked for Fort Montagu to succeed Isaacs. When Turnquest was defeated for the Clarence Town, Long Island, nomination – another of the party's safe seats, currently held by Michael Lightbourn, who sat as an independent after being expelled from the FNM – matters came to a head. The party's seven MHAs and three of its senators, together with fifteen members of the party's central council, called on Wallace-Whitfield to resign as leader. He refused and retained the support of a majority on the central council. The party divided down the middle; the party secretary, Clifford Cooper, and the women's branch backed the parliamentary wing, while the party treasurer, A. D. Farquharson, joined Wallace-Whitfield. At a specially convened party convention Wallace-Whitfield gave the parliamentary members fourteen days to reconsider their position; they countered by choosing Senator Henry Bostwick as "parliamentary leader", a post additional to those held by Tynes in the House and Turnquest in the Senate.

In December, after attempts by Sir Roland Symonette to negotiate

Cecil Wallace-Whitfield (Courtesy of *Guardian*)

Henry Bostwick (Courtesy of *Tribune*)

a settlement had failed, the parliamentary wing of the FNM formed the Bahamian Democratic Party (BDP) with the support of a number of former MHAs of the old UBP. Bostwick was designated leader of the opposition in the Senate, but Tynes remained leader of the opposition in the House even though Isaacs had returned to the chamber several months earlier. At the BDP's inaugural conference Turnquest gave the keynote address; Moxey was a guest speaker, and subsequently joined the party. A new party paper, the *Democrat*, was started under the editorship of Foulkes. A further round of negotiations failed, and both the BDP and FNM pressed on with the selection of candidates for the general election. Two of the earliest chosen by the BDP were Bostwick for Fort Montagu and Michael Lightbourn for Marsh Harbour.

The PLP managed its selection of candidates more efficiently, but not without problems. Only two sitting MHAs retired voluntarily, but seven others failed to secure party endorsement: Speaker Butler, the party whip Cadwell Armbrister, Carlton Francis, who had been one of the party's senior ministers, Lionel Davis, Franklyn Wilson, Earl Thompson, and Oscar Johnson. Johnson later claimed that he had actually been endorsed by a majority of the National General Council, but the decision had been reversed after Pindling, Hanna, and other ministers had threatened to resign. A redistribution of constituencies a few months earlier assisted the party leadership in its purge, and incidentally abolished one anti-PLP safe seat, the City, and merged two others, Harbour Island and St John's. A third seat was created at Grand Bahama in recognition of the huge enrolment that had built up at Freeport.

The general election was called for 19 July 1977. In their campaigns both the BDP and the FNM emphasized the level of unemployment and the allegations of corruption in the government. The PLP countered by claiming that the BDP was merely a revival of the UBP, but on the eve of the poll Pindling deemed it advisable to offer some promises: customs duties would be cut to bring down the cost of living, real property taxes would be adjusted according to family size, and the old age pension would be increased to forty dollars a month. Such concessions had not been necessary. Although the PLP's share of the total vote fell still further, to 57.2 per cent in New Providence and 50.4 per cent in the Out Islands, it still won all but two of the twenty seats on New Providence, and twelve of the eighteen Out Island seats. The BDP retained two seats on New Providence, where it had 28.5 per cent of the total vote compared with the FNM's 11.5 per cent, and four on the Out Islands, where it had 23.9 per cent of the vote to the FNM's 23 per cent. The FNM managed to carry only two of the three Grand Bahama seats. Of the seven purged PLP MHAs who stood for re-election, five were roundly defeated with less than 5 per cent of the

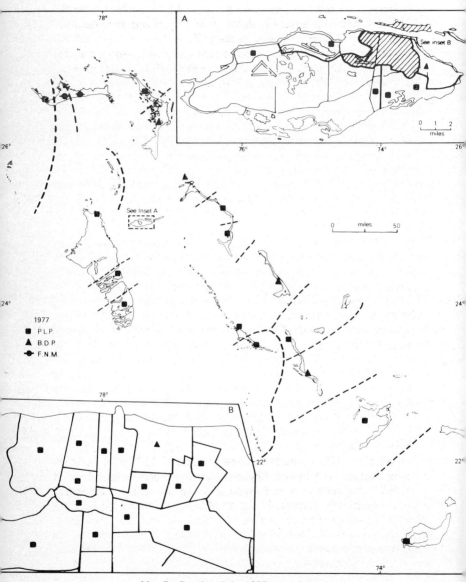

Map 7.   Results of the 1977 general election

votes each; only Moxey, who had the BDP ticket, and Francis, who was not opposed by the BDP, managed a respectable vote. Once more the PLP had survived an extensive shake-up of its parliamentary membership and come through unscathed at the polls.

After the election Pindling claimed that a united opposition would have had an even worse defeat, and he might well have been correct. Only one constituency, Bimini and West End, Grand Bahama, might have been lost had the BDP not broken away from the FNM, and even there the evidence is complicated by the intervention of a disgruntled PLP member who stood as an independent. The PLP had the chance of picking up another seat, Marsh Harbour, where Wallace-Whitfield's vote left Lightbourn with a majority of only four votes ahead of the PLP's Edison Key. On the disputed ballots Key had the possibility of winning by one vote. The result was not challenged, however, because of the legal costs involved; the PLP still had a debt of more than forty thousand dollars from the previous disputed return case at Long Island at the 1972 election.

The PLP chose three new ministers: Kendal Nottage, who secured the portfolio of Youth, Sports and Community Affairs and became government leader in the Senate in place of Paul Adderley, who had moved to the House of Assembly again; Philip Bethel, who went to Transport replacing Clifford Darling, who became Speaker; and Perry Christie, a former senator, who went to Health. The party dropped four of its senators, including E. J. Rolle, Ira Curry, who had been one of the party's longest-standing supporters, and Maillis; another five had moved to the House of Assembly. By insisting on its own choices for the three Senate places supposedly filled after consultation with the opposition, the PLP effectively chose nine new senators to join the three who remained there: the president, Doris Johnson, the deputy president, Lochinvar Lockhart, and Mizpah Tertullien. Two of the recruits to the Senate were former MHAs, Scherling Bootle, who had retired at the 1977 general election, and a former minister, Jeffrey Thompson, who had withdrawn from politics in 1972; another two, Kendal Nottage and Edison Key, had been unsuccessful candidates at the 1977 election and were thought likely to try again for the House when opportunity permitted. The FNM's request that they be given Senate representation was rejected; the Constitution did not require it, and their representation in the House of Assembly was too small to justify making special provision. The BDP nominated four Negroes: Turnquest, Foulkes, Moxey, and Henry Bostwick's wife, Janet, so now the only white senator was the PLP's Edison Key.

The leadership of the BDP, concerned that their party's association with the defunct UBP had been a severe handicap, began to review their position. After a post-mortem lasting four days, it was agreed that a new image was needed. In 1977 the party had elected four whites and two Negroes to the House; at the next election candidates would have to "more accurately represent the racial balance in the country".[67] Upon the retirement, shortly before his death, of Sir Roland Symonette as MHA for Shirlea, the party chose Keith Duncombe to succeed him, and one of the last links with the old UBP leadership was broken. However, when a merger of the BDP with the FNM was negotiated in October 1979, a new schism began. Under the terms of the merger, the FNM's Wallace-Whitfield would be recognized as party leader, but Henry Bostwick would remain parliamentary leader until the next election. Norman Solomon left the BDP, charging that he would not serve in a party led by Wallace-Whitfield, and three other MHAs followed him out, Lightbourn, Duncombe, and James Knowles. Bostwick resigned as leader of the opposition, and Solomon was recognized in his place. To Bostwick's charge that the UBP was re-forming once more, Solomon replied that he had been one of those instrumental in winding up the UBP and he had no intention of trying to bring it back. The 1977 election had returned an opposition divided between the BDP with six seats and the FNM with two; it now comprised a nameless group behind Solomon comprising four members, three in the BDP–FNM group and one independent, Ervin Knowles, who had previously left the BDP. The country was no nearer to a united and effective opposition to the PLP than it had ever been.

NOTES

1. *Tribune*, 28 April 1972.
2. *Guardian*, 2 August 1972.
3. *Tribune*, 30 June 1971; the report was serialized from 1 to 7 July 1971.
4. *Guardian*, 9 July 1971.
5. Ibid., 14 May 1971.
6. Ibid., 26 November 1971.
7. Ibid., 8 and 10 April 1972.
8. Ibid., 29 July 1972.
9. Ibid., 23 and 29 September 1972.
10. Ibid., 13 and 15 June 1972.
11. *People*, 9 December 1972.
12. *Guardian*, 15 June 1977.
13. *Guardian* and *Tribune*, 25 August 1973.
14. *Guardian*, 28 February 1974.
15. *Tribune*, 13 December 1973.
16. *Guardian*, 10 January 1974.
17. Ibid., 19 and 21 September 1973; *People*, 29 September 1973; see *Guardian*, 7 August 1973, for a more hostile version from the *Miami Herald*. When the public disclosure of the private interests of MHAs and senators began, it became possible to update such figures; at the end of December 1978 the prime minister had assets worth $1,335,002 and liabilities of $358,195, for

a net worth of $976,807, and an income totalling $133,905, of which $102,000 was official salary, $27,700 income from securities, and $4,205 other income (*Guardian,* 3 November 1979).

18. *Tribune,* 4 October 1972.
19. *Guardian,* 12 September 1974.
20. Ibid., 16 January 1975.
21. Ibid., 5 August 1977.
22. Ibid., 12 December 1974.
23. *Tribune,* 11 July 1974.
24. *People,* 24 February 1973.
25. *Tribune,* 22 December 1973.
26. *Vanguard,* February 1973.
27. *Guardian,* 24 March 1973.
28. *Tribune,* 2 June 1973.
29. *Guardian,* 17 June 1971.
30. Most recently, Daniel J. Crowley, *I Could Talk Old-Story Good: Creativity in Bahamian Folklore* (Berkeley: University of California Press, 1966); see pp. 4–5 for earlier collections.
31. *Guardian,* 1 August 1972.
32. Ibid., 14 August 1972.
33. *Tribune,* 8 July 1971.
34. Ibid., 10 June 1972.
35. *Guardian,* 2 February 1971.
36. Ibid., 22 February 1971.
37. Ibid., 15 June 1971.
38. Ibid., 4 March 1972.
39. *Tribune,* 16 February 1971.
40. Ibid., 8 July 1971.
41. *Guardian,* 20 June and 10 July 1971.
42. *Tribune,* 25 March 1971.
43. Ibid., 3 November 1971, 2 September 1972.
44. *Guardian,* 16 July 1971.
45. *Tribune,* 11 June 1971.
46. *Guardian,* 28 July 1971.
47. *Vanguard,* October 1971.
48. *Guardian,* 19 October 1971.
49. Ibid., 5 October 1971.
50. *Torch,* 18 December 1971.
51. *Guardian,* 26 February 1971.
52. *Tribune,* 28 June 1972.
53. *Guardian,* 11 August 1972.
54. Ibid., 16 September 1972.
55. For the CLP programme, see the *Guardian* of 7 September 1972.
56. *People*, 23 September 1972.
57. *Guardian,* 24 March 1973.
58. Ibid., 21 September 1974.
59. Ibid., 10 October 1973.
60. Ibid., 30 May 1974.
61. Ibid., 16 October 1973.
62. Ibid., 22 October 1974.
63. *Tribune,* 30 November 1972.
64. *Guardian,* 14 May 1975.
65. Ibid., 23 May 1975.
66. Ibid., 19 April 1975.
67. *Tribune,* 30 October 1979.

8

Symbolic Politics in a Radically Divided Society

The preceding chapters have traced successive stages in the transformation of the Bahamas. In the simplest terms, that transformation was the replacement of the political, social, and economic hegemony of a white bourgeoisie by a hegemony of a black bourgeoisie that is complete in the political sector, largely complete in the social sector, but still incomplete in the economic sector, where the white bourgeoisie retains a predominant share. It can also be seen as the history of the rise of a political party *cum* nationalist movement, the Progressive Liberal Party, and its leader, Lynden Pindling, and of the transfer of power from the colonial power, Great Britain, and its local allies, the "Bay Street Boys", to an independent black government. The approach has been historical and focused on change and the means by which change was brought about. There is still need for another study by a political scientist, of the Bahamian polity as it now is, to describe the machinery of government in detail: how the legislature works, the structure and staffing of the public service, cabinet government in operation, and the like; and the machinery of party politics too: the formal organization of the PLP and its rivals, their policies and doctrines, the recruitment and activities of party members, and the electoral process displayed in constituency contests and the voting decisions of individual voters. Although there is an urgent need for such a work, there is good reason to be pessimistic about its early publication; for none of the larger West Indian countries — Jamaica, Trinidad and Tobago, Guyana, or Barbados — has yet secured such a study, though some portions are already available, mainly in the journal *Social and Economic Studies* and in publications associated with the University of the West Indies.

In an article surveying political science research in the Caribbean, J. E. Greene noted first, that much of the literature seeks to highlight "different independent societal variables as critical determinants of political activity",[1] and, second, that the chief variables so employed are colonialism, social stratification, and race. In this book race has been given pride of place.

Colonialism in the Bahamas was muted as political factor, partly because under the Old Representative System the Bahamas enjoyed *de facto* internal self-government and possessed a constitutional structure that could be converted to *de jure* self-government and independence with a minimum of institutional alteration, partly because the winding up of empire was far advanced by the time a government seeking independence was elected in the Bahamas. To put things that way is to take a narrow meaning of colonialism, confining it to political and constitutional relationships. There is a wider sense, employed by Philip Mason:

> It is the essence of colonialism . . . that the few impose on the many a spiritual yoke which comes to govern their day-to-day actions, more constantly and pervasively, if less obtrusively, than the physical force which lies in the background. Nowhere did this happen more completely than in the Caribbean. Whole societies were persuaded to imitate a way of life that was quite unfamiliar to them, one they had little hope of attaining and not in itself particularly estimable; what was more serious, they came to despise themselves and their own way of life.[2]

In that meaning of the word, the Bahamas had an intensely colonial experience.

Social stratification is more of a problem, because of its close association with racial division. Greene asks generally: "A major question . . . remains unanswered, viz. Is race as a physical and mental force with political and cultural thrusts taking the place of class as a factor in contemporary politics? Or, is it a complementary factor of class?"[3] The Bahamian experience suggests that, for the years of transformation at least, race was more significant than class in shaping political conflict in general and party competition in particular. This may not always be the case, but the signs for the future are ambiguous. Given the capacity for occupying the middle ground Pindling and most of the PLP's leaders have displayed so far, it is quite possible that their combination of middle-class leadership and working-class electoral support can survive another decade or more. Greene argues that such alliances of national bourgeoisie and working class continue within one movement only so long as one aspect of change, the constitutional, provides some hope of social and economic transformation, but the remaining tasks of Bahamianization of the workforce and the economy – which according to Pindling's own timetable will extend to 1985 (see chapter 7) – could well continue to be perceived as part of that process, especially if the level of economic prosperity can be maintained and probably even if it declines slowly.

Over the twenty years between the formation of the PLP and the achievement of independence, the party and its leader exercised considerable skill in practising what Murray Edelman calls "politics as symbolic action":[4]

> Political myths fall into a small number of archetypical patterns, though they vary widely in detail. Either they define an enemy who is plotting against the national interest and may need to be exterminated; or they define a savior-hero-leader of a popularly or divinely sanctioned social order who is to be followed and obeyed and for whom deprivation, suffering, or sacrifice are gratifying. All sorts of specific political concerns are translated into these forms.[5]

The political myths that have shaped Bahamian political disputation have been framed in racial terms: the enemy has been the *other* race, the saviour-hero-leader has been the racial leader. Quoting Edelman again:

> Politics is for most of us a passing parade of abstract symbols, yet a parade which our experience teaches us to be a benevolent or malevolent force that can be close to omnipotent. Because politics does visibly confer wealth, take life, imprison and free people, and represent a history with strong emotional and ideological associations, its processes become easy objects upon which to displace private emotions, especially strong anxieties and hopes.[6]

As Timothy McCartney observes in the Bahamian context, the internalization of racial prejudice leads to grave conflicts both within the individual personality and in the individual's relationships with his environment.[7] Oliver Cox puts it incisively:

> A premium is put upon degrees of whiteness among the people of color. Degrees of color tend to become a determinant of status in a continuous social-class gradient, with whites at its upper reaches. Thus, assuming cultural parity among the group, the lighter the complexion, the greater the economic and social opportunities. In this situation, then, there are significant color distinctions among the colored people themselves. Usually a color scheme is established, with generally recognized names for the different shades; and color problems of a more or less momentous nature come into being.
>   The system tends to generate among even those of light complexion a painfully morbid bitterness against fate, a diffused attitude of hatred and despair, the basis of which appears to be without social definition. The colored people as a whole tend to become perennially preoccupied with the problem of degrees of pigmentation and lament the luck of their dusky progenitors.[8]

Colour shame is intensified when the relationship is maintained under the surveillance and control of the whites, and it may be further intensified when displayed in a more extreme form by a large, economically and culturally dominant neighbour — for the Bahamas the United States.

An encapsulation of several symbols loaded with personal and political significance occurs in the cartoon reproduced here which appeared in the *Herald* numerous times in the 1950s and up to the 1962 general election. The frightful white figure can be identified with particular UBP politicians – e.g., the eye-patch with the fact that Stafford Sands was blind in one eye, the side-whiskers with Roy Solomon, who wore such before they became fashionable; the spiked club and boots are no more than standard science fiction artwork. What is more surprising is the cowering, perspiring Negro figure, which appears to have been copied from some ancient American cartoon strip. It is

PLP cartoon

difficult to understand why a PLP journal should choose to identify the Bahamian Negro with so unheroic a figure, and to do so many times – unless to some extent the representation embodied doubts about the reliability of the Bahamian to stand up for himself, to use the weapon which was already to hand. Certainly the balance between the two figures is a strange contrast to, say, the manly worker and the bloated exploiter of most socialist-labour cartooning, when there is no hint of fear on the part of the oppressed.

Such "strong anxieties and hopes" as racial prejudice induces are projected onto politics in an especially potent and lasting form. Edelman distinguishes between *referential* symbols, which refer to objective elements in objects or situations, such as economic indicators (which for the Bahamas could be either the annual number of tourists or the number of expatriates in the workforce), and *condensation* symbols, which evoke emotions associated with a situation: "They condense into one symbolic event, sign, or act patriotic pride, anxieties, remembrances of past glories or humiliations, promises of future greatness: some one of these or all of them."[9] As the Bahamian examples show, referential symbols can also act as condensation symbols, and this is so not only in a racial situation – for example, miners' accidents may do the same when they symbolize a threat to life and family security.

> For the spectators of the political scene every act contributes to a pattern of ongoing events that spells threat or reassurance. This is the basic dichotomy for the mass public. The very fact that the same act which one grouping favors looms ominously for another reinforces each side in its perceptions for it seems to make it all the more clear that the enemy is really there, fighting against the good life or against life itself.[10]

In recent Bahamian history five events are highpoints of this process: the 1942 riot, the 1956 House of Assembly resolution against discrimination, the 1958 general strike, the 1965 mace incident, and the 1967 election. Each warrants consideration.

The West Indian riots of 1934–38 triggered off a process of political and constitutional change when demands that had previously been the preserve of a handful of middle-class politicians, answerable to restricted electorates, and of a few trade union leaders, heading small and ill-organized labour movements, were transmuted into mass political movements. The Nassau riot of 1942, partly because the Colonial Office was reluctant to intervene in Bahamian affairs, partly because the Negro politicians of the day were unable to convert a momentary outburst of raw energy into a political movement, had no such immediate consequence. A demand for political change did not emerge for another ten years; it took a further fifteen to achieve the first goal, control of the elected part of the legislature. In Jamaica the period of transition from riot to electoral victory lasted only six years.

Long after the event, and when political victory had been won, a PLP politician–historian could ask:

> Did that band of disgruntled labourers – Bahamian labourers – realize that their actions virtually constituted a declaration of war against the white minority in power – the Conchy Joes as they were scurrilously called? Did they foresee that this vigorous revolt against one of many practices of inequality would cause stirrings in the hearts of the poor and the not-so-poor Bahamian, in the young and the not so young Bahamian – in the people who were destined to change the course of the Colony's history? Could they know, as they protested that particular discrimination, that they had taken hold of

a power — the power of political awareness — which would eventually enable them to shape their own destinies?[11]

The answer to these rhetorical questions, for the marchers and looters
of 1942, must be "No". Nevertheless, the historical fact of the riot
remained, embodied in the jaunty folksong, "Burma Road Declare War
on the Conchy Joe". To the whites it was a constant reminder of their
physical powerlessness against mob violence, to be revived fearfully
during the general strike (see chapter 4) and whenever violence erupted
at election meetings. To the Negroes, once a political movement had
finally started, it provided martyrs and a heroic moment which was
never again required.

Dupuch's anti-discrimination resolution in January 1956 has an
uncertain place in present political mythology. Thus Doris Johnson
explains its timing by the growing strength of the PLP, then observes
that it did not go far enough and was not pressed to the statute book,
while conceding:

> But the resolution was enough to kindle the courage of thousands
> of black Bahamians. Jubilantly, they converged on Bay Street
> almost at once and began testing the anti-discrimination proposal
> by entering places forbidden to them until now. Many registered in
> hotels and enjoyed one night of comparative luxury before returning
> to their small wooden houses "over the hill". It was true, the barriers
> had begun to fall. The PLP had created a climate in which almost
> miraculous things could happen. Sweetly encouraged, the black
> Bahamian was walking tall in his homeland at last.[12]

Not surprisingly, Sir Etienne Dupuch sees it differently. The resolution
"was destined to revolutionize the entire social and economic structure
of the colony".[13]

> Things moved very rapidly after the anti-discrimination resolution
> passed the Legislature with a unanimous vote. Almost overnight the
> whole structure of the colony passed through a complete revolution
> without a single disturbance, not an arrest was made, not a single
> drop of blood was shed.
> As I expected, all kinds of coloured people flocked to the hotels.
> But most them went only once. They could not afford this luxury;
> many of them were not comfortable in this environment. All they
> wanted was to be sure the barriers were down. The managers of
> these public establishments showed a great deal of common sense
> during this period. They were very tolerant and exercised consider-
> able restraint, and the whole situation adjusted itself naturally after
> a few weeks.[14]

These two extracts indicate, first, that there was a general recognition that something important had happened, and, second, that as a
practical matter very little was changed. Certainly for the well-to-do

Negroes, steadily increasing in number, it was a real gain to be able to visit hotels and restaurants from which they had previously been excluded. For all Negroes the incident showed that a show of determination — and force, for twice the crowd had made its presence felt around the House of Assembly — could make Bay Street back down. It also exploded the claim that Jim Crow practices were necessary to maintain the economy; tourists continued to go to desegregated hotels and restaurants. But it reinforced belief in the obduracy of the white community and its politicians, their unwillingness to give an inch, and their readiness to manipulate legal procedures, in this case the selection of a committee bound to defeat the motion, to secure their own ends.

The third incident, the general strike of 1958, has also attracted some questionable history. Doris Johnson, after describing the start of the general strike, writes:

> The PLP held an emergency meeting and threw its strength behind the strikers. The party called mass meetings at the Southern Recreation Ground and collected money which it turned over to the Taxicab Union. PLP officials conferred with the Governor and the Secretary of State for the Colonies, who had flown to Nassau in an attempt to deal with the crisis first hand.
>
> Seizing the extraordinary opportunity, the PLP held additional talks with the Secretary of State for the Colonies during his stay, and persuaded him to recommend certain constitutional changes for the Bahamas.[15]

In fact Lennox-Boyd's visit was in April, well after the strike had ended, and the PLP's support for the strike had been hesitant, if not grudging. What was significant was that labour unrest had set off a conditioned reflex in governor and Colonial Office that now something had to be done about the Bahamas.

So far we have been looking at Bahamian politics as a bilateral contest in which white and Negro politicians sought to mobilize and deploy electoral support in their respective constituencies. But it was also potentially a triangular affair, with the governor/Colonial Office being both an additional contestant and, in the last resort, holding the ring and settling the rules for the other two. Thus the direction of political communications could also be towards London to secure intervention in or abstention from the local contest, and the effect of the general strike was to bring the third party in at last in an open declaration of what should be done. For the white community, the strike was confirmation that the forces unleashed by politics and trade unionism would wreck the economy. The *Guardian* claimed at the time that the strike was not really a labour dispute but a political act, the culmination of class and race hatred (see chapter 4), and even Doris Johnson accepts the argument about economic harm: "The Florida press and radio had exaggerated the disturbance in Nassau, effectively diminishing the tourist trade. This caused unemployment among construction and hotel workers. But the far-reaching results of the strike placed it among the most advantageous events of the era."[16] Once again the subsequent obduracy of the UBP cost them such tactical advantage as the strike had offered by their unsuccessful attempts to draw new electoral boundaries to their own advantage and to delay the enfranchisement of women, the image of them as implacable enemies was further reinforced.

The view of politics as drama being employed in these pages is endorsed by Johnson's opening paragraph on the mace incident:

> In 1965 the curtain rose on the second act of the political drama set in the aquamarine islands of the Bahamas. The directors and producers, who had long guided the play according to their own whims, had become increasingly wary of several new actors who had appeared in the last scenes of Act I. These new actors, now waiting in the wings, were about to lift the drama from the humdrum to a climax of worldwide significance.[17]

As Kenneth Burke puts it: "It is a principle of drama that the nature of acts and agents should be consistent with the nature of the scene."[18] For almost ten years the PLP had been battling the enemy in the parliamentary theatre. Dupuch had shown how effective use could be made of the House, not by scoring victories but by defying authority in a good cause and at personal risk. In 1956 Dupuch ignored the Speaker's order to sit down; when in 1962 Butler challenged the Speaker he was given an extension of time — the UBP had learned that much at least — and Pindling had three extensions. It was only after the PLP's amendments to the UBP's electoral proposals had been voted on and defeated that Pindling attacked the supreme symbol of authority in the House, the mace.

> Obedience to the reigning symbols of authority is in itself natural and wholesome. The need to reject them is painful and bewildering. The dispossessed struggle hard and long to remain loyal — but by the nature of the case, the bureaucratic order tends simply to "move in on" such patience and obedience. Eventually, sectarian divergence becomes organized (as thinkers manipulate the complex forensic structure, to give it a particular emphasis in one direction). But those in possession of the authoritative symbols tend to drive the opposition into a corner, by owning the priests (publicists, educators) who will rebuke the opposition for its disobedience to the reigning symbols. The opposition abandons some of the symbolic ingredients and makes itself "ready to take over" other symbolic ingredients.[19]

Burke's analysis can have had fewer more explicit illustrations. Pindling seized the mace and threw it through the window to the crowd outside saying: "This is the symbol of authority and authority on this island belongs to the people, and the people are outside! Yes, the people are outside, and the mace belongs outside too!" Whether or not Pindling had in mind Cromwell's example at the dissolution of the Long Parliament, a latterday Venetian ambassador could have echoed the earlier report that "the dissolution [was] viewed with admiration rather than surprise and [gave] general satisfaction". For the majority in the House and their supporters this was one more example of the lawlessness and anarchy, the denial of parliamentary tradition and the contempt for property, which the PLP embodied. For the parliamentary minority and their supporters it was the necessary stroke to break the unjust rules which bound a true expression of the people's will that would be expressed in a fair election. Pindling's readiness to operate at another level of political debate, perhaps equally effective with the masses, is shown in the placard he wore at a demonstration immediately after the mace incident: "How Much Commission Boundary Commission Got".[20]

The fifth, and final, episode was the PLP's first electoral victory on 10 January 1967. In political mythology it was the tenth day of the first month when the Lord began the freeing of the Israelites from their Egyptian bondage (Exod. 12: 1–3). The use of biblical imagery had long been a feature of Bahamian political debate. The Bible was *the* book, the one book with which all were familiar, closely familiar; it told of a people who escaped from slavery and subjugation to alien rulers to restore their own kingdom. As Doris Johnson puts it:

> Thus it was that on "the tenth day of the first month", black Bahamians emerged from the centuries-old domination of a white power group and crossed over to the promised land of "milk and honey", on which they could grow more and more able to shape their destiny. They could walk tall and proud in their own land as never before, and humble too, as their deeply religious sense attributed their Glory in victory, to the mysterious ways of their God.[21]

It happens to be the case that Bahamians resort to scriptural authority in unusual contexts; for example, "An Irate Taxi Driver" denounces the provision of a government bus to the airport: "Let me warn the ministers of government and government as a whole, God is watching you! He will soon make a decree against your subtle and evil ways. Daniel 4:13, 17. Remember the heaven rules the earth. Dan. 4: 26."[22] The escape from Egypt to the Promised Land is so powerful a myth, one that has been so long sustained among American Negroes as their hope for the future, that its adoption to the Bahamian scene was inevitable, suggesting perhaps that white Methodists are not as close students of the scriptures as black Baptists. Consider the elaboration of the myth by the Reverend Theophilus Duncombe, writing from Long Bay Cays in Pindling's constituency:

> . . . the victory the PLP got in 1968 on April 10, didn't come by force or power from man, but this was the power from God as when the destroying angel passed through the land of Egypt and the PLP stands the only pattern for the modern Israelites and the U.B.P. is the modern Egyptians.
>
> If you don't believe that these two parties are a pattern of the former flight out of bondage, watch the murmurers and complainers who murmur against their leader. See how they already out as fast as they raise up. It is that they are not satisfied with what God do for them. The ancient Israelites could have reached the promised land in 40 days, but they took 40 years and all who came out of Egypt by the leading of Moses died in that wilderness except two and that was Caleb and Joshua.
>
> So I want all the UBP supporters to know that God the Creator set in the kingdom of man from creation and he take up whom he chose and put down whom he will.[23]

Burke explains: "Poetic image and rhetorical idea can become subtly fused — a fusion to which the very nature of poetry and rhetoric makes us prone. For the practised rhetorician relies greatly upon images to affect men's ideation (as with current terms like 'power vacuum' and 'iron curtain') and a poet's images differ from sheerly senstory images precisely by reason of the fact that a poet's images are saturated with ideas."[24]

The choice of this image of the escape met an immediate and deeply felt response from the great majority of Negro Bahamians. In *The Souls of Black Folk,* W. E. B. DuBois wrote of the Negro church of his day as "the social centre of Negro life in the United States", providing the focus for a wide range of voluntary organizations and fund-raising activities: "At the same time this social, intellectual, and economic centre is a religious centre of great power. Depravity, Sin, Redemption, Heaven, Hell, and Damnation are preached twice a Sunday with much fervour . . . Back of this more formal religion, the Church often stands as a real conserver of morals, a strengthener of family life, and the final authority on what is Good and Right."[25] Until quite recently, the Negro churches of the Bahamas, primarily Baptists and more fundamentalist sects, occupied a comparable place in Bahamian society, and within the democratically organized churches the final source of authority was the Bible.

As a source of guidance and inspiration, however, the Bible has been more helpful in effecting the escape from Egypt than in running the Promised Land. The charisma that attached to the party and the leader through their identification with that myth enabled them subsequently to reject the authority of the churches, most obviously in government's growing involvement with gambling. As the Bahamian Negro bourgeoisie have grown in numbers and self-confidence, as in the United States,[26] they have begun to reject the popular culture of the masses and its dominant strain of religiosity; at the same time a substantial part of working class youth has been alienated from the churches' influence. The question thus arises: What can be the source of the new myth to sustain society in the years of independence?

As yet there is little sign of Pindling or the PLP producing an ideology to fill the gap. The most ambitious statement of Pindling's political philosophy was his pamphlet, *Building a Nation through Peace, Understanding and Love,*[27] distributed to the 1970 convention which saw the secession of the Free PLP. It genuflects to Kenneth Kaunda and proclaims a philosophy of Humanism:

> This philosophy is founded in the belief that Man is the prized creation of the Creator. On this belief is based the corollary that Man is more important than things: and is so important, in fact, that he should be permitted to live in a situation where he is free from exploitation by his fellow men and can develop his talents unimpeded by the artificial barriers of race, colour, religion and class.
>
> Our heritage in the Bahamas has not been one that was dedicated to the upliftment of Man. Indeed, it has been just the contrary: it has been dedicated to the dehumanisation and exploitation of Man. We are the results of one of the most cruel examples of dehumanisation in the history of the World: it is scarcely three centuries since we were *de jure* recognised as human beings and the fight for *de facto* recognition still goes on. We have been taught to despise ourselves and our own.
>
> These deep wounds have left tremendous scars which we must eradicate by every means at our command – political, economic and social – so that, in our time, we can help the World to realise the true worth of Man as a Human Being developing a new and full sense of self-reliance.

Kaunda's humanism, however, was closely tied to what he calls the African philosophy of man derived from the African's close relationship with nature and the psychological impact of centuries of tribal life. In particular, the tribal society was a *mutual* society which discouraged individualism, it was an *accepting* community which did not reject the less successful, especially in material things, and it was an *inclusive* society in which the web of relationships involving mutual responsibility was widely spread.[28] Pindling's pamphlet begins with the affirmation that the structure of Bahamian society is in need of fundamental change, and goes on to warn that "some of us" – presumably in his PLP audience – are aware of this but others are not. So there is a gap between the two groups, the aware and the unaware, just as everywhere in modern society there are gaps that can widen and turn into a gulf. When that happens there is an explosion, violent revolution. But when a gap can be closed, there is peace; the tools of peace are understanding and love.

The PLP may be the leaders of a revolution, but they have not yet begun to think about remoulding society. Kaunda could build on a society which, despite the industrialization of the Copper Belt, is still whole; tribal society is there to provide the foundations for African humanism — or African socialism. As Pindling recognizes, Bahamian society for the majority of its members has been created by separating the people from their own language and culture, but instead of tackling the fundamental question of national and cultural identity at that point his pamphlet turns to nuts-and-bolts questions under a series of headings:

- human values: abolish primogeniture, provide equal rights for illegitimate children and equal remedies for men and women under the divorce laws;
- housing: public housing and urban redevelopment of the worst slums;
- land: division of public lands for low-cost housing, tax on undeveloped land;
- labour: stronger unions, the agency shop but not the closed shop or the union shop which are not "democratic or humanistic";
- cost of living: price control and finding cheaper sources of supply;
- new instruments of national policy to maintain Bahamian control of the development and utilisation of Bahamian resources: the Bahamas Development Corporation; the Central Bank; the Bahamas Banking Corporation; the Bahamas Insurance Corporation; a Bahamian flag carrier airline; a gaming corporation to run the casinos; the Bahamas Electricity Corporation to take over private companies on Out Islands;
- new sources of national income: which reduces to the very limited proposition that the Bahamas misses out under double-taxation agreements by not having an income tax;
- independence: a target period should be set not earlier than 1972 or later than 1974, and a mandate secured at an election.

Building a Nation through Peace, Understanding and Love is essentially a reformist programme. It is certainly not a radical philosophy. It looks outwards to cut back external intervention in and control over the Bahamian economy rather than inwards to redistribute wealth or power within the existing Bahamian society. In sum it is archetypical of the "nationalist bourgeoisie" approach to the needs of a small polity/ economy/society.

David Lowenthal echoes many other commentators on the West Indian scene when he writes:

> A striking feature of West Indian identity is the low esteem in which it is locally held. West Indians at home often wish they were not West Indian. This desire permeates Caribbean life not only because life is for many inflexibly hard, but also because West Indians genuinely believe their identity can be altered. The wish is often realized in imagination; they easily persuade themselves they are something else. This delusion is most prevalent in the elite and middle class, but the desire extends throughout the social order; both Kingston suburbanites and West Kingston Ras Tafari believe themselves to be citizens of some remote land. Even for non-Rastas conventional allegiance entails private dissent. Instead of rejecting the system, West Indians deny their own identity. Indeed, the greatest conformists have the strongest yearning not to be West Indian.
>   West Indian self-negation has two principal components, colour and nationality. As a consequence of slavery and colonialism, black and coloured Creoles strive to be both white and European.[29]

In certain respects the Bahamian quest for identity is even more complicated than for most West Indians. A century of alternating boom and bust left a get-rich-quick philosophy of life which was intensified by the post-war boom during which most Bahamians now alive grew up, by the conspicuous consumption of tourists, and by close association with American values through proximity to Florida. Only Trinidad, the wealthiest of the former British West Indies, comes close, and Trinidad was the original model for the "basket of crabs" metaphor that has been extended to all West Indian middle-class society. (Land crabs, a great delicacy, can be easily kept in a shallow container, for as soon as one manages to climb part way up the side others will rush to make their escape by clambering over him — and pull him back down to the bottom.) Franklin Frazier wrote of a similar phenomenon in the United States among the Negro bourgeoisie who created a world of make-believe to protect themselves from the realities of social discrimination and economic powerlessness:

> They seek an escape in delusions involving wealth. This is facilitated by the fact that they have had little experience with the real meaning of wealth and that they lack a tradition of saving and accumulation. Wealth to them means spending money without reference to its source . . . Moreover, the attraction of the delusion of wealth is enhanced by the belief that wealth will gain them acceptance in American life. In seeking an escape in the delusion of wealth, middle-class Negroes make a fetish of material things or physical possessions.[30]

At one stage Bay Street politicians played on such sentiments. Their statistical presentations of Bahamian economic advantages over the West Indies carried the message that the political advances of the West Indies were less important, or might even have been secured at the cost of economic achievement, but they opened the way to more invidious comparisons closer to home. If material values were paramount, why should Negro Bahamians have less than white Bahamians or expatriates? The easiest answer was that whites were abler or worked harder, but even by the mid-1950s that was too blatant. Instead the issue was partly sublimated by equating demands for change with an economic threat:

> There is an indefinable atmosphere which is created in part by the physical attributes of Nassau, but in the greatest measure by the feeling of harmony among all sections of the people and traditions of living which combine the best of both worlds. The preservation of this Bahamian way of life is an important asset to a Colony which relies, almost entirely, upon tourism to provide its annual revenue. Indeed, the creation of disharmony and a violent change in the political climate would serve only to destroy in a very short time the whole structure of our vast tourist industry.[31]

The "traditions of living" and the "Bahamian way of life" in this context meant social segregation. When they were overturned without any apparent ill effect, the argument then became the incapacity of PLP politicians to run the economic machine: "The PLP, after all, has not produced leadership that, should they gain power, could induce confidence in the economic future of the Colony on the part of individuals seeking a place to deposit investment capital. They are unskilled and untutored in the business of government, and some individuals in their party have already exposed themselves as being completely irresponsible."[32]

In putting forward such arguments, white politicians were not manufacturing slogans which they did not believe themselves. Rationalizations of this sort derived naturally from the myth of white supremacy which had dominated the Bahamas for centuries. When aiming at the cupidity of black Bahamians, white Bahamians were merely expressing their own values in selecting what they believed were the most effective arguments. Meeting such arguments, the PLP were equally prisoners of a set of values that transcended racial divisions. They had to claim to be able to administer the economic miracle equally well and to accept certain basic rules of the economic game, such as no income tax or death duties, encouraging foreign investment, and maintaining a climate of free enterprise primarily because of its attractiveness to foreign capital. Only when, in the 1970s, the boom faltered and the rising cost of welfare policies began to press on revenue did the PLP have to face potential conflict between an economic philosophy they had inherited from their predecessors and the political reality of their working-class support. Even then, the solidly middle-class composition of the parliamentary party, the electoral ineffectiveness and even more right-wing stance of the official opposition, and the absence of an effective trade union movement cushioned and concealed the conflict. Growing government involvement in the economic sector either took the form of advantaging party supporters, as with airlines, or held out the promise of ultimate reconversion to capitalism, as with hotels. Such redistribution as the government attempted was framed in nationalist terms — the displacement of expatriates from the workforce.

The statement on economic development in the White Paper on independence displays this approach:

Basic Premises
96.   The Government is convinced that Independence for the Commonwealth of the Bahama Islands must be based on the economic independence of the Bahamian people. To achieve this end, the Government bases its policy on:
(a)   an effective level of control over the national economic environment
(b)   the maximisation of the benefits to the Bahamas arising from both domestic and foreign investment
(c)   an increase in Bahamian ownership and/or participation in business activity where this is feasible.
National Effort
97.   To implement such a policy our total skills must be directed towards:
(a)   developing or stimulating a style of growth which will progressively improve and broaden our economy
(b)   instituting programmes which will enable us to control and direct such improvements so that a satisfactory level of benefit to the Bahamas is obtained
(c)   maintaining an economic climate which will encourage both domestic and foreign enterprise of a type which is sensitive to the social and emotional needs of the people and to the physical environment which must be protected as one of our greatest natural assets . . .
Investment: Incentives and Conditions
134. The future economic growth of our Commonwealth is largely dependent on commercial and industrial investments and the Government's policy is to encourage such investments whether the initiative comes from domestic or foreign enterprise. It is realised that one of the prime motivations in business is profitability. But it is also realised that, as a developing Nation, particular attention must be paid to the attitudes and sense of responsibility organisations adopt in regard to the needs of the Bahamas. In the past, certain private institutions have taken the viewpoint that they can dictate

their own terms; even that they are doing us a favour simply by setting up an interest within our shores. Such attitudes amount to gross irresponsibility and cannot be justified. It must be appreciated that if any commercial venture is to be acceptable in our Country, it must abide by the regulations necessarily laid down to protect our best interests.

Incentives

135. The Commonwealth of the Bahamas shall continue to provide what is among the best range of incentives for the development of private enterprise anywhere in the world, and nationalisation shall not be an instrument of the Government's economic policy.[33]

To achieve these objectives, investors would have to be prepared to make "a proper contribution" to the economic and social development of the Bahamas, prepare a full statement showing the benefit the proposed investment would bring to the country, indicate plans to train Bahamian personnel, and "if applicable", offer shares to Bahamians, and whenever possible seek partnership with Bahamians, including the possibility of participation by the Bahamian government. Such a statement is undoubtedly more forceful than a UBP government would have made had it been in power on the eve of independence, but as a statement of economic nationalism it is certainly as bland as the most nervous international investor could ever expect to see. Foreshadowing it in the Green Paper on independence, the government had promised:

79. As envisaged, the policy will . . . define the extent to which the Government will wish to control public utilities and act in partnership with the various elements in the private sector. However, by this it should under no circumstances be construed that the Government is likely to adopt any measure which may upset the public or private sectors of the economy.[34]

It is arguable that the government sought, also, not to upset the Bahamian electorate.

One may turn to the Green and White papers for the PLP's thinking on the political and social implications of independence as well. The initial argument set out in the Green Paper can be summarized thus: Dependent territories have their own problems, the solution of which requires "intimate local knowledge and strong national motivation"; the government's responsibility must be "to advance the well-being and prosperity of the Commonwealth of the Bahamas and its peoples and to safeguard the Nation's security". Therefore it had been concluded "that, for the individual and for our Country as a whole, the greatest and most desirable benefit will be derived through independent status".

Most clearly established is that development can only come from within. Only by this means can a nation attain a true sense of unity and develop a character and philosophy on which to base its future growth and stability. In the final analysis, no outside agency can assume this responsibility.

Independence is the natural and logical outcome of growth that has been going on for years:

> It would be unnatural if the Bahamas did not achieve independence at this time, just as it would be abnormal for an adolescent to fail to reach manhood. The Country's constitutional evolution, the Government's record, and the fact that Bahamians are increasingly assuming responsible Government and business posts — these and similar factors illustrate the point.
>
> It is impossible to quantify emotion, but there can be no doubt that, psychologically, we are at the final staging post before self-determination. This is evidenced in a number of ways, most notably in the almost tangible growth of pride in the fact of being Bahamian. There has emerged a consciousness of nationality distinct from all others; a blossoming of those characteristics which unequivocally demonstrate. that, as a people, we have attained a very special and previous sense of unity which can only be given voice through statehood.

From that positive affirmation, the Green Paper goes on to demolish the arguments against independence: size — there are smaller states in existence, economic — no country is commercially self-sufficient, the Bahamas has substantial resources, and independence can be a positive incentive to economic development. But what was the foundation of "the consciousness of nationality", the "pride in the fact of being Bahamian"?

In an ingenious paper entitled "The Island of Ireland: A Psycho-Analytical Contribution to Political Psychology", read to the British Psycho-Analytical Society in 1922, Ernest Jones argued that the psychology of islanders is different.[35] As befitted the biographer of Freud, Jones linked this to the Oedipus complex, but one need not accept that part of his argument to agree with his conclusions. The geographical fact of insularity, reinforced by a variety of historical associations with European metropoles, produces the present political fragmentation of the Caribbean within which the comic-opera secession of Anguilla from St Kitts was only an extreme statement of a general predisposition. Some of the reasons for local peculiarities were suggested in chapter 1. The absence of sugar, the very brief experience of a plantation economy and the scale of its operation, the substantial white population, the reliance on the sea for a livelihood, the close ties with the United States, all contributed to make a Bahamian, whatever his colour, somewhat different from any West Indian. The retention of the Old Representative System, combined with the protracted political domination of the white community despite the broad franchise which left power dangling before the majority who failed to snatch it, made for significant political differences. If one compares the social and political situation in Barbados, where sugar remained king and the plantation dominated the economy, the significance of the numerical size of the white community is demonstrated,[36] but in many respects Barbados was closer to the Bahamas than was any other British West Indian colony.

The intention of Bay Street whites to maintain their political position ensured the out-of-hand rejection of an invitation to attend the Montego Bay conference of 1947, which set in train a decade and a half of closer association in the West Indies, culminating in the abortive federal government. But it would probably be true to say that Bahamian Negroes shared to a considerable extent, though for different reasons, the white Bahamians' distrust of West Indians. Turks Islanders, because of their proximity, ancient association, and small number, were a qualified exception, but West Indians were generally perceived as snooty like the Barbadians, or quarrelsome like the Jamaicans, and invariably ready to undercut a Bahamian for a job. An essay on the meaning of Bahamianization by a final year sociology student at the University of the West Indies, Mark Anthony Wilson, defined it as "the Bahamas for Bahamians first", and explained why West Indians were expatriates who could not take part in shaping national norms and attitudes:

> The West Indian is, in many senses, a brother wrongly guided. He comes from a social and cultural milieu similar to that which exists in the Bahamas, so similar in fact that he fails to recognize that there are also differences, and these differences are the focus of conflict between the West Indian and Bahamian.
>
> The major difference is that Bahamians are generally more charitable towards each other than other West Indians, with the result that West Indians coming to the Bahamas often feel that Bahamians sit and let opportunities pass them by. They therefore display a characteristic which is described by the Bahamian term "GRABALICIOUS" and which is held in rank contempt by the Bahamian people.[37]

In opening new connections with West Indian governments and political parties, the PLP had to move cautiously; to have declared a common interest or identity would have been foolhardy.

It has been easier to affirm an Afro-Bahamian identity than to claim to share in a common West Indianness. The early efforts of whites to smear the first signs of Negro assertiveness with the primitiveness of pre-colonial Africa and the excesses of post-independence African regimes produced an inevitable reaction. Black Bahamians were pushed into a more emotional identification with Africa than they might have chosen on their own, but it was merely identification with a vague notion of Africa the homeland rather than a detailed acquaintance with particular pan-African ideologies or any developed philosophy of negritude. Much of the message of race pride came by way of the United States. The black heroes whose portraits and potted biographies figured in the Nassau newspapers, ultimately even the *Guardian*, were chosen by American press agencies; they were the heroes of the civil rights movement of the United States rather than the heroes of African independence movements. So the PLP used black American entertainers and even as dubious a politician as Adam Clayton Powell to give respectability and authority to its campaign to break down the same social barriers as American Negroes were attacking. But once this part of its struggle was over, the inappropriateness of the American connection was obvious. Bahamian Negroes were the majority in their own country; American Negroes could only hope to be an accepted minority in theirs. The radical strain in American Negro protest was more violent than the respectable middle-class leaders of the PLP could stomach, and it was hardly appropriate to a black government controlling a black police force.

So, by a process of elimination, the only possible identity left was that of Bahamian. In their classic study of political cultures, Almond and Verba asked the question, "Speaking generally, what are the things about this country that you are most proud of?" and found substantial differences among the five countries where the survey was conducted. Thus in the United States the overwhelming majority, in Britain half, and in Mexico almost one-third of respondents cited governmental and political institutions, but in Germany only 7 per cent and in Italy only 3 per cent. However, in Italy, Mexico, and Germany many more mentioned the physical characteristics of their country than in Britain or the United States, and many more in Germany, Mexico, and the United States mentioned the achievements of the economic system than did so in Britain or Italy.[38] We have no comparable survey data for the Bahamas, but if one Bahamian's guesses have any evidentiary value, the matters in which Bahamians take national pride would be the beauty of their country, in particular the shallow seas which gave the archipelago its name,[39] and the colourful history that begins with Columbus's discovery of the New World and proceeds melodramatically through Puritans and pirates, Loyalists and wreckers, blockade-runners and bootleggers. In an editorial on the surrender of Biafra, the *Bahamian Times* wrote: "There are many things that have been done and that will have to be done to bring true nationhood to the people of these islands. The foremost among these is the development of an awareness of our history and the fact that solutions to our problems must be arrived at purely in the context of what is good for us — not necessarily for any other people."[40]

But Bahamian history as it has been written so far is very much the history of the dominant white community;[41] when it is eventually expanded to include the social and economic history of slaves, spongers, and peasant farmers and fishermen, that part will lack the Saturday matinee glamour which attached to the earlier, incomplete version. Nor will it be easy to make "the quiet revolution" of electoral and parliamentary competition that occurred between 1953 and 1973 into a historical rhetoric of struggle comparable, say, to the Jamaican experience.[42]

Archie Singham distinguishes between the two types of political heroes that have emerged in the West Indies:

> On the one hand there is the middle-class hero, claiming that he has sacrificed his career for the sake of helping the people; often he argues that he might have been an international lawyer or scholar of some repute. On the whole, this type of leader has tended to stress constitutional advance. On the other hand there is the hero who comes from humble origins and bases his claims to political leadership on his role as a trade union leader. In spite of the differences in their class origins and their leadership style, however, these two types share certain similarities: they tend to develop personal organizations which are essentially authoritarian.[43]

So far Pindling has been closer to the middle-class hero type; yet despite the complaints of those who have broken with the PLP over the years, he has avoided the personal authoritarianism which might be expected to attach to a new Moses. This is due in part no doubt to his personal moderation and pragmatism in politics, but also perhaps to the absence of any effective challenge to his leadership either within the party and government or from outside. Should the demands of independence, the problems of a flagging economy, or the appearance of powerful working-class aspirations bring that leadership into question, then one might expect an increased emphasis on his charisma to preserve the regime, and with it a deliberate rewriting of Bahamian history to elevate still further his role in it. That could well be the means whereby the majority of Bahamians find their place in Bahamian history, through identification with the man who fought and won the racial battle which was the most significant chapter in that long story.

NOTES

1. J. E. Greene, "A Review of Political Science Research in the English Speaking Caribbean: Toward a Methodology", *Social and Economic Studies* 23 (1974): 3.

2. Philip Mason, *Patterns of Dominance* (London: Oxford University Press, 1971), p. 274.
3. Greene, "Review of Political Science Research", p. 7.
4. Murray Edelman, *Politics as Symbolic Action* (Chicago: Markham, 1971).
5. Ibid., p. 15.
6. Murray Edelman, *The Symbolic Uses of Politics* (Urbana: University of Illinois Press, 1972), p. 5.
7. Timothy O. McCartney, *Neuroses in the Sun* (Nassau: 1971), p. 55.
8. Oliver C. Cox, *Caste, Class and Race* (New York: Monthly Review, 1971), p. 361.
9. Edelman, *Symbolic Uses of Politics,* p. 6.
10. Ibid., p. 13.
11. Doris L. Johnson, *The Quiet Revolution in the Bahamas* (Nassau: Family Islands Press, 1972), p. 15.
12. Ibid., p. 34.
13. Etienne Dupuch, *Tribune Story* (London: Benn, 1967), p. 147.
14. Ibid., pp. 151–52.
15. Johnson, *Quiet Revolution in the Bahamas*, p. 35.
16. Ibid., p. 36.
17. Ibid., p. 51.
18. Kenneth Burke, *A Grammar of Motives* (Berkeley: University of California Press, 1969), p. 3.
19. Kenneth Burke, *Attitudes Toward History* (Los Altos, Cal.: Hermes, 1959), p. 226.
20. Johnson, *Quiet Revolution in the Bahamas,* p. 54.
21. Ibid., p. 111.
22. *Guardian,* 16 March 1974.
23. Ibid., 13 April 1971.
24. Burke, *Attitudes Toward History,* pp. xii–xiii.
25. W. E. Burghardt DuBois, *The Souls of Black Folk* (Greenwich, Conn.: Fawcett, 1961), p. 143.
26. E. Franklin Frazier, *Black Bourgeoisie* (New York: Collier-Macmillan, 1962), p. 98.
27. Printed in full in the *Guardian* of 4 November 1970.
28. Kenneth Kaunda, *A Humanist in Africa* (London: Longmans, 1966), chap. 1.
29. David Lowenthal, *West Indian Societies* (London: Oxford University Press, 1972), p. 250.
30. Frazier, *Black Bourgeoisie,* p. 189.
31. *Guardian,* 12 November 1954.
32. Ibid., 26 February 1960.
33. *Independence for the Commonwealth of the Bahamas: Presented to Parliament by The Prime Minister 18th October 1972,* (Nassau: 1972).
34. *Independence for the Commonwealth of the Bahamas: Presented to Parliament 8th March 1972,* (Nassau: 1972).
35. Ernest Jones, *Essays in Applied Psycho-Analysis* (London: Hogarth, 1951).
36. Mason, *Patterns of Dominance,* pp. 282–83; Raymond W. Mack, "Race, Class, and Power in Barbados: A Study of Stratification as an Integrating Force in a Democratic Revolution", in *Social Change in Developing Areas,* ed. Herbert R. Barringer et al., (Cambridge, Mass.: Shenkman, 1965), pp. 131–54.
37. *Guardian,* 10 January 1972.
38. Gabriel A. Almond and Sidney Verba, *The Civic Culture* (Princeton, N.J.: Princeton University Press, 1963), chap. 3.

39. The first sentence of Doris Johnson's *The Quiet Revolution* quotes the American astronaut, Russel Schweikert, "Of all the beautiful sights I saw from the spacecraft, the waters of the Bahamas stick in my mind as the most spectacular of all."

40. *Bahamian Times,* 14 January 1970.

41. See an article by the Guild of Graduates of the U.W.I. critical of the books by Paul Albury and Michael Craton as "white man's history", *Guardian,* 22 July 1975.

42. E.g., Rex Nettleford, "Aggression, Violence and Force: Containment and Eruption in the Jamaican History of Protest", in *Violence and Aggression in the History of Ideas,* ed. Philip P. Weiner and John Fisher, (New Brunswick, N.J.: Rutgers University Press, 1974), pp. 133–57.

43. A. W. Singham, *The Hero and the Crowd in a Colonial Polity* (New Haven, Conn.: Yale University Press, 1968), p. 152.

Appendix: Election Result Statistics

GENERAL ELECTION RESULTS 1956-77

NEW PROVIDENCE [1]

1956	1962	1967	1968	1972	1977
					_6
CITY (1,887)	CITY (1,887)	CITY (1,139)	NASSAU CITY (1,468)	NASSAU CITY (1,266)	
S.L. Sands (UBP) 264	S.L. Sands (UBP) 1,220	S.L. Sands (UBP) 764	C.E. Adderley (UBP) 687	C.E. Adderley (FNM) 645	
R.W. Sawyer 194	R.W. Sawyer (UBP) 1,028	M.B. Butler, jr 249	B.A. Nichols (PLP) 538	N.R. Gay (PLP) 431	
J. Burnside (PLP) 103	R.F.A. Roberts (PLP) 533				
	G.C. Cash 341				
WEST (5,998)	WEST (5,998)	KILLARNEY (2,624)	KILLARNEY (1,408)	KILLARNEY (3,195)	DELAPORTE (2,107)
M.B. Butler (PLP) 726	P.L. Adderley (PLP) 3,531	E.L. Donaldson (PLP) 1,366	E.L. Donaldson (PLP) 1,091	C.C. Armbrister (PLP) 1,894	P.D. Pinder (PLP) 960
G.C. Cash 685	M.B. Butler (PLP) 3,179	D.L. Brown (UBP) 925	N.F. Arahna (UBP) 147	E.L. Donaldson (FNM) 1,019	A.A. Foulkes (BDP) 530
P.E. Christie (PLP) 282	S. Oakes (UBP) 1,696	H.G. Smith (NDP) 141			B.A. Nichols (FNM) 402
M.H. Bethel 240	B.A. Cambridge (UBP) 886				
C.L. Adderley (UBP) 233		FORT CHARLOTTE (1,102) 886	GAMBIER (2,598)	GAMBIER (2,862)	CARMICHAEL (2,449)
A.P. Maillis (UBP) 174			C.T. Maynard 1,744	C.T. Maynard 1,503	D.L. Adderley 1,173

P.L. Adderley   191
(NDP)

BAINS TOWN (971)
M.B. Butler   816
(PLP)
P.A. Hepburn   49
(UBP)

FORT CHARLOTTE (1,468)
C.C. McMillan   1,086
(PLP)
L.T. Chea   113
(UBP)

BAINS TOWN (1,620)
M.B. Butler   1,549
(PLP)
C.E. O'Brien   27
(UBP)
A.P. Bain   18

FORT CHARLOTTE (1,357)
E.V. Thompson   741
(PLP)
C.C. McMillan   401
(FNM)

BAINS TOWN (1,401)
M.B. Butler   992
(PLP)
W.E. Brown   200
(FNM)

F.H. Watson   330
(FNM)

YELLOW ELDER (1,745)
C.T. Maynard   1,075
(PLP)
E.D. Barrett   322
(BDP)
R.A. McSweency   200
(FNM)

FORT CHARLOTTE (2,176)
V. Grimes   1,028
(PLP)
G.C. Bain   475
(FNM)
A. Humes   336
(BDP)
E.V. Thompson   85
(BDP)

BAINS TOWN (2,349)
N.R. Gay   1,459
(PLP)
S. Johnson   310
(FNM)
E.A. Theophilus   225
(BDP)
D.H. Knowles   13
(VNSP)

1956	1962	1967	1968	1972	1977

1956

SOUTH
- R.F. Fawkes (PLP) — 1,440
- L.O. Pindling (PLP) — 1,334
- B.A. Cambridge — 235
- O.H. Bode — 199
- C.R. Walker — 121

1962

SOUTH (6,205)
- S.S. Bethel (PLP) — 2,615
- R.F. Fawkes (Lab) — 2,501
- C.A. Dorsett (PLP) — 2,348
- A. Klonaris (U3P) — 1,429
- C.R. Walker (Lab) — 548
- A. Roberts — 87

SOUTH CENTRAL (3,386)
- L.O. Pindling (PLP) — 2,187
- O.A. Turnquest (PLP) — 2,165
- I. Allen — 818
- A. Cambridge (UBP) — 425

1967

ST AGNES (1,196)
- C.V. Wallace-Whitfield (PLP) — 916
- L.H. Lockhart (NDP) — 72
- F.B. Bowe (UBP) — 52

GRANTS TOWN (1,045)
- A.A. Foulkes (PLP) — 902
- O.A. Turnquest (NDP) — 152
- J.T. Mills (UBP) — 20

FORT FINCASTLE (1,212)
- J.M. Thompson (PLP) — 902
- R.H. Lobosky (UBP) — 152
- H.H. Minnis (NDP) — 24

ST MICHAELS (1,057)
- J.J. Shepherd (PLP) — 854
- J. Klonaris (UBP) — 76
- O.A.L. Burnside (NDP) — 14

1968

ST AGNES (1,434)
- C.V. Wallace-Whitfield (PLP) — 1,114
- F. Bowe (UBP) — 58

GRANTS TOWN (1,571)
- A.A. Foulkes (PLP) — 1,275
- G.R. Symonette (UBP) — 62

FORT FINCASTLE (1,863)
- J.M. Thompson (PLP) — 1,442
- J.F. Greenidge (UBP) — 106

ST MICHAELS (1,563)
- J.J. Shepherd (PLP) — 1,280
- G.E. Weir (UBP) — 46

ST BARNABAS (1,583)
- R.F. Fawkes (Lab) — 823
- W.H. Heastie — 452

COCONUT GROVE (1,936)

1972

ST AGNES (1,332)
- B.C. Braynen (PLP) — 691
- C.V. Wallace-Whitfield (FNM) — 393
- B.L. Lunn (CLP) — 18

GRANTS TOWN (1,376)
- F.R. Wilson (PLP) — 918
- A.A. Foulkes (FNM) — 247
- A.C. Kemp — 195

FORT FINCASTLE (1,808)
- A.T. Maycock (PLP) — 1,098
- C.M. Cooper (FNM) — 411
- O. Frazier — 7

ST MICHAELS (1,393)
- G.W. Mackey (FNM) — 856
- J.J. Shepherd (PLP) — 239
- E.A. Theophilus (BDP) — 32
- J.L. Rolle (CLP) — 29
- S. Mitchell (CLP) — 18

ST BARNABAS (1,491)

1977

ST AGNES (2,165)
- B.C. Braynen (PLP) — 942
- C.E. Adderley (BDP) — 431
- S. Quant (FNM) — 412
- B.L. Lunn — 16

GRANTS TOWN (2,083)
- S.A. Morris (PLP) — 1,073
- A.C. Kemp (FNM) — 678

FORT FINCASTLE (2,403)
- A.T. Maycock (PLP) — 1,582
- R.N. Dorsett (BDP) — 363
- B.J. Mortimer (FNM) — 117

ST MICHAELS (2,144)
- G.W. Mackey (PLP) — 1,180
- J.A. Ramsey (BDP) — 382
- J. Wood — 247
- J.T. McCartney (VNSP) — 24

R.F. Fawkes (Lab) 847
W.K. Duncombe (UBP) 45

COCONUT GROVE (1,453)
E.S. Moxey (PLP) 1,092
A. Klonaris (UBP) 93
M.N. Taylor (Lab) 79
S.S. Bethel (NDP) 33

ENGLERSTON (1,374)
C. Darling (PLP) 1,067
D.K. Sands (UBP) 70
A.W. Gibson (Lab) 56
C.A. Dorsett (NDP) 39

C.M. Dorsett (UBP) 62

ENGLERSTON (2,232)
C. Darling (PLP) 1,895
K. Knowles (UBP) 89

SOUTH BEACH (2,002)
C.E. Francis (PLP) 1,554
K.H. Moss (UBP) 3CO

(PLP)
I.G. Stubbs (FNM) 159
R.F. Fawkes (CLP) 146

COCONUT GROVE (1,691)
E.S. Moxey (PLP) 1,223
R. Greene (FNM) 213

ENGLERSTON (2,317)
C. Darling (PLP) 1,610
S.S. Bethel (FNM) 308
A. Smith (CLP) 17

SOUTH BEACH (3,207)
C.E. Francis (PLP) 1,986
J.H. Bostwick (FNM) 901

S.S. Outten (PLP)
I.G. Stubbs (PLP) 1,384
E.S. Moxey (BDP) 699
C. Taylor (FNM) 201
E.K. Mesitumbo (VNSP) 8

ENGLERSTON (2,374)
C. Darling (PLP) 1,362
A. McPhee (BDP) 511
E.H. Bullard (FNM) 158
L. Carey (VNSP) 10

BAMBOO TOWN (2,625)
L. Minnis (PLP) 1,296
G.W. Pinder (BDP) 663
C.M. Hunt (FNM) 377
C. Armbrister 39
D.A. Bullard 2

SOUTH BEACH (2,946)
E. Glinton (PLP) 1,619
C.E. Francis 851
J.J. Shepherd 145

1956	1962	1967	1968	1972	1977
EAST	EAST (5,338)	CENTREVILLE (1,177)	CENTREVILLE (1,984)	CENTREVILLE (1,918)	CENTREVILLE (2,189)
R.T. Symonette 1,352	A.D. Hanna 2,481	R.T. Symonette 558	R.F.A. Roberts 1,169	R.F.A. Roberts 900	P.P. Christie 1,154
S.L. Isaacs 1,235	(PLP)	(UBP)	(PLP)	(PLP)	(PLP)
(PLP)	G.A.D. Johnstone 2,258	R.F.A. Roberts 511	G.W. Arnett 546	O.A. Turnquest 772	O.A. Turnquest 724
A.E.J. Dupuch 1,188	(UBP)	(PLP)	(UBP)	(FNM)	(BDP)
G.A.D. Johnstone 990	A.A. Foulkes 2,208	W.H. Aranha 32			R.P. Knowles 78
W.G. Cash 121	(PLP)		SHIRLEA (1,290)	SHIRLEA (1,132)	(FNM)
	P. Dupuch 1,909	SHIRLEA (1,635)	R.T. Symonette 790	R.T. Symonette 776	
		U. McPhee 777	(UBP)	(FNM)	SHIRLEA (2,266)
	EAST CENTRAL (5,024)	(PLP)	S.S. Outten 267	M. Tertullien 193	R.T. Symonette 1,392
	R.T. Symonette 2,644	J.R. Morley 668	(PLP)	(PLP)	(BDP)
	(UBP)	(UBP)			B.B. Roberts 577
	E.A.P. Dupuch 2,340	P.P.T. D Arville 29	CULMERVILLE (1,582)	CULMERVILLE (1,622)	(PLP)
	H.M. Taylor 1,823	J.E. Purkiss 11	A.G. Butler 1,009	A.G. Butler 845	
	(PLP)	(NDP)	(PLP)	(PLP)	SALEM (1,873)
	S.L. Isaacs 1,721		E.P. Albury 367	T.A. Robinson 559	D.A. Knowles 851
	(PLP)	PALMDALE (1,203)	(UBP)	(FNM)	(PLP)
		G.D.F. Clarke 592		J.T. Mills 8	T.A. Robinson 687
		(UBP)	FREETOWN (1,603)		(BDP)
		A.G. Butler 527	S.L. Bowe 1,037	FREETOWN (1,622)	L. Moree 88
		(PLP)	(PLP)	S.L. Bowe 844	(FNM)
			R.W. Key 344	(PLP)	A.G. Butler 70
		ANNS TOWN (1,483)	(UBP)	L.S. Moree 531	(FNM)
		A.D. Hanna 1,126		(FNM)	ANNS TOWN (2,161)
		(PLP)			

G.A.D. Johnstone 962
(UBP)
L.L. Davis 406
(PLP)
WINTON (2,146)

C.E. Francis 1,231
(PLP)
J.B. Farrington 723
(UBP)

A.A. Munroe 159
(UBP)
FORT MONTAGU (1,565)

G.A.D. Johnstone 991
(UBP)
D.M. Williams 326
(PLP)
FOX HILL (1,371)

L.L. Davis 763
(PLP)
N.E.J. Jones 382
(UBP)

A.D. Hanna 1,089
(PLP)
N.J. Smith 288
(FNM)
E.A. Hepburn 10
(DLP)
FORT MONTAGU (1,568)

K.G.L. Isaacs 1,079
(FNM)
M.B. Butler, jr 272
(PLP)
FOX HILL (1,593)

L.L. Davis 765
(PLP)
F.S. Ramsey 645
(FNM)
P. Galanos 17
(CLP)

P. Galanos 61
(FNM)
PINEDALE (2,423)

M.B. Butler, jr 1,244
(PLP)
J.G. Bostwick 877
(BDP)
J.M. Thompson 115
(FNM)
MONTAGU (3,095)

J.H. Bostwick 1,618
(BDP)
J.O. Brown 996
(PLP)
R.C. Thompson 192
(FNM)
FOX HILL (2,535)

F.L. Edgecombe 1,264
(PLP)
F.S. Ramsey 853
(BDP)
E.A. Knowles 146
(FNM)
L.L. Davis 26

ANDROS

1956	1962	1967	1968	1972	1977
ANDROS	**ANDROS (2,756)**	**NICHOLLS TOWN and BERRY IS. (891)**	**NICHOLLS TOWN and BERRY IS. (1,141)**	**NICHOLLS TOWN and BERRY IS. (1,383)**	**NICHOLLS TOWN and BERRY IS. (1,532)**
C.St.J. Stevenson 492 (PLP)	C.A. Bain 1,348 (PLP)	W.McP. Christie 414 (UBP)	A.L. Roker 572 (PLP)	A.L. Roker 664 (PLP)	A.L. Roker 778 (PLP)
C.A. Bain 487 (PLP)	C.St.J. Stevenson 1,343 (PLP)	A.L. Roker 383 (PLP)	W.McP. Christie 389 (UBP)	W.McP. Christie 603 (FNM)	W.McP. Christie 645 (BDP)
P.D.G. Bethell 297	K.M. Thompson 740 (UBP)	**MANGROVE CAY (978)**	**MANGROVE CAY (1,171)**	**MANGROVE CAY (984)**	O.C. Munnings 5 (FNM)
B.H. McKinney 295	N. Aranha 662 (UBP)	C.A. Bain 450 (PLP)	C.A. Bain 776 (PLP)	D.E. Rolle 729 (PLP)	**MANGROVE CAY (1,064)**
	O. Bode 140	N. Aranha 353 (UBP)	C.A. Dorsett 145 (UBP)	B.O. Neymour 141 (FNM)	D.E. Rolle 772 (PLP)
		U. Cargill 3 (NDP)			B.O. Neymour 131 (FNM)
		KEMPS BAY (748)	**KEMPS BAY (816)**	**KEMPS BAY (884)**	N.F. Aranha 48 (FNM)
		L.O. Pindling 386 (PLP)	L.O. Pindling 597 (PLP)	L.O. Pindling 643 (PLP)	**KEMPS BAY (943)**
		C.St.J. Stevenson 283	E. Albury 129 (UBP)	G.W. Pinder 178 (FNM)	L.O. Pindling 713 (PLP)
				E.G. McPhee 1 (CLP)	M.I. Lundy 155 (FNM)

GRAND BAHAMA

1956	1962	1967	1968	1972	1977
GRAND BAHAMA	**GRAND BAHAMA (2,239)**	**BIMINI and WEST END (942)**	**BIMINI and WEST END (2,012)**	**BIMINI and WEST END (2,071)**	**BIMINI and WEST END (2,654)**
C.W.F. Bethell unopposed	H. DeGregory 819	W.J. Levarity 514 (PLP)	W.J. Levarity 1,496 (PLP)	H.J. Bower 1,113 (PLP)	H.J. Bowen 875 (PLP)
	W.J. Levarity 612				

GRAND BAHAMA

(NDP)
G.W. Rolle (BDP) — 149

PINE RIDGE (1,827)
G.J. Levarity (FNM) — 871
M.W. Pinder (PLP) — 722

HIGH ROCK (4,093)
M.E. Moore (FNM) — 1,867
K.W. Nottage (PLP) — 1,582
Dr Roop — 107

GRAND BAHAMA (2,968)
K.W. Nottage (PLP) — 1,450
M.E. Moore (FNM) — 1,140

GRAND BAHAMA (3,083)
M.E. Moore (PLP) — 1,630
A. Russell (UBP) — 314

E.J. Outten (NDP) — 17

GRAND BAHAMA (1,444)
M.E. Moore (PLP) — 513
P.A. Russell (UBP) — 352
B.H. Grey (Lab) — 310
R.M. D'Arville (NDP) — 38
A.K. Neely (NDP) — 4

ABACO

COOPERS TOWN (1,422)
H.A. Ingraham (PLP) — 892
C. Parker (BDP) — 347
E.W. Brown (FNM) — 53

MARSH HARBOUR (1,401)
C.M. Lightbourn (BDP) — 507
E.M. Key (PLP) — 503
C.V. Wallace-Whitfield (FNM) — 280

COOPERS TOWN (1,241)
S.C. Bootle (PLP) — 562
L.M. Thompson (FNM) — 558

MARSH HARBOUR (1,278)
E.W. Watkins (FNM) — 883
R.G. Hudson (PLP) — 283

COOPERS TOWN (1,193)
S.C. Bootle (PLP) — 592
R. Thompson (UBP) — 400

MARSH HARBOUR (1,348)
S. Archer (UBP) — 672
J.H. Bostwick (PLP) — 286

ABACO (1,905)
J.H. Bethell (UBP) — 1,254
L.M. Thompson (UBP) — 1,247
F.H. Christie (UBP) — 1,176
S.C. Bootle (PLP) — 758
C.B. Archer (PLP) — 176
C.L. Rees — 168
R.I. Sawyer — 107

ABACO (2,097)
L.M. Thompson — 497
F.H. Christie (UBP) — 478
J.H. Bethell (UBP) — 212
C.L. Rees — 212
R. Sawyer — 169

ABACO
F.H. Christie — 1,400
L.M. Thompson — 1,331
H. Johnson — 1,183
C.L. Rees — 652
J. Butler (PLP) — 404

HARBOUR ISLAND

1956	1962	1967	1968	1972	1977
HARBOUR ISLAND	**HARBOUR ISLAND (1,372)**	**HARBOUR ISLAND (1,385)**	**ST GEORGE and DUNMORE TOWN (950)**	**ST GEORGE and DUNMORE TOWN (1,013)**	**ST JOHNS (1,708)**
J.T. Albury 469	J.T. Albury (UBP) 803	N.S. Solomon (UBP) 740	N.S. Solomon (UBP) 638	N.S. Solomon (FNM) 799	N.S. Solomon (BDP) 899
A.R. Braynen 382	G.D.F. Clarke (UBP) 633	A.R. Braynen (UBP) 715	A.P. Maillis (PLP) 166	A.P. Maillis (PLP) 145	C. Neilly (PLP) 505
G.D.F. Clarke 316	A.R. Braynen 609	J.T. Albury (UBP) 652			G.G. Newbold (FNM) 197
R.N. Higgs 313	N.S. Solomon 487		**ST JOHNS (688)**	**ST JOHNS (643)**	
C.A. Dorsett (PLP) 165	G. Rogers 287		A.R. Braynen 341	N.S. Roberts (FNM) 320	
	C. Cavill (PLP) 107		N. Roberts (UBP) 222	A.R. Braynen 249	
				J.B. Barry 21	

ELEUTHERA

1956	1962	1967	1968	1972	1977
ELEUTHERA	**ELEUTHERA (2,270)**	**ELEUTHERA (1,882)**	**GOVERNORS HARBOUR (1,185)**	**GOVERNORS HARBOUR (1,313)**	**GOVERNORS HARbOUR (1,470)**
C.T. Kelly 626	G. Baker (UBP) 1,391	G.L. Thompson (PLP) 1,004	G.L. Thompson (PLP) 744	P.M. Bethel (PLP) 701	P.M. Bethel (PLP) 918
G. Baker 515	C.T. Kelly (UBP) 1,312	G. Baker (UBP) 900	D. Sands 328	G.L. Thompson (FNM) 511	G.L. Thompson (FNM) 443
A.H. Pritchard 457	U. Baker (UBP) 1,055	P.H. Albury (PLP) 815	**ROCK SOUND (1,188)**	**ROCK SOUND (1,424)**	**ROCK SOUND (1,430)**
C.V. Wallace-Whitfield (PLP) 396	C.V. Wallace-Whitfield (PLP) 715	C.T. Kelly (UBP) 712	P.H. Albury (PLP) 615	P.H. Albury (PLP) 739	P.H. Albury (PLP) 681
W. Curry 348	D. Johnson (PLP) 499	U. Baker (UBP) 582	G. Baker (UBP) 427	G. Baker (FNM) 563	G. Baker (BDP) 566
U. Baker 218	A. Lofthouse (PLP) 468	S.A. Pritchard 492			A. Allen (FNM) 81
	P.H. Albury (PLP) 315				

CAT ISLAND

CAT ISLAND		CAT ISLAND (1,198)		CAT ISLAND (920)		CAT ISLAND (1,102)		CAT ISLAND (1,041)		CAT ISLAND (1,042)	
H.G. Christie	259	G.K. Kelly (UBP)	691	G.K. Kelly (UBP)	552	O.N. Johnson (PLP)	602	O.N. Johnson (PLP)	596	E. Knowles (BDP)	473
G.K. Kelly (UBP)	244	H.G. Christie (UBP)	690	H.J. Bowen (PLP)	320	G.K. Kelly	347	J.A. Ramsey (FNM)	341	C.A. Smith (PLP)	432
G. Thompson	137	O.N. Johnson (PLP)	407							O.N. Johnson	32
H. White (PLP)	118	H.R. Culmer (PLP)	403								
A.D. Hanna (PLP)	53										
G.E. O'Brien (PLP)	7										
C. Reeves (BDL)	2										

EXUMA

EXUMA		EXUMA (1,329)		EXUMA (1,353)		ROLLEVILLE (684)		ROLLEVILLE (748)		ROLLEVILLE (838)	
F.H. Brown	196	R.H. Symonette (UBP)	693	R.H. Symonette (UBP)	620	G.A. Smith (PLP)	388	G.A. Smith (PLP)	428	G.A. Smith (PLP)	464
R.H. Symonette (UBP)	194	F.H. Brown (UBP)	669	F.W. Brown (UBP)	598	F.H. Brown (UBP)	220	S.J. Smith (FNM)	258	G.G. Brown (BDP)	290
D.B. McKinney	159	L.B. Johnson (PLP)	455	L.N. Coakley (PLP)	543					W. Pyfrom (FNM)	0
H.J. Bowen (PLP)	128	H. Smith (PLP)	437	G.A. Smith (PLP)	445						
				F.N. Bowe (NDP)	75						
				S. Gray	32						

GEORGE TOWN and RAGGED ISLAND 2 (337)		GEORGE TOWN and RAGGED ISLAND (822)		GEORGE TOWN and RAGGED ISLAND (808)	
L.N. Coakley (PLP)	484	L.N. Coakley (PLP)	552	L.N. Coakley (PLP)	481
G. Lightbourn (UBP)	253	J.G. Scavella (FNM)	204	R.C. Symonette (BDP)	267
				S.P. Ferguson (FNM)	2

SAN SALVADOR

1956	1962	1967	1968	1972	1977
SAN SALVADOR R.M. Solomon 87 R.I. Butler 23 (PLP)	SAN SALVADOR (365) R.M. Solomon 286 (UBP) L. Lockhart 48 (PLP)	SAN SALVADOR (298) R.M. Solomon unopposed (UBP)	–[3]	–	–

LONG ISLAND

1956	1962	1967	1968	1972	1977
LONG ISLAND D.E. D'Albenas 356 P.D. Graham 355 (UBP) H.M. Taylor 233 (PLP) L. Lockhart 178 (PLP)	LONG ISLAND (1,626) P.D. Graham 1,199 (UBP) D.E. D'Albenas 1,157 (UBP) J. Purkiss 289 (PLP)	LONG ISLAND (1,484) P.D. Graham 1,378 (UBP) D.E. D'Albenas 1,329 (UBP) R.I. Butler 200 (PLP)	NORTH LONG ISLAND, RUM CAY and SAN SALVADOR (955) P.D. Graham 507 (UBP) R.I. Butler (PLP) CLARENCE TOWN (986) D.E. D'Albenas 662 (UBP) S. Carroll 208 (PLP)	NORTH LONG ISLAND, RUM CAY and SAN SALVADOR (1,059)[5] C.S. Fountain 473 (FNM) P.P. Smith 473 (PLP) CLARENCE TOWN (930) C.M. Lightbourn 667 (FNM) S. Carroll 173	NORTH END, LONG ISLAND (1,001) P.P. Smith 560 (PLP) C.S. Fountain 350 (BDP) CLARENCE TOWN (1,014) J.F. Knowles 487 (BDP) E.W. Watkins 291 T.A. Wells 155

CROOKED ISLAND

CROOKED ISLAND	CROOKED ISLAND (7794)	CROOKED ISLAND (694)	CROOKED ISLAND (812)	CROOKED ISLAND (699)	CROOKED ISLAND (609)
E.A.P. Dupuch (BDL) 116	B.T. Kelly (UBP) 419	B.T. Kelly unopposed	W.A. Moss (PLP) 385	C.F. Tynes (FNM) 340	W.A. Moss (PLP) 319
B.T. Kelly 72	A.L. Roker (PLP) 218		B.T. Kelly (UBP) 292	W.A. Moss (PLP) 292	C.F. Tynes (BDP) 219
H.H. Heastie 31					

INAGUA

INAGUA	INAGUA (632)	INAGUA (612)	INAGUA (706)	INAGUA (608)	INAGUA (666)
G.A. Bethell 119	B. Dupuch (UBP) 297	B. Dupuch (UBP) 331	J.R. Ford (PLP) 300	J.R. Ford (PLP) 273	J.R. Ford (PLP) 324
A.L. McKinney (BDL) 111	A.L. McKinney (PLP) 274	J.R. Ford (PLP) 196	B. Dupuch (UBP) 290	V.J. Symonette (FNM) 238	A.D. Farquharson (FNM) 246
				C.H. Taylor 50	

1. Grouped approximately to original four districts.
2. Transferred from Long Island.
3. Transferred to Long Island.
4. Set aside by the election court; at subsequent by-election B.T. Kelly (UBP) 337, W.A. Moss (PLP) 290.
5. Referred to election court; meanwhile a by-election was held and boycotted by the FNM: P.P. Smith (PLP) 573; C.S. Fountain 4; on a recount of the general election by the election court which became the final result: C.S. Fountain (FNM: 475, P.P. Smith (PLP) 471.
6. Abolished.

Name Index

Subject Index

Abaco Independence Movement, 193
Abaco secession, 183, 191, 193
Africa, 71-72, 104-5, 115-16, 137, 158, 219, 225-26
Afro-Bahamian. *See* Africa
agriculture, 1-2, 3-6, 8, 12, 14-16, 88, 114, 148-49, 169-70
airlines, 14, 82, 151, 173-74
anthem. *See* national symbols
aragonite industry, 149
Arawaks. *See* Lucayans

Bahamas Business League, 166
Bahamas Christian Council. *See* churches
Bahamas Democratic League (BDL), 40-41, 50
Bahamas Federation of Labour (BFL), 48, 57, 59, 63-65
Bahamas Federation of Youth. *See* Progressive Liberal Party (PLP), youth organizations
Bahamas Observer, 134
Bahamas Workers' Council, 196
Bahamian Christian Social Democratic Party, 197
Bahamian Democratic Party (BDP), 197, 203, 205-6
Bahamian Federation of Trade Unions (BFTU), 155, 195
Bahamian Times, 82, 119, 124, 132, 137, 139, 142-43, 159, 161, 184
Bahamian Trades Union Congress (TUC), 65, 107
Bahamian history. *See* national culture
"Bay Street Boys", 17, 29, 35-36, 41, 51-52, 57, 59, 72. *See also* United Bahamian Party (UBP)
"belongers". *See* immigration

biblical language in politics, 40, 138, 162, 183, 216-17
Black Power, 131-32, 156-57, 182, 186, 198-99
bootlegging, 14-15
British officials, 28-29
British troops, 63, 76, 82
building industry, 86-87, 114, 166
by-elections: Abaco, 59; Bains Town, 195; City, 131, 133; Crooked Island, 129; Eastern and Southern, 67, 70, 78-79; Eleuthera, 39-41; Grand Bahama, 74-75; Mangrove Cay, 187; North End Long Island, 194; St Barnabas 196

Caribbean. *See* West Indies
casinos. *See* gambling
Cat Island land case, 103-4
Christian Democratic Party, 36, 38
churches, 38-39, 111, 119, 156-57, 172, 175, 182, 217-18
civil service, 74, 100, 104, 145
coat-of-arms. *See* national symbols
Coconut Grove Freedom and Justice Committee, 198
Collins Wall, 41-42, 81
Colonial Office, 32, 36, 55-57, 59-60, 64, 66, 69, 80, 95-97, 119-20, 136-37, 141-42, 182, 214
colonialism, 208-9
Committee on Colonialism. *See* United Nations
Commonwealth Labour Party, 189, 196
Commonwealth of the Bahama Islands, 141
Commonwealth of the Bahamas Trade Union Congress (TUC), 195
Commonwealth People's Party, 160

Union (SEIU), 155
single-member constituencies, 97, 136
slavery, 4–8, 21–23, 27, 77, 87–88, 92
Socialist Democratic Party, 160
social services, 71, 166–67, 177, 189
social stratification, 209
Spain, 3–4
Speaker. *See* House of Assembly, Speaker's role
sponge industry, 12–13, 15
symbolic action, 210–11

tax haven. *See* finance industry
Taxi Cab Union, 46, 62–64
Teamsters Union, 83
Torch, 184
tourist industry, 1, 13, 15–16, 32, 34, 45, 47–48, 62, 81, 88, 92–93, 127–28, 146–49, 151, 162, 165, 170–71
trade unions, 17, 47–48, 57, 65–66, 102, 154–56, 222
Tribune. See Nassau Tribune
Turks and Caicos Islands, 8–9, 168

"Uncle Tom", 99–100
unemployment, 84, 88, 101–2, 177
Unicomm. *See* Progressive Liberal Party (PLP), youth organizations
United Bahamian Party (UBP), 66, 80–81, 103, 126, 160, 195. *See also* "Bay Street Boys"
United Nations, 107, 110, 116
United States. *See* North American influence

Vanguard, 186
Vanguard Nationalist and Socialist Party (VNSP), 179, 186–87

Wall Street Journal, 116–17
way of life, Bahamian, 4, 47–48, 115, 120, 148–49, 168, 221
West Indies, 6, 20, 26, 29, 43, 47, 65, 78, 220, 225, 227
Windsor Field blockade, 62
women, votes for. *See* franchise
workforce. *See* immigration
wrecking, 8–9, 12